San Diego Christian College
2100 Greenfield Drive
El Cajon, CA 92019

STROLLS WITH PUSHKIN

Russian Literature and Thought
Gary Saul Morson, *Series Editor*

Abram Tertz
(Andrei Sinyavsky)

STROLLS WITH PUSHKIN

Translated by
Catharine Theimer Nepomnyashchy and
Slava I. Yastremski

Introduction by
Catharine Theimer Nepomnyashchy

Notes by
Slava I. Yastremski

Yale University Press
New Haven and London

Designed by James J. Johnson and set in Linotype Walbaum by Tseng Information Systems, Durham, North Carolina. Printed in the United States of America by Edwards Brothers, Ann Arbor, Michigan.

Library of Congress Cataloging-in-Publication Data

Siniavskiĭ, A. (Andreĭ), 1925–
[Progulki s Pushkinym. English]
Strolls with Pushkin / Andrei Sinyavsky (Abram Tertz) ; translated by Catharine Theimer Nepomnyashchy and Slava Yastremski ; introduction by Catharine Theimer Nepomnyashchy ; notes by Slava Yastremski.
   p.   cm.
Includes bibliographical references.
ISBN 0-300-05279-0

1. Pushkin, Aleksandr Sergeevich, 1799–1837—Criticism and interpretation.   I. Nepomnyashchy, Catharine Theimer.   II. Yastremski, Slava.   III. Title.
PG3356.S51313   1993
891.71'3—dc20   93-13718

A catalogue record for this book is available from the British Library.

The paper in this book meets the guidelines for permanence and durability of the Committee on Production Guidelines for Book Longevity of the Council on Library Resources.

10 9 8 7 6 5 4 3 2 1

CONTENTS

INTRODUCTION

To the Western reader, Andrei Sinyavsky's—or, more accurately, Abram Tertz's—*Strolls with Pushkin* must seem an unlikely contender for the title of most controversial book published in the Soviet Union during the glasnost period. Appearing just as censorship was entering the final stages of collapse, which allowed Soviet readers access to a bewildering profusion of sensational historical revelations and previously repressed literature, this slim, playful, stylistically difficult and esoteric work devoted to a nineteenth-century poet should, one would think, have gotten lost in the shuffle. Yet when the journal *October* printed a four-page excerpt from *Strolls with Pushkin* in April 1989, it unleashed a storm of outrage, which polarized the literary intelligentsia in Moscow and Leningrad and spilled over into the popular press. Cries that Sinyavsky was a "russophobe" who had "defiled Russia's national treasure" sounded repeatedly in the press and at writers' meetings throughout the autumn of 1989. One of Sinyavsky's most outspoken critics even compared him to Salman Rushdie, appealing to the Russian readership to emulate the example of those Muslim fundamentalists who had protested the publication of the *Satanic Verses* and stopping just short of approving the Ayatollah Khomeini's call to murder the author.[1] The vehemence of the reaction to this first Soviet publication of *Strolls with Pushkin* bears witness to the sensitivity of the topic as well as to its author's gift for challenging the status quo and for performing virtuoso linguistic juggling tricks with the sacred cows of Russian and Soviet culture.

Sinyavsky's career began quietly enough. He studied literature at Moscow University during the postwar years and in 1952, the year before Stalin's death, he completed the requirements for his candidate degree (roughly equivalent to an American doctorate) and went on to receive an appointment at the prestigious Gorky Institute of World Literature in Moscow, embarking on a promising career as a literary scholar and critic. By the middle of the next decade he was publishing

---

1. Igor Shafarevich, "Fenomen emigratsii," *Literaturnaya Rossiya*, no. 36 (September 8, 1989): 5.

essays and reviews in the Soviet Union's premier literary journal, *New World* (Novy mir), had co-authored books on early Soviet poetry and on Picasso, and had written a lengthy introduction to a new edition of Pasternak's poetry, establishing his reputation as a rising liberal voice in Soviet cultural life.

In the mid-1950s, however, Sinyavsky literally began leading a double life. Disillusioned with the Soviet system—because of attempts to recruit him as a KGB informer, the arrest of his father, and the growing divergence between his own tastes in literature and art and those prescribed by the regime—he took the decision to have certain of his writings that could not be published in his homeland smuggled out of the country for publication abroad. The first of these works to appear in the West was a literary manifesto of sorts entitled *What Is Socialist Realism*, which was published in 1959. The essay is an ironic tour de force in which Sinyavsky's narrator poses as a defender of the officially sanctioned Soviet approach to art subsumed under the label *socialist realism* in order, ultimately, to turn the tradition upside down by subverting it from within. Pointing out the internal inconsistencies in the practice of socialist realism, Sinyavsky concludes by rejecting its subordination of literature to an extraliterary purpose—furthering the building of communism—and ends the essay with what might be considered his literary credo:

> In the given case, I place my hopes on a phantasmagoric art with hypotheses instead of a purpose and grotesque in lieu of realistic descriptions of everyday life. It would correspond more fully to the spirit of our day. Let the exaggerated images of Hoffmann, Dostoevsky, Goya, and the most socialist of them all, Mayakovsky, and of many other realists and nonrealists teach us how to be truthful with the help of absurd fantasy.
>
> In losing our faith, we did not lose our ecstasy at the metamorphoses of God that take place before our eyes, at the monstrous peristalsis of his intestines—the convolutions of the brain. We don't know where to go, not having understood that there is nothing to be done, we begin to think, to construct conjectures, to suggest. Perhaps we will think up something amazing. But it will no longer be socialist realism.[2]

Following this essay, between 1959 and 1965 three novellas, six short stories, and a brief collection of aphorisms by Sinyavsky appeared in

2. Abram Tertz, "Chto takoe sotsialistichesky realizm," in *Fantastichesky mir Abrama Tertsa* (New York: Inter-language Literary Associates, 1967), 446.

Western publications under the pseudonym Abram Tertz. The fictional works were, in essence, exemplars of the purposeless, phantasmagoric art invoked at the end of *What Is Socialist Realism,* what Sinyavsky would later come to call (using a term apparently coined by Dostoevsky) fantastic realism. This approach to literature is in turn intimately related conceptually to Sinyavsky's pseudonym. Borrowed from Abrashka Tertz, a legendary Jewish bandit whose exploits are celebrated in an Odessa thieves' song, the pseudonym identifying the writer as an outlaw has remained Sinyavsky's trademark and alter ego long since it outlived its practical usefulness as a blind protecting him from detection by the Soviet authorities.[3]

The dodge worked for six years, but in October 1965 Sinyavsky was arrested along with his friend Yuly Daniel, who, with Sinyavsky's help, had also secretly sent works abroad for publication under the pseudonym Nikolai Arzhak. The trial, which lasted four days in February 1966, drew the battle lines between the government, which was tightening its controls over cultural life after the Khrushchev "thaw," and the burgeoning dissident movement. It was preceded by a virulent press campaign painting the two writers, whose works were completely unknown to average Soviet readers, as turncoats who had betrayed their Soviet homeland and sold out to the ideological interests of the West. The authorities were evidently trying to script a show trial reminiscent of the Stalin years, but the key actors failed to play their parts docilely. In the wake of the relative freedom of the Khrushchev years, a certain segment of the Soviet intelligentsia refused to submit quietly to the official line and rallied in support of Sinyavsky and Daniel, and the two defendants, even after more than four months of pre-trial incarceration, staunchly pleaded innocent at the trial, delivering eloquent speeches in their own defense.[4]

Despite protests both at home and abroad, Sinyavsky and Daniel were found guilty of "anti-Soviet agitation" under article 70 of the Soviet penal code and sentenced, respectively, to seven and five years at hard labor. The two writers were transported to different labor

3. For a more thorough discussion of the significance of Sinyavsky's pseudonym, see Catharine Theimer Nepomnyashchy, "Sinyavsky/Tertz: The Evolution of the Writer in Exile," *Humanities in Society* 7, no. 3–4 (Summer-Fall 1984): 123–42.

4. Sinyavsky has maintained: "For example, *Strolls with Pushkin* was for me to a certain extent a continuation of my closing speech at the trial." Catharine Theimer Nepomnyashchy, "An Interview with Andrei Sinyavsky," *Formations* 6, no. 1 (Spring 1991): 11.

camps in the Dubrovlag system near Potma in Mordovia. Daniel served out his sentence there, and Sinyavsky was released a year later, in 1971.

Perhaps the greatest irony of Sinyavsky's career is that he wrote what would become his most controversial book while imprisoned in Dubrovlag. In a 1990 interview, Sinyavsky explained how he managed to write *Strolls with Pushkin* and send it out in letters to his wife, Mariya Rozanova, while under constant surveillance by the authorities:

> I realized that I had to come up with something, and I thought up the idea of incorporating my writing into letters. Letters are usually written at one sitting, and in this I was aided by a misfortune. There was a restriction on letters—you could mail only two letters a month. Fortunately, there was no restriction on their length. Of course it was forbidden to send a very long letter, but you could write twenty pages in tiny but very neat handwriting, so that it would be easier for the censor to read. And I realized that these letters were getting through and even suited the camp authorities and the censor. What is the most criminal thing you can do in the camps? There are two things: to criticize the Soviet government and to meddle in politics or describe the horrors of camp life: to complain that you're badly fed, you're sick all the time, etc.—that was forbidden. And I used the ploy . . . well, sometimes, so as not to forget completely, I would betake myself to talk about Pushkin—in the guise of what looked to be random thoughts, but were in fact an already thoroughly conceived book—and Mariya caught on to this and separated out all of these passages and collected them together. I came back from the camp, and the book was already done.[5]

In the same fashion, Sinyavsky completed the first chapter of a book on Gogol while imprisoned, and when he returned home to Moscow after his release he compiled an introspective camp memoir also out of passages from his letters to his wife.

These works represent both a continuation and a further development of Sinyavsky's earlier writings. *Strolls with Pushkin* in effect initiated a new literary genre: fantastic literary scholarship (*fantasticheskoe literaturovedenie*). Sinyavsky has described this approach to writing about literature as a departure from traditional scholarly writing in which the writer can develop whimsical hypotheses and, in relation to accepted convention, deliberately do things "wrong":

5. Ibid., 11–12.

When a person takes up the study of art, he can write an academic work or he can act just as he would in fantastic realism. After all art is the same objective reality as reality is. That means that it can be portrayed in different ways, emphasizing some things, exaggerating, sometimes turning them upside down. By the way, that's why people say that everything is wrong in those works [Sinyavsky's books on Pushkin and Gogol]. But sometimes it's done wrong consciously. It was simply amusing to write a scholarly monograph on Pushkin while in a labor camp. But some things I simply broke first, the way you break a toy, and glued them back together a new way.[6]

This playful and, from the point of view of traditional literary studies, perverse approach to literature brought down on Sinyavsky the ire of those in his culture who had an investment in things being done "right."

In 1973 Sinyavsky was allowed to emigrate with his wife and son to France. The family took up residence in the small town of Fontenay-aux-Roses just outside Paris, and Sinyavsky was offered a professorship at the Sorbonne, where he has taught Russian literature ever since. He has also continued, now openly, to pursue his double career as Professor Andrei Sinyavsky and writer-outlaw Abram Tertz, signing his own name to what he terms "academic" works, as well as to overtly polemical political writings, and his pseudonym to works he considers "fantastic" or "exaggerated." His camp works were published in the West in the years following his emigration—*A Voice from the Chorus* (his camp memoir) in 1973 and *Strolls with Pushkin* and *In the Shadow of Gogol* in 1975. In emigration Sinyavsky has written two books published under the Tertz pseudonym, the novella *Little Tsores* and the novel *Goodnight!,* and three books published under his own name, a scholarly monograph on the philosopher Vasily Rozanov and studies of Russian and Soviet culture entitled *Soviet Civilization* and *Ivan the Fool: An Essay on Russian Popular Faith.*

Although both of Sinyavsky's personae have continued in emigration to carry on active and productive careers, even in the West neither Sinyavsky's nor Tertz's life has been free of controversy. Initially welcomed by the Russian emigre cultural establishment, Sinyavsky increasingly found himself at odds with some of its more powerful figures over their Russian chauvinism and antisemitism. In 1978, disgusted with the politics of emigre journalism, Mariya Rozanova began pub-

6. Ibid., 10.

lishing the journal *Syntax* out of the Sinyavsky house. Originally conceived as an outlet solely for Sinyavsky's works, *Syntax* from the beginning attracted contributors from both the emigration and the Soviet Union. The enterprise soon expanded to include a publishing house of the same name, which also operates out of the Sinyavsky home. In publishing not only Sinyavsky's articles and books but also works by authors who fall outside the mainstream of emigre publishing, the journal and publishing house have earned Sinyavsky and Rozanova a reputation as renegades from the emigre cultural establishment. Sinyavsky has contributed to that reputation by writing articles directed against the conservative nationalist camp, in particular polemicizing with the most visible exponent of its platform, Aleksandr Solzhenitsyn. By the same token, just as Sinyavsky's political articles have turned him into something of a pariah in the emigre community, so too his Tertz works have drawn fire and none more than *Strolls with Pushkin*. Its original publication in Russian in the West called forth indignant protests from emigre critics, who, in viewing the book as an attack on Pushkin, forestalled the later Soviet response.

Thus, over the course of a quarter century Sinyavsky-Tertz has three times found himself at the center of a scandal that polarized Soviet or emigre Russian culture. Beginning with his trial and continuing through the blowups over the publication of *Strolls with Pushkin* in emigration and in the USSR—he has been accused of hating and betraying his homeland, of "trampling on all that is most holy" in its culture.[7] The tenor and intensity of the accusations leveled at Sinyavsky over the years are particularly surprising considering that his Tertz works strive neither for political sensationalism nor for a mass audience. Clearly he has managed—most successfully in *Strolls with Pushkin*—to touch a very sensitive nerve in Russian culture, whether emigre or Soviet. The beginning of an answer to the riddle of the explosive nature of *Strolls with Pushkin* is embedded in the title of the work itself. "Strolls" denotes aimless movement—not subordinated to some higher purpose—which may violate official borders and therefore may end in trespassing on forbidden territory. In fact, Sinyavsky's work is built completely on these principles, the text rambling over boundaries and treading on space traditionally held sacred in Russian culture. Sinyavsky himself

7. This is from Sinyavsky's own description at his trial of the accusations made against him: "Sinyavsky topchet vsyo samoe svyatoe, vplot do materi." "Poslednee slovo Andreya Sinyavskogo," in *Tsena metafory ili prestuplenie i nakazanie Sinyavskogo i Danielya* (Moscow: Kniga, 1989), 475.

has said, "I only find it interesting to write if there is a prohibition, a taboo."[8] To understand the taboo that he violates in *Strolls with Pushkin,* let us survey the ground that Sinyavsky is traversing—the life and works of his companion in his strolls, Aleksandr Pushkin, and Pushkin's afterlife in Russian culture.

Aleksandr Sergeevich Pushkin was born in Moscow on May 26, 1799,[9] into a boyar family that could trace its lineage back for centuries. Throughout his life, Pushkin was proud to the point of hypersensitivity of his aristocratic pedigree and did not suffer what he considered social slurs lightly. In 1830 he wrote that "the names of my ancestors are met with every minute in our history,"[10] and he on occasion incorporated references to his forebears into his works. In this connection by far Pushkin's most colorful ancestor, and the one who apparently most vividly engaged the poet's imagination, was his maternal greatgrandfather Ibrahim Hannibal. According to family legend, Hannibal was the son of an Abyssinian prince. In 1705 a Russian envoy found him living as a hostage at the court of the Turkish sultan and took the boy back to Petersburg as a gift to Peter the Great. The tsar made Hannibal his godson, sent him to France for military training, and after Hannibal's return to Russia appointed him an officer in his own crack Preobrazhensky Regiment. Hannibal lived to a ripe old age—according to Pushkin into his nineties—and in the course of his military career attained the rank of general. For his services he was granted by Peter's daughter the Empress Elizabeth a number of estates, including the estate at Mikhailovskoe, which was to play such an important role in Pushkin's own life.

Pushkin's fascination with his African ancestry remained a leitmotif of his life and work. In the first chapter of *Evgeny Onegin,* his narrator speaks of "sighing for gloomy Russia under the sky of my Africa," and his first attempt at prose was a fictionalized biography of his greatgrandfather, *The Blackamoor of Peter the Great.* Though there is some disagreement among contemporary descriptions of Pushkin, reference to his "Negroid features" was standard, as evidenced by an incident

8. "Interview with Andrei Sinyavsky," 9.

9. The dates of Pushkin's life are given in this introduction according to the Julian calendar, observed in Russia during the poet's lifetime, rather than the Gregorian.

10. A. S. Pushkin, "Rodoslovnaya Pushkinykh i Gannibalov," cited in V. Veresaev, *Pushkin v zhizni,* 7th ed. (1936; rpt. Chicago: Russian Language Specialties, 1970), 1:22. Sinyavsky read Veresaev's compendium while in Lefortovo prison.

from the poet's early life: "In his childhood years Pushkin was not a robust child and had all the African features of physiognomy he had as an adult; but when he was a little boy, his hair was so curly and so elegantly crimped by his African nature that one day [the poet] I. I. Dmitriev said to me: 'Look, he is a real little Moor.' " [11]

Pushkin grew up in Moscow, spending summers at the estate of his maternal grandmother, Marya Alekseevna Hannibal, at Zakharovo. Marya Alekseevna was noted for her elegant command of Russian, and it is apparently from her that Pushkin received his first real exposure to his native tongue since, following the custom of the time, French was the dominant language in the Pushkin home. Pushkin never recorded his memories of his childhood, but by virtually all accounts his mother and father left much to be desired as parents. His mother, Nadezhda Osipovna, a capricious and moody woman, was a noted society beauty who was often referred to by the nickname "the beautiful creole." His father, Sergei Lvovich, was reputed to be extremely tightfisted while at the same time squandering money on gambling and social pursuits and allowing himself to be robbed by his peasants.

Yet although Pushkin may have received little real nurturing from his parents, the ambiance created by his family must certainly have fostered his literary interests. His father was an assiduous raconteur known in society circles for his wit, and seems even to have written poetry in French. Pushkin's mother, for her part, ceded little to her husband in either social graces or knowledge of French literature. Moreover, Pushkin's uncle Vasily Lvovich Pushkin was a minor poet in his own right, known primarily for his epigrams and fables, and as much of a social gadfly as his brother. Through his uncle, Pushkin as a child met a number of the most famous literary figures of the day, including the prose writer and historiographer Nikolai Karamzin and the poet Konstantin Batyushkov. More important, perhaps, Pushkin had access to his father's extensive library, which consisted primarily of French classics of the seventeenth and eighteenth centuries, and from an early age he became a voracious reader.

In June 1811 Pushkin left his family home, apparently with few regrets, for Petersburg, to be enrolled as a member of the first class to attend the newly founded lycée at Tsarskoe Selo, an institution conceived with the goal of training the sons of the nobility for service to the

---

11. M. N. Makarov, "A. S. Pushkin v detstve," cited in Veresaev, *Pushkin v zhizni*, 1:55.

state. The official opening of the lycée, attended by the tsar and other dignitaries, was held on October 19, a date that Pushkin commemorated in his poetry to the end of his life. Pushkin remained at the lycée for six years, until his graduation in June 1817. As his continuing devotion to the institution testified, these years were among the happiest of Pushkin's life, and the friends he made there—among them Baron Anton Delvig, Wilhelm Kyukhelbeker, and Ivan Pushchin—became a surrogate family to him.

An indifferent student, excelling in those subjects he liked and doing poorly in those he found uninteresting, Pushkin soon gained a reputation for his literary gifts, and his devotion to poetry was looked on indulgently by at least some instructors, as Ivan Pushchin recalled:

> All the professors looked on in reverence at Pushkin's growing talent. In mathematics class Kartsev once called him to the blackboard and gave him a problem in algebra. For a long time Pushkin shifted from one foot to the other, all the time writing some kind of formulas. Kartsev finally asked him, "Well, what is the answer? What is x equal to?" Pushkin, smiling, answered, "Zero!" "Good! In my class everything with you ends in zero. Go back to your seat and write verses."[12]

Moreover, Pushkin's reputation as a poet soon spread beyond the lycée. In 1814, at the age of fifteen, he published his first poem, and some thirty of his poems appeared in print during his school years. While still in school, he also began to gain recognition from some of the literary lights of the time, including the grand old man of Russian poetry, ode writer to Catherine the Great, Gavriil Derzhavin. So impressed was Derzhavin by the boy's early poems that he told an acquaintance, "This is who will replace Derzhavin."[13] But not everyone who came in contact with Pushkin during these early years was convinced of his promising future, and one of the harshest criticisms of the young poet came from the director of the lycée, Egor Antonovich Engelhardt:

> Pushkin's highest and ultimate aim is to shine, and precisely through poetry; but it will hardly find a solid foundation in him, because he fears all serious study, and his mind, having neither penetration nor depth, is a completely superficial, French mind. That is moreover the best that can be said of Pushkin. His heart is cold and empty; there is

12. I. I. Pushchin, cited in Veresaev, *Pushkin v zhizni*, 1:78.
13. F. N. Glinka, *Vospominanie o piiticheskoi zhizni Pushkina*, cited in Veresaev, *Pushkin v zhizni*, 1:77.

neither love nor religion in it; perhaps it is as empty as ever a youthful heart has been. Tender and youthful sensations are abased in him by an imagination defiled by all the erotic works of French literature.[14]

Engelhardt may have had a personal animus against Pushkin, however. Relations between the director and the student, who was precocious in affairs of the heart as well as in poetry, had apparently soured when Pushkin made untoward advances to a widow living with the Engel-hardt family.

Upon his graduation from the lycée, Pushkin was awarded the rank of collegiate secretary in the civil service and received a position as a clerk in the Ministry of Foreign Affairs. This largely nominal appointment left him free to immerse himself in the social life of the capital, attending balls, frequenting the ballet and theater, and indulging in amorous escapades with actresses and dancers. He wrote to a friend in 1819: "Thank God, there's plenty of champagne—and actresses as well—the one we drink, the other . . ." [15]

Pushkin's enjoyment of the amusements that the imperial capital had to offer shaded over into his literary life. His growing reputation as a poet as well as his uncle Vasily's connections gained him entrée into the foremost literary groupings of his day—Arzamas, into which he was accepted as a member while still a student at the lycée, and its successor, the Green Lamp. Coteries of this sort flourished in Russia at the time. Literature, on the eve of the appearance of a new commercial audience, was still largely confined to such friendly associations, which explains the fondness for such intimate genres as verse epistles, epigrams, and verses written for ladies' albums.[16] The meetings of the societies to which Pushkin belonged seem to have combined literary discussions with drinking bouts and (at least in the case of the Green Lamp) political radicalism.

Despite all the distractions of Petersburg social and literary life, Pushkin continued writing poetry. At the beginning of April 1820 he completed his first long narrative poem, *Ruslan and Lyudmila,* and gave a reading of it at the home of the noted poet and translator Vasily Zhukovsky. Zhukovsky was so taken with the new poem that he gave

14. From V. Raevsky, *Pushkin v litsee,* cited in Veresaev, *Pushkin v zhizni,* 1:83–84.
15. A. S. Pushkin, *Pis'ma,* ed. B. L. Modzalevsky (1926; Moscow: Kniga, 1989), 1:9.
16. On the literary institutions of Pushkin's time, see William Mills Todd III, *Fiction and Society in the Age of Pushkin* (Cambridge, Mass.: Harvard University Press, 1986).

Pushkin a copy of his portrait with the inscription: "To the victorious pupil from the vanquished teacher." [17]

Ruslan and Lyudmila is a light-hearted and largely parodic work in the tradition of the European and Russian mock epic. Throughout the poem Pushkin pokes fun at his sources, deflating the conventions of the fairy tale and sentimentalist poetry, particularly Zhukovsky's maudlin "Lyudmila. A Russian Ballad," from which his title character borrows her name. The prologue to the poem, which remains among the most beloved of Pushkin's verses, was added only in the second edition, which came out in 1828. It opens on an oak tree standing on a curved seashore and goes on to describe a land filled with fantastic creatures, characters from Russian folklore and fairy tales. A "learned cat" walks back and forth along a golden chain wrapped around the oak, singing songs and telling stories, and in its final version *Ruslan and Lyudmila* becomes one of the cat's tales.

Before he could enjoy his success and within weeks of the completion of the poem, Pushkin found himself under threat of exile to the Solovetsky Monastery on the White Sea. For some time unpublished poems by Pushkin of a politically sensitive nature, notably his ode "Liberty," had been circulating surreptitiously in Petersburg. Moreover, the young poet was fond of improvising epigrams directed at highly placed figures, including even the powerful Count Aleksei Arakcheev and Alexander I himself. By the spring of 1820 the situation had provoked the tsar to the point of taking action. Only because of the intercession of the poet's friends was Pushkin sent out of Petersburg not as a political exile but as a government servant, and not to the far north but to the south, to the chancellery of General Inzov in Ekaterinoslav.

Pushkin arrived in Ekaterinoslav in mid-May. His new superior was apparently inclined to view the poet's past political indiscretions with indulgence and almost immediately granted him a leave of absence to travel with the family of General Nikolai Raevsky to take the waters in the Caucasus, and then to journey on with them to the Crimea. Pushkin became fast friends with Raevsky's elder son, Aleksandr, who introduced him to the poetry of Byron, which was briefly to exert a powerful influence on Pushkin's own writing. Scholars have spent a good deal of effort trying to decide which of the general's four daughters Pushkin fell in love with during their travels.[18] What is certain

17. Cited in Veresaev, *Pushkin v zhizni*, 1:135.
18. The two contenders are Ekaterina, the oldest daughter, and Mariya, who was only fourteen at the time. Mariya has drawn particular attention from Soviet Pushkin-

is that Pushkin was fond of the whole family, and, as he wrote to his brother shortly thereafter, "I spent the happiest minutes of my life in the midst of the family of the honorable Raevsky." [19]

By the time Pushkin rejoined General Inzov in September, his head-quarters had been transferred to Kishinyov, the capital of Bessarabia. Pushkin remained there for almost three years, until he was finally allowed in July 1823 to transfer to the more cosmopolitan Odessa. There he was attached to the staff of the governor general of the region, Count Mikhail Vorontsov. Pushkin's relations with his new superior degen-erated soon enough, in part perhaps because of the incompatibility of their temperaments and in part because of Pushkin's amorous pur-suit of the count's wife, with whom he may have had an affair. In July 1824, Vorontsov, having intercepted a letter from Pushkin to a friend in which the poet wrote that he was "taking lessons in pure atheism," [20] used this evidence of impiety to secure Pushkin's dismissal from the government service and the transfer of his place of exile to the family estate at Mikhailovskoe.

While in Kishinyov, Pushkin completed two very different narrative poems—*The Prisoner of the Caucasus* and *The Gabrieliad*—and started another, *The Robber Brothers*, which he left unfinished. He also began what was to become his most famous work, the "novel in verse" *Evgeny Onegin*, shortly before his move to Odessa. In Odessa he completed the first two chapters of *Onegin* as well as a third narrative poem, *The Fountain of Bakhchisarai*, and began writing a fourth, *The Gypsies*, which he finished only at Mikhailovskoe.

Among Pushkin's "southern" poems *The Gabrieliad* stands alone as a throwback to the mock epics of the preceding century. It is a bawdy retelling of the Annunciation, which has Mary seduced by the snake and the angel Gabriel before giving herself to God, who comes to her in the shape of a dove. The blasphemous subject made the poem unpub-lishable in Pushkin's lifetime, although it did circulate anonymously in manuscript.

Pushkin's other long works from the period reflect his infatuation

---

ists, because she later married the Decembrist Sergei Volkonsky and followed him into Siberian exile.

19. A. S. Pushkin to L. S. Pushkin, September 24, 1820, *Pis'ma*, 1:12.

20. A. S. Pushkin to P. A. Vyazemsky (first half of March 1824, Odessa), *Pis'ma*, 1:74–75. There is some disagreement as to who was the addressee of the letter, and in the English translation of Pushkin's letters the addressee is identified as Kyukhelbeker. *The Letters of Alexander Pushkin*, trans. J. Thomas Shaw (Madison: University of Wisconsin Press, 1967), 156.

with and subsequent repudiation of European romanticism, especially Byron. The romantic settings and plots of the poems, in which themes of captivity and exile figure prominently, converge with Pushkin's own situation. The protagonist of *The Prisoner of the Caucasus* is a nameless Russian taken captive by Circassian tribesmen. A Circassian maiden falls in love with him and eventually helps him escape. *The Fountain of Bakhchisarai* is based on the legend surrounding the "fountain of tears" at Bakhchisarai, which Pushkin visited in the company of the Raevskys. It recounts the tale of a Polish woman, Maria Potocski, who was abducted and held hostage by the khan of the Crimean Tartars, Girei. According to the legend, another of Girei's wives, Zarema, murdered Maria out of jealousy over Girei's love for her. The poem culminates not in the murder, which is left shrouded in innuendo, but in the dramatic confrontation between the two women from different cultures. In *The Gypsies* a disenchanted young Russian who has fled or been exiled from the north comes across a gypsy camp. He falls in love with a gypsy woman, Zemphira, and "marries" her, joining her and her father and the gypsy band in their travels. Soon enough, however, Zemphira tires of the romance and dallies with another man. Enraged, the Russian exile murders the lovers and is consequently expelled from the gypsy camp. In his concluding speech the old gypsy, Zemphira's father, who is something of a "noble savage," chastises the Russian for wanting freedom for himself while not knowing how to grant it to others. This ending has been read as Pushkin's deflation of the conceit of the Byronic hero, and the poem as a whole certainly marks the end of Pushkin's "Byronic" period.

Pushkin's exile at Mikhailovskoe lasted slightly more than two years. When he first arrived at the estate in August 1824, his parents were there with his brother and sister, and initially the family reunion seemed happy enough. However, Pushkin's father agreed to help the local authorities keep watch on his wayward son by opening his letters. This situation ultimately precipitated a violent argument, in the wake of which the family departed for Petersburg, leaving Pushkin alone. His primary source of companionship was his old nanny, Arina Rodionovna, and the Osipov family living at the neighboring estate of Trigorskoe: "My isolation is complete—idleness is triumphant. I have few neighbors nearby. I am acquainted with only one family and I see them fairly seldom. I spend the whole day on horseback, and in the evening I listen to the fairy tales of my nanny, the original of Tatyana's nanny. I think you saw her once. She is my only girlfriend—and only

with her am I not bored."[21] He had at least one other "girlfriend," however: a niece of Praskovya Osipova, Anna Petrovna Kern, who arrived
for a visit at Trigorskoe in June 1825. Pushkin had met her briefly in
Petersburg in 1819, and her reappearance in his life was the occasion
for the writing of what is generally considered to be his greatest love
poem, "To —" ("I remember a wondrous moment"), inspired by the
memory of their first meeting.[22]

Relative isolation left Pushkin ample time for his writing, and during his stay at Mikhailovskoe he continued work on *Evgeny Onegin*
and wrote the comic poem *Count Nulin* and the historical drama *Boris
Godunov*. Both of the longer works Pushkin completed during his
Mikhailovskoe exile bear, in very different ways, the imprint of the
poet's reading of Shakespeare. *Count Nulin* is a travesty of *The Rape
of Lucrece*, in which the initial situation is turned upside down by the
comic outcome. Nulin, whose name is derived from the Russian word
for zero, is a modish young nobleman. While on his way to Petersburg,
his carriage breaks down and he seeks shelter at a provincial estate.
The mistress of the house, Natalya Pavlovna, a devotee of sentimental novels whose husband is away hunting, flirts with him over dinner,
but indignantly rebuffs his advances when he sneaks into her room
later the same night. The next day Natalya's husband returns, and the
chastened Nulin departs. True to the comic spirit of the poem, Pushkin
leaves the reader with sly hints that Nulin may, during the night, have
found consolation with Natalya's maid and that the apparently virtuous
Natalya may herself be having an affair with a neighbor.

Boris Godunov is closer in spirit to the Shakespearean historical
dramas that inspired its loose scenic structure and eschewal of melo-
drama. The play draws on the persistent belief that Boris Godunov—
who succeeded Tsar Fyodor, the last ruler in the Ryurik dynasty, and
ruled Russia from 1598 to 1605—was responsible for the death of the
likely successor to the throne, Ivan the Terrible's youngest son, Dmitry.
Pushkin portrays Godunov as a tragic figure haunted by his crimes.
His hold on power is threatened by social unrest and challenged by

21. A. S. Pushkin to D. M. Shvarts (draft), A. S. Pushkin, *Polnoe sobranie sochinenii v shesti tomakh* (Moscow: Khudozhestvennaya literatura, 1938), 6:91. Tatyana is
the heroine of *Evgeny Onegin*.

22. One subtext that may have been on Sinyavsky's mind in writing *Strolls with
Pushkin* is the discrepancy, which many have found disturbing over the years, between
the elevated diction of the poem and Pushkin's less than reverent reference to Anna Kern
as the "whore of Babylon" in a letter of May 1826.

the forces of the False Dmitry, supposedly a fugitive monk named Grigory Otrepev who claimed to be the tsarevich and did briefly succeed Godunov before himself being murdered in 1606.

Pushkin's exile at Mikhailovskoe caused him—fortunately, it would seem—to miss one of the most famous events in Russian history. In the wake of the death of Alexander I, on December 14, 1825, a group of disillusioned army officers, with little or no popular support, staged what came to be known as the Decembrist revolt on Senate Square in Petersburg. The rebellion, along with hopes for the institution of a constitutional monarchy in Russia, was immediately quashed, and those who took part in it were harshly punished. Five of the ringleaders were hanged, and the others were imprisoned or sent into exile. Several of the insurrectionists were close friends of Pushkin, most notably his lycée classmates Kyukhelbeker and Pushchin, and he was acquainted with a number of others, including, by some accounts, all five who were executed.[23] It was reported that poems by Pushkin were found among the papers of all of the arrested Decembrists, and Pushkin clearly had grounds for fearing that an attempt would be made to implicate him in the conspiracy. The investigation into the uprising eventually cleared the poet, however, or at least the new tsar, Nicholas I, decided that it would be politic to start his reign—clouded from the outset by rebellion—with a gesture of apparent tolerance. In the middle of the night of September 4, 1826, a special courier was sent to escort Pushkin to Pskov, whence he was sent on with a new escort to Moscow for a personal meeting with the tsar. One account, which purports to record Pushkin's own words, gives the high points of the meeting:

> They took me, all covered with dirt, into the office of the emperor, who said to me, "Hello, Pushkin, are you glad to be back?" I answered appropriately. The sovereign talked to me for a long time, then asked, "Pushkin would you have taken part in December 14, if you had been in Petersburg?"
>
> "Without question, sovereign, all my friends were in the conspiracy, and I could not not have taken part in it. Only my absence from Petersburg saved me, for which I thank God!"

23. Given the extent to which in the Soviet period the stories of the Decembrists and Pushkin have become intertwined, Soviet commentators have been ingenious in searching out ties between Pushkin and the Decembrists, on occasion perhaps stretching the evidence. What seems clear is that, whatever his personal and literary ties to the Decembrists, Pushkin was never taken into the conspirators' confidence, probably because he was not considered sufficiently cool-headed and discreet.

"You have played the fool long enough," the emperor retorted. "I hope that now you will be reasonable, and we will quarrel no longer. You will send me everything that you write; henceforth I will be your censor." [24]

This interview marked the end of Pushkin's exile. His apparent reconciliation with the new tsar and the tsar's offer to serve as his personal censor (freeing him from the ordinary censorship) seemed to promise a less constrained period in the poet's life. As it turned out, however, Pushkin was to find himself in an increasingly complicated and ultimately unbearable position of powerlessness and dependency on the tsar. This was in part because, as the poet soon learned, he was to deal with Nicholas not so much directly as through his chief of gendarmes, Aleksandr Benkendorf. Ultimately he found his ability to publish and his freedom of movement even more constricted than before by this arrangement. He was now required to show all of his works to the tsar through Benkendorf before he could submit them for publication, and he had to request, again through Benkendorf, permission before he traveled anywhere.

Throughout much of 1827 and 1828 the poet found himself under investigation by the Third Section (the tsarist secret police), which Benkendorf headed, for works he had written years before: the lyric poem "André Chenier" (circulated among Decembrist sympathizers under the title "December 14") and *The Gabrieliad*. After twice denying under interrogation his authorship of the latter poem, Pushkin only managed to put the matter to rest in October 1828 by writing a letter to Nicholas, the contents of which are unknown but in which he apparently admitted he had composed the poem and asked for clemency.

Pushkin's difficulties with the authorities along with the distractions of the capital, to which he was returning after so many years of exile, took their toll on his writing. Yet if these years were not among Pushkin's most productive, they did mark a significant shift in his literary concerns. *The Blackamoor of Peter the Great*, begun in 1827 and never completed, was Pushkin's first attempt at prose. The novel also evidenced Pushkin's growing interest in the epoch of Peter the Great and particularly in the figure of Peter himself, to whom Pushkin would return in his works again and again.[25] Peter the Great also appears as a

24. As reported by A. G. Khomutova, cited in Veresaev, *Pushkin v zhizni*, 1:314.
25. Pushkin is said to have worked on his unfinished *History of Peter the Great* on the morning of his fatal duel.

character briefly, but memorably, in the only major work that Pushkin completed during this period, *Poltava*. The text of *Poltava*, which is the longest of Pushkin's narrative poems, interweaves historical events and personal drama, playing out its central love intrigue against the background of Peter's victory over the Swedes at Poltava.

Shortly after his return from exile, Pushkin made his first marriage proposal to a distant relative, who turned him down. Another young woman Pushkin seriously considered marrying, Anna Olenina, recorded in her diary a description of the poet:

> Having given him a singular genius, God did not reward him with an attractive exterior. His face was expressive of course, but a certain malice and sarcasm eclipsed the intelligence that could be seen in his blue, or rather, glassy eyes. The Negro profile he inherited from his mother's line did not enhance his face. And add to that his terrible sidewhiskers, his disheveled hair, his nails long as claws, his short stature, his mincing manners, the insolent way he regarded the women whom he favored with his love, the strangeness of his natural and constrained disposition, and his unlimited vanity—these are all the *merits*, bodily and spiritual, that high society attributed to the Russian poet of the nineteenth century.
>
> People also said that he is a bad son, but it is impossible to know everything in family matters; that he is a dissolute man, but then all the young men of the time are almost the same.[26]

Appearance and morals aside, Pushkin was a less than desirable suitor despite his renown as a poet because of his reputation as a political scapegrace and his relatively meager and unstable income. Olenina later claimed that she did not marry Pushkin "because he had no position in society, and because he was poor."[27]

Pushkin first met the woman who ultimately did become his wife, Natalya Nikolaevna Goncharova, at a ball in December 1828. He became smitten with the sixteen-year-old beauty almost immediately and proposed in the late spring. Given his precarious financial and social position, Pushkin was pleased when he was put off rather than turned down. He left Moscow on May 1, 1829, to visit his brother, Lev, who was on active service with the Russian army in the Caucasus. On his way south Pushkin visited the retired general Aleksei Ermolov in Oryol, and

26. Anna Olenina, *Dnevnik Anny Alekseevny Oleninoi*, ed. Olga Oom (Paris, 1936), 10–11.

27. Cited in David Magarshack, *Pushkin: A Biography* (New York: Grove Press, 1969), 217.

then followed the Russian troops fighting the Turks under the command of General Ivan Paskevich into the Turkish town of Erzerum. Pushkin over and over requested permission from the tsar to travel abroad, always unsuccessfully, and this trip was the closest he ever came to leaving Russia. In his travel sketch *Journey to Erzerum* he described his first sight of the Turkish border: "To me the border had something mysterious about it; since childhood my fondest dream had been to travel. For a long time thereafter I led a nomadic life, wandering now to the south, now to the north, and I had not yet escaped from the boundaries of immense Russia. I gaily rode into the cherished river, and the kindly horse carried me to the Turkish bank. But that bank had already been taken; I was still in Russia."[28]

When Pushkin returned to Moscow, his suit was once again rebuffed by Goncharova's mother, who apparently hoped that her daughter could make a better match. By the spring of 1830, however, when no other suitors had materialized, Pushkin's proposal was accepted, and the engagement went forward, although negotiations between Pushkin and his future in-laws over finances kept the arrangement rocky almost up to the wedding.

In the midst of trying to reach an agreement with the relations of his dowerless bride, Pushkin left at the end of August for the family estate at Boldino. He had planned to stay there only a month, but a quarantine against a cholera epidemic kept him in the country until the beginning of December. This forced isolation resulted in one of the most productive periods of his career, and during this "first Boldino autumn" he completed *Evgeny Onegin* and all four of his "little tragedies," as well as writing *The Tales of Belkin* and some thirty short poems.

Evgeny Onegin, which Pushkin wrote over a period of eight years, is his signature work. The plot of the novel is flimsy. The title character is a young Petersburg dandy who goes to the country to tend to his dying rich uncle. While there, he becomes friendly with a sentimental young poet, Vladimir Lensky, who introduces him to the family of his fiancée, Olga Larina. Olga's sister, Tatyana, becomes infatuated with Onegin and writes him a letter confessing her feelings. Onegin responds coldly to Tatyana's naive outpouring of affection and in a fit of pique provokes Lensky's jealousy by flirting with Olga. The poet challenges Onegin to a duel and is killed. Sometime later Onegin again meets Tatyana, who

28. A. S. Pushkin, *Sobranie sochinenii* (Moscow: Khudozhestvennaya literatura, 1970), 8:241.

in the interim has married and become an elegant arbiter of Petersburg fashion. Now Onegin is lovestruck, but when he in his turn writes a letter to Tatyana professing his love, she spurns him, citing her wifely duty and reproaching him for his earlier insensitivity. The schematically symmetrical plot at times seems little more than an excuse for the "idle chatter" of Pushkin's garrulous narrator, who continually leaves the action hanging to hold forth on everything from the weather to metapoetics.

The virtuoso interplay of classically symmetrical plot and deceptively careless digressions finds its match in the intricate stanzaic form sustained throughout *Evgeny Onegin*. The structure and effect of this variant on the traditional sonnet, which was created by Pushkin and has come to be known as the Onegin stanza, was most memorably described by Vladimir Nabokov in his introduction to his translation of the poem. Nabokov compared the Onegin stanza to the "spin of a top," the "patterns" showing clearly in the opening lines, blurring during the "main spinning process" in the central lines, and reappearing with stunning effectiveness in the concluding couplet.[29]

The comic narrative poem, *The Little House at Kolomna*, shares with *Evgeny Onegin* such features as a talkative narrator and slim reliance on plot. The poem revolves coyly around the suggestive situation of a hussar who, disguised as a female cook, moves into the house where a maiden named Parasha lives with her mother. The mother, suspecting that their new servant plans to rob them while they are out, rushes home from church to find the "cook" shaving. Pushkin ends his poem with a "moral":

> It's dangerous to hire a cook for free;
> It is strange and futile for one who was born a man
> To dress up in a skirt;
> Sometime he will have to shave,
> Which is incompatible
> With a woman's nature . . . Nothing more
> Will you squeeze out of my story.[30]

In contrast, the dramatic scenes known as the "little tragedies" are masterpieces of verbal economy, concentrated explorations of extremes of human psychology. *The Covetous Knight* portrays the confrontation

29. A. S. Pushkin, *Eugene Onegin*, translated from the Russian with a commentary by Vladimir Nabokov (Princeton: Princeton University Press, 1973), 10.

30. Pushkin, *Sobranie sochinenii*, 4:341.

between a miserly baron, who hoards his riches and dreams of returning from the grave "like a watchful shade to sit on my trunk and guard my treasure from the living,"[31] and his resentful son. *Mozart and Salieri,* based on the rumor that Mozart was poisoned by the Italian composer Antonio Salieri out of jealousy, explores the proposition that genius and villainy are incompatible. *The Stone Guest,* the longest of the "little tragedies," is Pushkin's version of the Don Juan story. *Feast in Time of Plague* is a close translation of an excerpt from John Wilson's *The City of the Plague.* Pushkin's rendition, however, rises above the original, focusing the emotional intensity of the revels of the characters in the city ravaged by disease and death.

In the Belkin tales Pushkin again tried his hand at prose. The five short stories of the collection are attributed to "the late Ivan Petrovich Belkin," who is represented in the publisher's preface—playfully signed A. P.—as a provincial landowner who for "lack of imagination" recorded stories related to him by others. The five stories differ markedly from one another, ranging from fantasy and comic farce to muted pathos, and are only loosely bound together by narrative structure and recurring leitmotifs.

Pushkin at last married Natalya Goncharova on February 18, 1831. The marriage between the teenaged beauty and the poet had all the earmarks of a mismatch, and Pushkin himself seems to have had few illusions, as revealed in a letter he wrote shortly before the wedding:

> I am married—or almost. I have already thought over everything that you could say in defense of the bachelor life and against marriage. I have cold-bloodedly weighed the advantages and disadvantages of the state I have chosen. My youth passed tumultuously and fruitlessly. Up until now I have lived differently from the way people usually live. I have not been happy. *Il n'est de bonheur que dans les voies communes.* I am over thirty. At thirty people usually marry—I am acting as people do and will probably not regret it. Moreover, I am marrying without rapture, without juvenile infatuation. The future does not appear rosy to me, but in its complete nakedness. Sorrows will not surprise me: they are included in my domestic budget—Any joy will be unexpected.[32]

As it turned out, Pushkin's assessment was, if anything, overly optimistic. The marriage exacerbated problems in Pushkin's life that had predated it, most obviously the poet's increasingly complex relationship

31. A. S. Pushkin, *Sobranie sochinenii,* 4:146.
32. A. S. Pushkin to N. I. Krivtsov (February 10, 1831), *Pis'ma,* 3:12.

with the tsar. Goncharova's success in high society made her an asset in court circles, which is where Nicholas I was determined to keep her. To that end the tsar granted Pushkin a nominal post in the Ministry of Foreign Affairs, including a modest yearly salary and the right to work in archives. Then on the last day of 1833 Nicholas conferred on Pushkin the title of *Kammerjunker*, a position that made it possible for Goncharova to attend court functions with Pushkin as her escort. This "honor" was particularly irksome to the status-conscious poet, because the rank was generally granted to much younger men. Pushkin commented on the subject in his diary, perhaps with more moderation than he actually felt: "People ask me if I am satisfied to have been made a *Kammerjunker*. I am, because the sovereign intended to honor me, not to humiliate me." [33]

Although he received a salary and commanded extraordinary royalties for his writings by the standards of the time, Pushkin's income was far from sufficient to sustain the expenditures necessitated by his wife's social activities—not to mention his own gambling. His literary earnings were particularly unreliable since they depended not only on what he was able to write, but also on what the tsar and Benkendorf would allow him to publish. On occasion he was forced to go to Nicholas to plead for large loans from the state, which only deepened his galling dependency on the ruler. During the last years of the poet's life, the situation became so dire that Pushkin was periodically reduced to pawning family valuables. Twice he took serious measures to extricate himself from the worsening situation. In the summer of 1834, he requested official permission to resign his government post. Benkendorf communicated to him that his resignation would be accepted but he would lose access to the archives he needed for his historical research, so Pushkin withdrew his request. On June 1 of the next year, the poet made a final attempt to retire at least temporarily from the financially ruinous Petersburg social life. He wrote to Benkendorf: "I find myself in need of curtailing expenditures that only lead me into debt and are preparing for me a future of anxiety and worries, if not of destitution and despair. Three or four years of retirement in the country would make it possible for me to return to Petersburg and take up again the pursuits for which I am still indebted to the benevolence of His Majesty." [34] This time he was simply refused.

33. Pushkin, "Dnevnik," cited in Veresaev, *Pushkin v zhizni*, 2:191.
34. A. S. Pushkin to A. Kh. Benkendorf (July 1, 1835), A. S. Pushkin, *Polnoe sobranie sochinenii* (Izdatel'stvo Akademii nauk SSSR, 1949), 16:31.

The problems that dogged Pushkin's life after marriage emanated, at least in part, from the ambiguity of his position as a writer at a time when literary institutions were in a period of transition. The old system of court patronage, of which Pushkin's tortured relationship with Nicholas I may perhaps be seen as a vestige, was giving way to a new professionalism among writers and a new commercialism among publishers seeking to appeal to a growing readership. The ascendancy of the intimate salon culture of the "gentleman poets" was coming to an end as poetry ceded to prose as the dominant literary form. Though Pushkin may have been Russia's first "professional" writer—that is, the first writer to depend largely on the income derived from his literary works for his livelihood—he was also, ironically, the first victim of these changes. His contemporaries increasingly saw him as a literary dinosaur, an aristocrat, and already in the late 1820s his literary reputation began to decline. Thus, Vissarion Belinsky, who was to become Russia's most influential critic, wrote in his first large article in 1834: "Pushkin reigned for ten years: *Boris Godunov* was his last great feat; in the third part of the complete collection of his poems the sounds of his harmonious lyre have died away. Now we do not recognize Pushkin: he has died, or, perhaps, only lost consciousness for a time."[35]

Belinsky's report of the poet's death as a writer was premature—Pushkin wrote some of what were to become his most famous works in the last years of his life. But the poet was having an ever more difficult time writing. Even before his marriage he had developed a pattern of fleeing Petersburg for the country to write and had conceived an almost superstitious belief in autumn as the season when he was visited by intense bursts of creativity. As we have seen, however, it was becoming harder and harder for Pushkin to get away from Petersburg. Nonetheless in 1833 he received permission from the tsar to travel for the purpose of pursuing his historical research, and in September he visited the area of the Urals that had been the site of the Pugachov rebellion under Catherine the Great. Pugachov, a Don Cossack who claimed to be Catherine's dead husband, Peter III, had in the autumn of 1773 amassed a force of some thirty thousand of Russia's dispossessed and disenchanted and managed to capture a number of large cities before he was apprehended by government forces and executed. Pushkin traveled to the centers of the revolt, Orenburg and Kazan, as

---

35. V. G. Belinsky, *Izbrannye sochineniya* (Moscow: Gosudarstvennoe izdatel'stvo khudozhestvennoi literatury, 1949), 32.

well as to other towns, interviewing eyewitnesses to the insurrection. He then spent the month of October at Boldino, where he completed his *History of Pugachov* and wrote several poetic works, most notably *The Bronze Horseman.* This "second Boldino autumn" was to be the last of Pushkin's productive periods. An attempt to seek inspiration yet again at Boldino the following year ended in failure, and he was never to find another chance to return there to write.

The Bronze Horseman is considered by many to be Pushkin's masterpiece. It relates the story of a petty clerk named Evgeny whose fiancée, Parasha, dies during the Petersburg flood of 1824. Evgeny's mind is unhinged by the incident and he wanders the city in a daze for a year. One night, when the foul weather recalls the flood, he finds himself on the square where the Bronze Horseman, the famous Falconet statue of Peter the Great on a rearing horse, stands. Blaming his misfortunes on Peter, who founded the city, Evgeny confronts the statue, which comes alive and chases the poor man through the streets of Petersburg. The poem ends with Evgeny lying dead on the ruins of Parasha's house. *The Bronze Horseman* occupies a central place among Pushkin's works and in the Russian literary tradition not only because of the brilliance of its poetry. It gave literary form to fundamental tensions of Russian culture, most notably the drama of confrontation between the individual and the state. Because of the tsar's objections, the poem could not be published in Pushkin's lifetime and in fact did not appear in print in its original form until the twentieth century.

"The Queen of Spades" was also, most likely, a product of the second Boldino autumn. In the story (which differs significantly from Tchaikovsky's opera) the central character, a russified German named Hermann, learns that an elderly countess holds the secret to three successive winning cards. When the countess refuses to divulge it, Hermann threatens her with a revolver, and she dies of fright. Several days later, she appears to him in a dream and tells him to play the three, the seven, and the ace. Hermann wins with the three and the seven, but when he plays the ace, the queen of spades is dealt to him instead. On the card, in place of the queen of spades, he sees the face of the old countess and goes mad.

Perhaps the brightest moment in the waning years of Pushkin's life came when in January 1836 the poet was granted permission to publish a quarterly journal, the *Contemporary.* For almost a decade Pushkin had nursed the desire to edit his own periodical but had been repeatedly refused permission. The *Contemporary* was unquestionably the finest literary periodical of its day, printing works by virtually every major Russian writer of the time. Among his own works that appeared in the *Contemporary*, Pushkin published his only completed prose novel, *The Captain's Daughter*. It is a fictionalized account of the Pugachov rebellion, centering around the narrator, a young officer named Grinyov, who meets Pugachov when the rebel leader is nothing more than a drunken tramp, and gives him a rabbitskin coat. This act of charity later prompts Pugachov, after his forces have seized the garrison in which Grinyov is serving, to spare his former benefactor's life. In the manner of Sir Walter Scott, historical events and personages—including Catherine the Great in house dress—are interwoven with the tale of Grinyov's life and love for the daughter of his superior officer. Despite the high literary quality of this and other works published in the *Contemporary*, the journal was not a commercial success (although it was to survive its founder by many decades) and did nothing to ease Pushkin's financial distress.

By 1836 Pushkin's situation was becoming intolerable. Aside from his mounting debts, his problems with Benkendorf and the tsar, and his waning literary fortunes, rumors had begun to circulate about the flirtation between his wife and a young cavalry officer, Georges d'Anthès, a French emigre and the adopted son of the Dutch ambassador, Baron van Heeckeren. Early in November Pushkin received, through unsuspecting friends, copies of an anonymous letter hinting transparently at a liaison between the poet's wife and the tsar. Either because he thought van Heeckeren was responsible for the letter or because he could not get at the tsar, Pushkin responded by challenging d'Anthès to a duel. Only after tense negotiations and an agreement that the Frenchman would marry Pushkin's sister-in-law, Ekaterina Goncharova, was the poet persuaded to back down. D'Anthès and Goncharova were wed on January 10, 1837, but it became clear soon enough that marriage was insufficient to restrain d'Anthès from public demonstrations of his attraction to his sister-in-law. Pushkin sent van Heeckeren a letter so insulting that it left d'Anthès no alternative but to issue a challenge, and the duel took place the next day, January 27. D'Anthès shot first, mortally wounding Pushkin, but the poet still managed to get off a shot. He hit his opponent but, as it turned out, the wound was not serious.

Pushkin died two days later in his apartment on the Moika Canal in Petersburg. One commentator, perhaps somewhat hyperbolically, marked an immediate change in public opinion about Pushkin: "All of

Petersburg began to talk about Pushkin's death, and the unfavorable opinion of him was immediately replaced by the most sincere enthusiasm: everyone turned to the bookshops—to buy the new miniature edition of *Onegin* that had just come out: more than two thousand copies were sold in three days."[36]

Pushkin's death prompted an unexpected public outpouring of emotion and served as a focus for the manifestation of deep-seated cultural rifts and allegiances. News of the poet's demise drew crowds of people to pay their final respects. A Prussian envoy even reported to his government that "as many as fifty thousand persons of all estates" viewed the body while it still lay in the Pushkin home.[37] Though that figure is most likely exaggerated, the mood of the public gave the authorities cause for concern, and measures were taken to prevent the situation from turning into an "indecent tableau of triumph of the liberals."[38] The body was carried out of Pushkin's home under police escort at midnight on the night of January 30–31 and taken to the Equerry's Church instead of St. Isaac's Cathedral, where the funeral was supposed to have been held. Despite the change of venue, there were crowds again in the church and on the square outside during the funeral on February 1. The emotional pitch of some of the mourners seems to have given rise to less than decorous behavior: "Respect for the memory of the poet in the huge crowds of common people, who were at his funeral service at the Equerry's Church, was so great that all the flaps of Pushkin's frock coat were torn to shreds, and he was left lying in little more than his jacket; his sidewhiskers and the hair on his head were carefully cut off by his lady admirers."[39] Pushkin's body was spirited out of Petersburg, again by the police in the middle

---

36. N. I. Ivanitsky, "Vospominaniya," cited in Veresaev, *Pushkin v zhizni*, 2:434.

37. Liberman, cited in Veresaev, *Pushkin v zhizni*, 2:451.

38. "Otchet o deistviyakh korpusa zhandarmov za 1837 god," cited in Veresaev, *Pushkin v zhizni*, 2:451. There seems to be evidence of popular anger among the lower classes against foreigners in general. One testimony rather eerily foreshadows the (Soviet) future: "The whole population of Petersburg, and especially the rabble and lumpen, were agitated, as if in convulsions, passionately desiring to take revenge on d'Anthès. No one, from small to great, wanted to agree that d'Anthès was not a murderer. They wanted to make short work even of the surgeons who had treated Pushkin, trying to prove that there was conspiracy and treachery here, that one foreigner had wounded Pushkin and other foreigners had been entrusted with the task of treating him." Stanislav Moravsky, "Vospominaniya," cited in Veresaev, *Pushkin v zhizni*, 2:436.

39. M. I. Semevsky, "K biografii Pushkina," cited in Veresaev, *Pushkin v zhizni*, 2:447.

of the night, and buried quietly with none of the poet's family and only a handful of his friends in attendance, at the Svyatogorsk Monastery near Mikhailovskoe on February 5.

The authorities also felt it prudent to keep a tight rein on newspaper accounts of the poet's death, and at least two papers were chastised for running brief notices acknowledging the poet's importance. The following obituary ran surrounded by a black border in the *Literary Supplement to the Russian Invalid:*

> The sun of our poetry has set! Pushkin has passed away, passed away in the flower of years, in the middle of his great pursuit! . . . We have no strength to say any more about this, and it is not necessary; every Russian heart knows the whole cost of this irreparable loss and every Russian heart will be torn to pieces. Pushkin! Our poet! Our joy, our national glory! . . . Can it really be that we no longer have Pushkin! It is impossible to become accustomed to this thought![40]

The editor of the newspaper, Andrei Kraevsky, was called before the president of the censorship committee, who had been delegated to convey to him the displeasure of Sergei Uvarov, the minister of education:

> Why is there a black border around the news of the death of a person who held no rank, who occupied no position in the state service? But that is nothing! What expressions! "The sun of poetry!!" Good gracious, such honor for what? "Pushkin passed away . . . in the middle of his great pursuit!" What pursuit? Sergei Semyonovich [Uvarov] precisely remarked: was Pushkin a general, a military leader, a minister, a statesman?! Finally, he died at almost forty! Writing verses does not mean, as Sergei Semyonovich expressed it, engaging in a great pursuit![41]

Ironically, the figure of Pushkin, fetishized in the collective memory, would ultimately overshadow "military leaders" and "statesmen" as a cultural hero for the Russian nation, putting down deep roots in the Russian consciousness and surviving the collapse of ruler cults and political systems.

It would be difficult to overestimate the spate and significance of the myriad associations that have accrued to the figure of Pushkin in

40. Cited in Veresaev, *Pushkin v zhizni*, 2:442.
41. Ibid., 2:443.

the culture of his native land during the century and a half since his death. Pushkin has served as a touchstone for definitions of national identity and of the function of literature in society and has been co-opted by virtually every ideology or faction that has had any voice in Russian and Soviet political, intellectual, or artistic life.[42]

The basic terms of the Pushkin myth were set during the poet's life-time and in the years immediately following his death. Nikolai Gogol was among the first to herald Pushkin as Russia's "national poet," in his 1834 article "Some Words About Pushkin." The essay begins:

> Pushkin's name immediately calls to mind the thought of a Russian national poet. In fact, none of our poets is superior to him or could be called more national; this right decisively belongs to him. In his works, as if in a dictionary, are contained all the wealth, strength, and flexibility of our language. More and farther than anyone else, he extended its boundaries and revealed its full expanse. Pushkin is an extraordinary phenomenon and perhaps the only manifestation of the Russian spirit; this is the Russian in his development, as he perhaps will appear in two hundred years. In him the Russian nature, the Russian soul, the Russian language, the Russian character are reflected

42. A number of American Slavists have done important work on the historical de-velopment of the Pushkin cult, and this introduction is greatly indebted to their labors. Readers who would like to learn more about the subject might explore the following works: Marcus C. Levitt's thoroughly researched and sharply reasoned study of the Push-kin celebration of 1880, which also briefly covers the later evolution of the Pushkin myth, *Russian Literary Politics and the Pushkin Celebration of 1880* (Ithaca, N.Y.: Cornell University Press, 1989); the anthology *Cultural Myths of Russian Modernism: From the Golden Age to the Silver Age*, ed. Boris Gasparov, Robert P. Hughes, and Irina Paperno (Berkeley and Los Angeles: University of California Press, 1992), which contains an ex-cellent selection of articles by leading scholars on Pushkin during the Symbolist period; Paul Debreczeny's thought-provoking reading of the history and role of the Pushkin cult to the present, "*Zhitie Aleksandra Boldinskogo:* Pushkin's Elevation to Sainthood in Soviet Culture," *South Atlantic Quarterly* 90, no. 2 (Spring 1991): 269–92; Victor Terras's interesting remarks on the vision of Pushkin as Russia's national poet, "Some Observa-tions on Pushkin's Image in Russian Literature," *Russian Literature* 14 (1983): 296–316; and Jeffrey Brooks's seminal studies on the history of literacy in Russia: "Russian Nation-alism and Russian Literature: The Canonization of the Classics," *Nation and Ideology: Essays in Honor of Wayne S. Vucinich*, ed. Ivo Banac, John G. Ackerman, and Roman Szporluk (New York: Columbia University Press, 1981), 315–34; "Readers and Reading at the End of the Tsarist Era," *Literature and Society in Imperial Russia, 1800–1914*, ed. William Mills Todd III (Stanford, Calif.: Stanford University Press, 1978), 150; and *When Russia Learned to Read: Literacy and Popular Literature, 1861–1917* (Princeton: Prince-ton University Press, 1985). I would also like to express my gratitude to Carol Ueland for helping out as always and allowing me to use the draft of her dissertation on Pushkin and the Symbolists.

with the same purity, the same purified beauty in which a landscape
is reflected on the convex surface of an optical glass.

His very life is absolutely Russian.[43]

Pushkin—both in his works and in his life—becomes the quintessen-
tial expression of Russianness, an apex of development that the average
Russian will not reach until far in the future. Gogol maintains that
even in the early works—many of which are set among non-Russian
peoples—Pushkin is "Russian," for he serves as the "voice" of the Russian people: "He was from the very beginning national, because true
nationality consists not in the description of sarafans but in the very
spirit of the people. A poet can be national even when he is describing a
completely foreign world, but looks at it through the eyes of his national
element, with the eyes of the whole people, when he feels and speaks
in such a way that it seems to his fellow countrymen as if they were
feeling and saying it themselves."[44] Gogol's insistence that Pushkin,
as an expression of the national spirit, can even appropriate the foreign, and his equation of Pushkin with a Russianness that transcends
social and economic divisions, ultimately became the cornerstone of
the Pushkin myth.

Pushkin's premature death added a new and compelling dimen-
sion to the premises of the myth outlined by Gogol. The circumstances
surrounding the duel and its fatal outcome were tailor-made to unleash the mythopoeic forces latent in Russian culture, and they have
continued to exercise the Russian imagination—sometimes, it seems,
more than Pushkin's poems themselves have—in the century and a
half that has elapsed since the event.

Aside from the popular response to the poet's death—the crowds
that flocked to pay their last respects and buy up the poet's works—
there came poetic responses as well. Virtually every prominent poet of
the day produced verses on the significance of Pushkin's demise. The
most famous of these poems—and the poetic interpretation that most
immediately grabbed the educated public's imagination—was Mikhail
Lermontov's "Death of a Poet," copies of which circulated in Petersburg in the days following Pushkin's death. In it Lermontov portrays

43. N. V. Gogol, "Neskol'ko slov o Pushkine," *Sobranie sochinenii v semi tomakh*
(Moscow: Khudozhestvennaya literatura, 1967), 6:68. Gogol published this article in the
same year that Belinsky pronounced Pushkin "dead." Perhaps it is not without founda-
tion to suggest that for any writer, being dead, whether literally or metaphorically, may
be a necessary condition for canonization.

44. Ibid., 70.

Pushkin as a victim of high society intrigue and makes the most of d'Anthès' foreign origin:

> From afar
> Like hundreds of refugees,
> In pursuit of fortune and status
> He was tossed here by the will of fate;
> Laughing, he boldly scorned
> The language and customs of a foreign country;
> He could not spare us our glory;
> He could not understand in that bloody moment
> What he had raised his hand against![45]

The presumed alliance between d'Anthès and the court of Nicholas casts Pushkin's death as a mythic conflict between "us" and "them," between Russia's glory and the menacing otherness of the European-ized upper classes. By the same token Lermontov and other poets who wrote poems commemorating Pushkin's death drew on hagiographic motifs to portray the poet as an innocent victim who went willingly to his death as a blood sacrifice to purge Russia's ills, thereby endowing Pushkin with an aura of religious martyrdom.[46]

"Death of a Poet" catapulted Lermontov from relative obscurity to notoriety, marking him as Pushkin's successor.[47] Henceforth virtu-ally every major Russian writer and literary critic would have to define himself in relation to Pushkin. Even Gogol, in his "Author's Confes-sion," written shortly before his death in 1852, pointed to Pushkin's encouragement of his literary career to validate his calling as a writer: "Perhaps, with the years and with the need to amuse myself this exu-

45. M. Yu. Lermontov, "Smert' poeta," in *Venok Pushkinu* (Moscow: Sovetskaya Rossiya, 1974), 31. This anthology, which tellingly opens with Pushkin's own "Monu-ment" poem, gives a good, although by no means exhaustive, sampling of poetry dedi-cated to Pushkin from his days at the lycée to the time of the book's publication. The collection contains a number of other poems commemorating—and interpreting—Push-kin's death, most notably Fyodor Tyutchev's "January 29, 1837," in which the poet equates d'Anthès with a royal assassin. Tyutchev's poem ends with lines that might be counted among the clichés of Pushkin lore: "You, like a first love,/Russia's heart will never forget." *Venok Pushkiny*, 40.

46. This argument is developed in Debreczeny, "*Zhitie Aleksandra Boldinskogo.*" Jeffrey Brooks argues in "Russian Nationalism and Russian Literature" (pp. 327–28) that the biographies of Pushkin and other Russian "classics" at the end of the nineteenth and the beginning of the twentieth centuries were cast in the mold of saints' lives to appeal to less-educated readers, who were more familiar with the conventions of the religious texts.

47. Lermontov would himself die in a duel only four years later.

berance would have disappeared and with it my writing career. But
Pushkin forced me to look at the business seriously. . . . He gave me his
own plot, out of which he wanted to make something on the order of a
long poem and which, he claimed, he would not have given to anyone
else. This was the plot of *Dead Souls*. (The idea for *The Inspector General* also belongs to him.)"[48] Pushkin had become the founding father
of the dynastic line of Russian literature from which, ultimately, future
writers and even literary traditions would draw their legitimacy.

Though all of the attributes of the Pushkin cult can be traced back
to the time of the poet's life and death, it was only much later in
the century that a forum for the myth capable of capturing the popular consciousness would be found. A massive retrospective in eleven
articles written by Belinsky between 1843 and 1846 reflects a certain
ambivalence about Pushkin's stature that was perhaps inevitable so
close upon the poet's death. Belinsky here modified his earlier view
and recognized Pushkin's greatness as an artist and the significance of
his historical role: "Pushkin's vocation was to be the first poet-artist of
Russia, to give it poetry as art."[49] Yet he was reluctant to follow Gogol
in conferring on Pushkin the status of national poet on a par with other
great writers of the world, arguing that Russia had not reached a level
of development where it could produce a writer of the first rank. In
the course of his argument Belinsky originated much of the stock in
trade of later Pushkin studies, including the claim that *Evgeny Onegin*
was a "picture that was true to the reality of Russian society in a certain epoch."[50] But this strength, the faithful depiction of reality, was
also the work's weakness, Belinsky maintained, for *Evgeny Onegin* had
already been bypassed by Russian society and appeared dated. By the
same token, while concluding his series of articles with the affirmation
that Pushkin would in the future be considered a "classic" in Russia,
Belinsky essentially relegated him to the past.

It was not until a new edition of Pushkin's works began to appear
in 1855—coincidentally, upon the death of Nicholas I and the end of
his repressive reign—that Pushkin's achievement and heritage were
seriously reconsidered. The ensuing debate, which continued for ten
years, pitted the "radical" critics, who claimed to be direct heirs of the
Belinskian tradition of socially committed criticism, against a varied
group of critics lumped together under the somewhat inaccurate label

48. Gogol, *Sobranie sochinenii*, 6:442.
49. Belinsky, "Stat'ya pyataya," *Izbrannye sochineniya*, 571.
50. Belinsky, "Stat'ya vos'maya," *Izbrannye sochineniya*, 635.

"aesthetes." In this polemic Pushkin was to some extent a pawn in a larger debate about the role of literature in society. While the aesthetes attempted to rehabilitate Pushkin's literary reputation by adopting him as a champion of the independence of art from political demands, their opponents countered with a utilitarian view of literature that subordinated art to social conscience and even questioned the value of art in society. The most extreme of Pushkin's detractors, the "nihilist" critic Dmitry Pisarev, claimed that Pushkin was no more than a "parody of a poet," whose place "is not on the writing desk of a contemporary worker, but in the dusty study of an antique collector, next to the rusty armor and broken harquebuses." Pisarev scathingly dismissed *Evgeny Onegin* as "nothing other than a vivid and brilliant apotheosis of the dreariest and most senseless status quo,"[51] to be swept aside to make way for a better Russia. For a time Pisarev seemed to have the final word, and once again discussion of Pushkin receded from the center-stage of cultural debate.

The turning point for Pushkin as a cultural icon came in 1880 with the unveiling of the now-famous statue of Pushkin by the sculptor A. M. Opekushin on one of Moscow's central streets.[52] The subscription drive to raise the funds for the statue—the first monument to a literary figure to be placed in a prominent location in any Russian city—dragged on for some two decades; the ceremonies surrounding the unveiling, perhaps the most ambitious private cultural enterprise ever undertaken in tsarist Russia, seemed at risk of falling apart almost until the last minute. But when the festivities did in fact come off, the response from the public and the popular press was beyond anything that could have been expected. The high point of the events was not the unveiling ceremony itself but the speech in honor of Pushkin delivered by Dostoevsky on the final day of the proceedings.[53] Dostoevsky, setting

51. D. I. Pisarev, "Realisty," *Sochineniya D. I. Pisareva: Polnoe sobranie v shesti tomakh* (St. Petersburg, 1894), 4:113. D. I. Pisarev, "Pushkin i Belinsky," *Sochineniya v chetyrekh tomakh* (Moscow: Gosudarstvennoe izdatel'stvo khudozhestvennoi literatury, 1956), 3:414, 357.

52. For the details of the Pushkin jubilee, see Levitt, *Russian Literary Politics*. The Pushkin monument was originally erected on Tverskoi Boulevard across the street from the Strastnoi Monastery. In 1931 the site on which the statue stood was renamed Pushkin Square, and shortly thereafter the monastery was demolished and the square made larger. In 1950, the statue of Pushkin was moved across Gorky (Tverskaya) Street to its present site on the enlarged Pushkin Square.

53. For an excellent and thorough discussion of Dostoevsky's Pushkin speech, see Levitt, *Russian Literary Politics*, 122–46. The chapter is appropriately titled "Dostoevsky 'Hijacks' the Celebration."

off from the vision of Pushkin outlined in Gogol's 1834 remarks,[54] went on to place him not on a par with but actually above the other great writers of the world:

> No, I state categorically that never has there been a poet with such a universal responsiveness as Pushkin. It is not only a matter of his responsiveness but also of its amazing depth, the reincarnation in his spirit of the spirit of foreign peoples, a reincarnation that is almost total and is therefore miraculous. Never has this phenomenon been repeated in any poet in the whole world. This we find in Pushkin alone, and in this sense, I repeat, he is a unique and unprecedented phenomenon, and, as far as we are concerned, a prophetic one . . . for it is precisely in this that his national, Russian strength was most fully expressed, in the national spirit of his poetry, the national spirit in its future development, the national spirit of our future, which is already concealed in the present and is expressed prophetically. For what is the strength of the Russian national spirit if not its striving, in its ultimate goals, for universality and common humanity? Having become fully a national poet, Pushkin immediately, as soon as he came in contact with the strength of the people, began to sense their great future vocation. In this he was a diviner and a prophet.[55]

It is therefore precisely Pushkin's ability to reincarnate himself in other nationalities that becomes a gauge of his Russianness, for the Russian spirit is defined by its aspiration toward universality: "To become a true Russian, to become completely Russian, perhaps, means only . . . to become a brother to all people, to become a *universal man*, if you will."[56] This conception of Russianness, of which Pushkin becomes a prophetic emblem, defines Russia's messianic mission in European history, which is "to strive to reconcile European conflicts once and for all, to show the way out of European ennui in our universally human and unifying Russian soul, to find room in it with brotherly love for all our brothers, and finally, perhaps, to utter the ultimate word of great, universal harmony, of ultimate brotherly accord between all tribes according to the law of Christ's Gospel!"[57]

54. Dostoevsky in fact opened with a quotation from Gogol's "Some Words About Pushkin."

55. F. M. Dostoevsky, "Pushkin (Ocherk)," *Polnoe sobranie sochinenii* (Leningrad: Nauka, 1984), 26:146–47.

56. Ibid., 147.

57. Ibid., 148.

In the ecstatic rhetoric of Dostoevsky's Pushkin speech all the elements of the Pushkin myth finally come together in an affirmation, legitimized by Pushkin, of the Russian nation's superiority to other nations. The wild enthusiasm with which Dostoevsky's words were greeted—especially as compared to the relatively subdued response to Turgenev's more measured and highbrow speech the preceding day—suggests that Dostoevsky was the first to tap the full potential of Pushkin as a cultural icon. By the 1899 centenary celebration of Pushkin's birth, both the tsarist government and the growing commercial sector of Russian society had recognized the value of Pushkin's name.[58] The authorities mobilized the vast bureaucratic structures at their disposal to take Pushkin—or at least a carefully orchestrated official version of Pushkin—to "virtually every corner of the empire."[59] The Pushkin of 1899 was, hardly surprisingly, presented as an apologist for autocracy and an obedient subject of the tsar, his biography sanitized and his works carefully screened for those that were most appropriate for presentation to "the masses." Copies of Pushkin's works as well as candy bars with Pushkin's image imprinted on them were passed out to schoolchildren, and enterprising businessmen produced "a spate of Pushkin products, which included Pushkin cigarettes, tobacco, rolling papers, matches, candy, steel pens, stationery, ink stands, liqueur, knives, watches, vases, cups, shoes, dresses, lamps, fans, perfume ("Bouquet Pouchkine"), a variety of portraits and postcards, plus a board game ("Pushkin's Duel," which was roundly criticized in the press as being in thoroughly bad taste)."[60]

The co-opting of Pushkin by the government and the growing mass readership did not sit well with the intelligentsia. Whereas representatives of the literary elite had dominated the 1880 Pushkin celebration—termed a "holiday of the Russian intelligentsia"—not a single major writer agreed to participate in the 1899 festivities. The "vulgarization" of Pushkin prompted a countermovement to reclaim him by the literary avant-garde, at the time under the sway of Symbolism. This trend gave a tremendous impetus to serious Pushkin scholarship, and some of the major poets of the Symbolist movement, notably Valery Bryusov, contributed textological studies that recovered some of Push-

58. For details of the 1899 celebration, see Marcus C. Levitt, "Pushkin in 1899," in *Cultural Mythologies of Russian Modernism*, 183–204.
    59. Ibid., 185.
    60. Ibid., 192–193.

kin's most significant works from the distortions perpetrated on them by the censorship and by well-meaning friends of the poet who posthumously "cleaned up" his works to get them into print. At the same time, the Symbolists responded to the "massification" and "politicization" of Pushkin by attempting to mold him to their own vision of the artistic process. Certainly, it was nothing new for literary (and literary *cum* political) critics to use Pushkin as a symbolic touchstone for their own theories of art (or of the derivative or secondary nature of art in society). A new development, however, was the impulse for writers, especially poets, to define themselves by creating personalized Pushkins—"my Pushkin"[61]—and to incorporate echoes of Pushkin's poetry and poetics as a sort of esoteric code into their own aggressively high-culture works unapologetically aimed at a narrow, intimate, exceptionally well educated audience of poet-readers. This diversification of Pushkin reflected the diversification of Russian culture itself as well as the appearance of competing claims for the powerful force of legitimization that had become embodied in the Pushkin myth.

At the end of the first decade of the twentieth century, the Russian Futurists, simultaneously challenging the Symbolists' hegemony over high culture and the official canonization of the nineteenth-century classics, launched an attack that was reminiscent of Pisarev's nihilist condemnation of Pushkin a half century before. In their 1912 manifesto, "A Slap in the Face of Public Taste," the Futurists rejected the Russian classical heritage as outmoded: "The past is constricting. The Academy and Pushkin are more incomprehensible than hieroglyphs. Throw Pushkin, Dostoevsky, Tolstoy, and etc. and etc. from the Steamship of contemporaneity." They demanded that the right of the poet "to an insurmountable hatred for all language that existed before him" be respected.[62] This radical repudiation of the culture of the past was a harbinger of the power struggle over how to define the newly emerging Soviet culture in relation to the past—and who was to define it—that shaped Bolshevik cultural policy during the first two decades after the Revolution.

In the wake of the Revolution the central terms of the debate over culture were redefined to focus on the issue of the creation of a proletarian culture. Should a distinctly proletarian culture be encouraged to develop and, if so, should it build on the cultural achievements of

61. The title, for example, of works by Bryusov and Marina Tsvetaeva.
62. D. Burlyuk, N. Burlyuk, A. Kruchyonykh, V. Kandinsky, B. Livshits, V. Mayakovsky, V. Khlebnikov, *Poshchyochina obshchestvennomu vkusu* (Moscow, 1912).

the past? In this struggle between "iconoclasts" and "preservers"[63] the Futurists, with the flamboyant Vladimir Mayakovsky in the lead, continued to be the most raucous spokesmen for the need to jettison the past and begin anew. At the other end of the spectrum, Bolshevik political leaders—Lenin first and foremost—tended to be more conservative in their tastes and inclined to mobilize prerevolutionary high culture as a source of legitimacy for the newly emerging Soviet culture.

In this context, the seemingly anomalous celebration of the eighty-fourth anniversary of Pushkin's death held on February 14, 1921, at the House of Writers in Petrograd stands out as a particularly poignant moment.[64] In his remarks on that occasion, the poet Vladislav Khodasevich clearly defined this off-year celebration of the poet's death as a sorrowful farewell to the old world of the Russian intelligentsia and its culture as embodied in Pushkin: "The former Russia, and therefore Pushkin's Russia, immediately and sharply moved away from us by an immeasurably greater distance than it would have moved away from us during the same period given an evolutionary movement of events. The Petrine and Petersburg period in Russian history has ended; no matter what stands ahead—the old will not return. A return is unthinkable both historically and psychologically."[65] Khodasevich went on to foresee the coming of a second "eclipse of the Pushkinian sun"[66] (the first having been during the era of Pisarev) and concluded his speech on a note of dark foreboding:

> That heightened interest in the poet that many have sensed in recent years arose, perhaps, out of a premonition, out of a pressing need: in part—to make sense of Pushkin before it was too late, before the link with his time was lost completely, in part—as a passionate desire to feel his nearness one more time, because we are living through the last hours of this nearness before parting. And our desire to make the day of Pushkin's death a day of universal celebration, partly, it seems to me, is prompted by this same premonition: we are coming to an agreement about by what name we are to hail one another in the darkness that is falling on us.[67]

63. These terms are from Richard Stites, *Revolutionary Dreams: Utopian Vision and Experimental Life in the Russian Revolution* (Oxford: Oxford University Press, 1989).
64. For a more thorough account, see Robert P. Hughes, "Pushkin in Petrograd, February 1921," in *Cultural Mythologies of Russian Modernism*, 204–13.
65. Vladislav Khodasevich, "Koleblemyi trenozhnik," *Sobranie sochinenii*, ed. John Malmstad and Robert P. Hughes (Ann Arbor: Ardis, 1990), 2:312.
66. Ibid., 2:313.
67. Ibid., 2:316.

Even as he symbolically bid farewell, Khodasevich suggested—prophetically, as it turned out—that Pushkin would remain a rallying point for the values of the intelligentsia in the years ahead.

Yet if it fell to Khodasevich on this occasion to pronounce the last rites over the prerevolutionary intelligentsia, it was Aleksandr Blok— cast by many of his contemporaries as the true heir to Pushkin's legacy —who spoke "on the calling of the poet" (as the speech was titled). Yet despite the ostensibly abstract nature of his speech, Blok's remarks, no less than Khodasevich's, used Pushkin to address the realities of his own time. Blok began by contrasting Pushkin to those who wield political and military power:

> Our memory preserves from infancy the cheerful name: Pushkin. This name, this sound fills up many days of our lives. The gloomy names of emperors, generals, inventors of weapons of murder, the torturers and martyrs of life. And next to them—this light name: Pushkin.
>
> Pushkin was able to carry his creative burden lightly and cheerfully despite the fact that the role of the poet is neither light nor cheerful; it is tragic.[68]

Blok argued that the poet's role was to bring harmony into the world out of the elemental chaos of being. He maintained that the internal part of the poet's labor could not be hindered by the outside world, but the final phase, when the poet's creations enter the world, put the poet at the mercy of the "rabble" (drawing his terms from Pushkin's 1828 lyric poem "The Poet and the Crowd"), "for whom a stove pot is more valuable than a god." Blok was careful to point out that the "rabble" were not the "common people" but "the court aristocracy, of which nothing remained in place of a soul except titles of nobility; but already before Pushkin's eyes the place of the hereditary aristocracy was rapidly being occupied by the bureaucracy. These clerks are our rabble as well."[69] Laying the guilt for Pushkin's tragic end squarely on the bureaucracy and censorship, Blok delivered a dark warning to the forces ranged against culture in the young Bolshevik state: "And it was not d'Anthès's bullet that killed Pushkin. He was killed by the absence of air. His culture died with him."[70] By a strange twist of fate,

68. Aleksandr Blok, "O naznachenii poeta," *Sobranie sochinenii v vos'mi tomakh*, ed. V. N. Orlov, A. A. Surkov, and K. I. Chukovsky (Moscow-Leningrad: Gosudarstvennoe izdatel'stvo khudozhestvennoi literatury, 1962), 6:160.

69. Ibid., 164.

70. Ibid., 167.

Blok, like Dostoevsky before him, survived his Pushkin speech by only a matter of months. As his last major public statement before his death and in the light of events to come, his remarks all the more profoundly entered the realm of the myth of the poet surrounding Pushkin as an epitaph to the spirit of the prerevolutionary intelligentsia.

This nostalgic and apprehensive gathering of intellectuals in Petrograd in 1921 stands in grim contrast to the 1937 jubilee marking the one hundred and fiftieth anniversary of Pushkin's death, which was the first major official commemoration of a Pushkin anniversary in the Soviet period. Symbolically, the year-long festivities consecrated the victory of conservative forces over iconoclasts in Soviet culture through a ritual recanonization of Pushkin as the founder of the dynastic line of Russian classical literature that had now been rechristened the line of succession leading directly to Soviet culture. There was a macabre irony in that these extravagant celebrations of Pushkin's death took place at the height of the Stalin purges, a coincidence that was rather too appropriately marked by the unveiling of a monument to the poet on February 8, the anniversary of Pushkin's duel with d'Anthès, in Leningrad on the site of that fatal confrontation.

The jubilee was an inverted mirror image of the 1899 tsarist celebration of the poet's birth, with the elements of the already well defined Pushkin mythology amplified and redefined to conform to the ideological exigencies of the Soviet period. An editorial entitled "Glory of the Russian People," which ran on the front page of *Pravda* on February 10, 1937, reads like a litany of the basic lineaments of the Soviet Pushkin cult. It opens with an invocation of the version of Pushkin's death that, harking back to Lermontov, would remain standard for the Soviet period: "A hundred years have passed since the greatest Russian poet, Aleksandr Sergeevich Pushkin, was shot by the hand of a foreign aristocratic scoundrel, a hireling of tsarism."[71] However, the article goes on to say, Pushkin lives on, and his immortal heritage—along with the cultural empowerment it entails—has now passed to the Soviet people: "Pushkin is completely ours, Soviet, for the Soviet power inherited everything that is best in our people, and it itself is the embodiment of the best aspirations of the people. . . . In the final analysis Pushkin's creation merged with the October socialist revolution as a river flows into the ocean." Pushkin, as the voice of his people, is now recast as an agent for bringing literacy to the masses—"Hundreds

71. "Slava russkogo naroda," *Pravda*, February 10, 1937:1.

of millions of people began to speak for the first time through Pushkin's lips"—and his traditional role as creator of the Russian literary
language is inflated into an expression of Russian cultural superiority:
"Pushkin elevated our language—by its nature rich and flexible—to
an extraordinary height, making it the most expressive language in the
world." Pushkin even serves as a justification for Soviet cultural imperi-
alism: "Pushkin is equally dear to the hearts of Russians and Ukrai-
nians, Georgians and Kalmyks, dear to the hearts of all the peoples
of the Soviet Union. . . . Pushkin long ago outgrew the boundaries of
his country. All progressive, cultured humanity stands on bended knee
before his genius." Pushkin had now been mustered into the service of
the new regime as proof of the importance of Russia's past and future
contributions to history.

The 1937 Pushkin jubilee established the premises of the Pushkin
myth as it was to function in Soviet society. Pushkin had been sacralized, forged into the center of a secular cult that nonetheless drew
its emotional force from the wellsprings of religious zeal. Around the
figure of Pushkin an entire cosmology was cultivated, a black-and-
white universe divided clearly between heroes and villains who were
defined ethically by their relations with Pushkin and served to validate
Pushkin politically through their own class allegiances. On the side
of evil were arrayed Pushkin's enemies—d'Anthès, van Heeckeren,
Nicholas, Benkendorf, and the aristocracy—characters associated with
the hated tsarist regime and pernicious foreignness. Featured most
prominently on the side of good were Pushkin's friends among the
Decembrists, close ties with whom added credence to Pushkin's image
as a revolutionary poet, and the poet's peasant nanny, Arina Rodionovna, who appeared as a surrogate mother to the son neglected by his
unfeeling, aristocratic parents and thus linked Pushkin to the "common people."

Yet it would be a mistake to imagine that there was only one "Soviet"
Pushkin. What we might term "Pushkin for the mass reader" was the
most widely propagated version—and, perhaps the one most closely
implicated in the official mythology. This was the Pushkin whose verses
every Soviet child began to memorize as soon as he or she began school,
if not before, and whose biography, reduced to something of a sim-
plistic catechism, was a standard part of the school curriculum. The
emphasis here, as in virtually all Soviet humanities schooling, was on
rote learning of canonic texts—favoring those of Pushkin's works that
could most easily be made to support the official image—and canonic

interpretations of those texts. This schoolbook Pushkin shades over into
the Pushkin of popular biographies, such as A. I. Gessen's *12 Moika
Embankment* (1969).[72] This book, which takes as its title the address
of Pushkin's last Petersburg apartment, is steeped in Pushkin lore and
written in a style overladen with saccharine sentimentality. The opening paragraph sets the tone and motivates the structure of the book:
"The antique clock on the fireplace in the study of Pushkin's last apartment shows 2:45. At this moment on January 29 (February 10), 1837,
the poet's heart stopped. And every year on this day, at this hour, gather
here the descendants of those who stood on that distant day before the
windows of Pushkin's apartment and holding their breath followed the
beating of the poet's pulse."[73] Gessen here begins from the end and,
tracing the events of the months that Pushkin lived in the apartment
on the Moika Canal, views the poet's life from the vantage point of his
death. This reverential approach invests every trivial incident with a
sort of ominous solemnity characteristic of popular discourse on Pushkin. Books like Gessen's, and the maudlin fascination with the details
of Pushkin's life—or, more accurately, death—to which they pander
seem to have met a serious demand, at least among a certain segment
of the Soviet readership.

At the other end of the social spectrum from these Pushkins for
the general reader stand scholarly Pushkin studies, the symbolic center
of which is the prestigious Pushkin House in St. Petersburg. Though
Pushkin scholarship in the Soviet Union suffered, especially during
the Stalin period, from the politicization of the Pushkin myth, it also
unquestionably drew impetus and resources from the pivotal role ac-
corded Pushkin in Soviet culture, producing valuable textological studies and research into the historical details of the poet's life. Nonetheless,
the very ponderousness of the academic apparatus devoted to Pushkin
confirmed his canonic status, and most Soviet Pushkin scholarship has
subscribed to the vision of Pushkin as a realist writer committed to
political reform.

All of these Pushkins to a greater or lesser extent participated in the
official cult of Pushkin. Yet the ability of the Pushkin myth to survive
with its basic legitimizing associations intact, under regimes represent-
ing radically different ideologies, testifies to what one commentator

72. I would like to thank Nadezhda Azhgikhina for having brought this book to
my attention.
73. A. I. Gessen, *Naberezhnaya moiki, 12: Poslednyaya kvartira A. S. Pushkina*
(Minsk: Narodnaya asveta, 1983), 7.

has termed the "multivalence" of the mythic structure.[74] The subversive potential of the myth among the intelligentsia became abundantly clear in the mid-1960s, when, beginning, ironically, with a demonstration against the arrest of Sinyavsky and Daniel on December 5, 1965, political dissidents adopted Pushkin Square in Moscow as the site of their protests. In line with the long-standing tradition of the poet as an opponent and even rival of political authority, oppositionists chose Pushkin, quite literally, as a rallying point. As Khodasevich had prophesied two generations earlier, Pushkin became a symbol—a sign of recognition—of intelligentsia values antithetical to the regime.

If the version of the Pushkin myth that implicitly empowered dissidents in their antigovernment activities shared a certain solemnity and reverence for Pushkin's authority with the official cult, there flourished another "unofficial" Pushkin, one that perhaps came into existence even during the poet's lifetime, that was impious in its very conception. This was the caricature of Pushkin that figured in *pushkinskie anekdoty*—various forms of verbal play ranging from obscene limericks to nonsense sayings and political jokes. This Pushkin coexisted peacefully with the sacralized Pushkin, perhaps serving as a sort of foil that simultaneously deflated and reinforced the myth.[75] Here is one example that subtly pokes fun at the Pushkin cult itself: Stalin is sitting in Heaven, and Pushkin comes to see him. "Look," he says, "I had a girlfriend named Anna Kern. Can she be transferred to Heaven?" Stalin calls Beria [head of the secret police] and tells him, "Kern has to be transferred to Heaven." Beria answers, "Well, you know, there's no room." And Stalin says to him: "But it's Pushkin who's asking!" "All right," Beria answers, "I'll do it!" Pushkin comes to Stalin again and again and asks for more and more favors until finally Stalin in exasperation calls Beria and says, "Ask d'Anthès to come here."[76]

Pushkin's role in Russian and Soviet society might best be conceived in spatial terms. The Pushkin myth removes Pushkin the poet and the man to a metaphorical sacralized space within the culture, a space marked by the exalted language that is the only officially accept-

74. See Debreczeny, "*Zhitie Aleksandra Boldinskogo*," 282.
75. On the concluding pages of her excellent study of the cultural mythology surrounding the eighteenth-century Russian poet and translator Vasily Tredyakovsky, Irina Reyfman suggests that Pushkin should be viewed as a "trickster." *Vasily Trediakovsky: The Fool of the "New" Russian Literature* (Stanford, Calif.: Stanford University Press, 1990): 253–54.
76. Based on a version told to me by Andrei Sinyavsky in October 1992.

able mode of discourse in speaking of him. This metaphor is realized in the consecration of specific spaces to Pushkin, beginning with the unveiling of the Pushkin statue in Moscow in 1880, which also heralded the beginning of Pushkin's apotheosis. In the Soviet period so-called "Pushkin places" (*pushkinskie mesta*) have proliferated, and virtually every locale linked with the poet's life, from the estate at Mikhailovskoe to the apartment where he died, was painstakingly restored and transformed into a museum, serving as a place of pilgrimage for the poet's admirers.[77] Seen in this light, the various incarnations of the official Pushkin exist in a cultural space separate from the irreverent manifestations of the anecdotal Pushkin, and an invisible but no less absolute boundary lies between them—a boundary that may be crossed only at one's peril.

It is precisely the boundary between the revered and the irreverent Pushkins that Sinyavsky transgresses from the very beginning of his *Strolls with Pushkin*. He sets off on his meanderings through the "sacred verses" of the poet with the Pushkin of *pushkinskie anekdoty* as his companion in hopes of circumventing the "wreaths and busts" that enshrine the canonic Pushkin and finding the "beautiful original." This initial border violation defines the course of Sinyavsky's strolls throughout. At every step he challenges accepted dividing lines—between writer and critic, author and character, sacred and profane, art and life—in order to undermine the commonplaces of the Pushkin myth as well as the understanding of literature as a reflection of reality that the myth entails. His project, moreover, rests on an internal contradiction. If strolling is by definition aimless motion, how can one stroll in search of something? This paradox is ultimately resolved when Sinyavsky reaches his goal only to discover that it is "zero," that it lies in the very imposture embodied in the anecdotal Pushkin with whom he began. His strolls have both attained their object and gone nowhere and thus become a paradigm for "pure art"—art that transcends purposes external to it and becomes an end in itself. As Sinyavsky observes, "Art strolls."

Thus, as much as it is about Pushkin, *Strolls with Pushkin* is also about the free play of language in the literary text, and the metaphor of strolling is enacted in the idiom and structure of the work itself. Sinyav-

77. On Pushkin places, see Stephanie Sandler, "Remembrance in Mikhailovskoe," in *Cultural Mythologies of Russian Modernism*, 231–50.

sky constantly breaches critical decorum, mixing lyrical effusions with colloquialisms and labor camp slang, playing havoc with chronology, and allowing his narrative to be carried along by the flow of metaphors that stand the clichés of the Pushkin cult on their heads.

The unorthodox gambols of Sinyavsky's language have sometimes bewildered and more often enraged Russian readers. Marya Rozanova, in a recent article on the response to *Strolls with Pushkin*, gives as a case in point two rather ludicrous reactions to what has become the most notorious line in the work: "Pushkin ran into high poetry on thin erotic legs and created a commotion":

> It began, of course, with the thin erotic legs. "Marya Vasilevna," a respected old doctor, stopped me one day in a Russian bookstore in Paris. "Where did Andrei Donatovich get the idea that Pushkin had thin erotic legs? After all, even in the notorious book *Pushkin's Don Juan List* there are no instructions to the effect that his legs were erotic." And I explained at length that since he was not running into a drawing room, but into poetry, these were not literal legs, but what is called a metaphor, and I consoled myself with rationalizations: well, he's old, well, he forgot. . . . But then not long ago the remarkable Russian writer Georgy Nikolaevich Vladimov asked: "Andrei Donatovich," he said, "where did you get the idea that Pushkin had thin legs? After all, it is well known that he was a very athletic person." It is some kind of sorcery: the man wrote a whole novel-metaphor and stumbled over those legs.[78]

Rozanova concludes that "the Russian people have unlearned how to read," that "after seventy years of realism—socialist or not socialist—many people have begun to read by syllables and only literally."

Even more disturbing, as the controversy over *Strolls with Pushkin* has revealed, is the extent to which Russian culture's investment in a realist aesthetic is tied to a deep-seated allegiance to language control. Two emigre articles published in the wake of the appearance of Sinyav-

---

78. Adapted from my translation of Marya Rozanova, "On the History and Geography of This Book," *Russian Studies in Literature* 28, no. 1 (Winter 1991–1992): 96–97. The issue in which Rozanova's article appears is entitled "The Return of Abram Tertz: Siniavskii's Reception in Gorbachev's Russia" and contains translations of a selection of articles on the controversy over *Strolls with Pushkin*. For a more thorough discussion of the attacks on Sinyavsky's work in both the emigration and Russia, see Catharine Theimer Nepomnyashchy, "Andrei Sinyavsky's 'Return' to the Soviet Union," *Formations* 6, no. 1 (Spring 1991): 24–44, and Stephanie Sandler's excellent discussion in "Sex, Death and Nation in the *Strolls with Pushkin* Controversy," *Slavic Review* 51, no. 2 (Summer 1992): 294–308.

sky's work in the West express the anger and even fear that language given free reign evokes in Russian readers.

The title of one early review of *Strolls with Pushkin*, "A Boor's Strolls with Pushkin," by Roman Gul, the editor of the New York–based *New Journal* (Novy zhurnal) vents the critic's disgust with Sinyavsky's book while also suggesting the deeper issues at stake. Gul plays throughout on the dual meaning of the Russian word *kham*, which signifies both "boor" and the biblical name Ham. In Genesis Ham sees his father's nakedness and tells his brothers, who rush to cover what he has seen. Gul writes, "I am using the word *kham* in the biblical sense—as the cynicism of man and mockery of that which in human society should not be mocked if society does not want to turn into a herd of orangutans."[79] Inveighing against Sinyavsky's "Smerdyakovish style" taken "directly out of the thieves' barracks at Dubrovlag," Gul maintains that it is not *"what* Abram Tertz wrote about Pushkin" but *"how* he writes about Pushkin"[80] that is so offensive. The crux of Gul's argument, then, lies in the accusation that Sinyavsky's use of language in *Strolls with Pushkin* is inappropriate to its subject, for "true art is *holy,* . . . the name . . . of Pushkin . . . for me is *holy.*"[81] The violation of linguistic decorum thus becomes a threat to society, because it challenges authority by revealing what should remain covered.

Solzhenitsyn's 1984 article on *Strolls with Pushkin*, ". . . Shakes Your Sacrificial Altar," draws its title from the concluding lines of Pushkin's famous 1830 lyric "To the Poet," in which Pushkin warns the poet to pay no heed to the fickle tastes of the crowd: "Are you satisfied with your work? Then no matter if the crowd abuses it/And spits on the altar where your fire burns,/And in childish playfulness shakes your sacrificial altar." It is Sinyavsky's "childish playfulness," which Solzhenitsyn views as sacrilegious in relation to the sacred person of the poet, that disturbs the writer. He repeatedly refers to *Strolls with Pushkin* as a "dance" that lacks a logical structure and leads nowhere. Observing darkly that it was only to be expected that once in emigration, and therefore freed from censorship, such "aesthetic nihilists" as Sinyavsky would immediately attack Pushkin in their attempt "to represent this universal irony, play, and license as a self-sufficient New Word,"[82] Sol-

---

79. Roman Gul, "Progulki khama s Pushkinym," *Novy zhurnal*, no. 24 (1976): 118.
80. Ibid., 126, 128, 120 (Gul's emphasis).
81. Ibid., 123.
82. Aleksandr Solzhenitsyn, ". . . Koleblet tvoi trenozhnik," *Vestnik Russkogo Khristyanskogo dvizheniya* 142 (1984): 152.

zhenitsyn insists that an attack on Pushkin is an attack on all authority. Language unrestrained thus becomes for Solzhenitsyn, as for Gul, a threat to the very foundations of society.

Following the publication of an excerpt from *Strolls with Pushkin* in the Soviet Union in 1989, Sinyavsky and his book became a symbolic focus for the anxieties and rancor unleashed by the collapse of the Soviet system. *Strolls with Pushkin* was perceived by Sinyavsky's detractors as an assault on one of the most fundamental legitimizing symbols of Russian national identity. When asked why Sinyavsky's work created such a furor in the author's homeland, one conservative critic told the following story in response:

> Not long ago I was in my native village, and I was standing in front of a church that had been destroyed. An old woman came up to me and I asked her when the church had been destroyed. She told me in 1932. She had still been a little girl and now she was an old woman and obviously the offense had festered in her soul for such a long time that she told me, a stray passerby, who happened to have gotten out of a car and gone up to the church . . . She told me, "I was a little girl and when they were destroying everything, I grabbed an icon and ran away with it, but when I was almost home, a man with a bag and with a revolver in his belt, tore the icon away from me and trampled it before my eyes." . . . When all of these holy things are trampled, when there are no more icons or very few, Pushkin is one of those icons. He is an icon equal to the icons of the church.[83]

So thoroughly had Pushkin become sacralized over the century and a half since his death, so profoundly had he become a symbol of Russia's national worth, that trampling the icon of Pushkin appeared tantamount to destroying Russia's culture and spiritual heritage.

Strolls with Pushkin is *not* an attack on Pushkin. It is, however, an assault on a particular image of Pushkin that is inextricably linked with the solemn and formulaic language of the Pushkin cult. The effect of *Strolls with Pushkin* might best be likened to the play of language in the Pushkin joke that runs: "I am washing, washing my Pushkin places."[84]

83. Ernst Safonov, editor of the newspaper *Literary Russia* (Literaturnaya Rossiya), where many of the Soviet attacks on Sinyavsky were published, cited from a taped transcript of a meeting with seven russophile writers and critics held at Columbia University on May 10, 1990. The group was visiting the United States under the auspices of the United States Information Agency.

84. "Moyus', moyus' po pushkinym mestam." I would like to express my gratitude to Greta Slobin for having told me this joke. Other commentators have identified this

Though the bawdy play on the conflation of "Pushkin places" and "private parts" comes through only weakly in English, we can nonetheless catch an echo of the linguistic subversion, the spice of which originates in the collapse of the boundary between sacred and profane. *Strolls with Pushkin*, like the joke, aims to shock, entertain, unsettle, and ultimately beguile the reader into a new, livelier appreciation of Pushkin and of the liberating potential of language.

---

as a Lenin joke ("my Lenin places"), which reveals the kinship between the Lenin and Pushkin cults. See Debreczeny, "*Zhitie Aleksandra Boldinskogo.*"

STROLLS WITH PUSHKIN

I often asked him: "Well, how's it going, Pushkin my friend?" "What can I say, my friend," he would answer: "I'm getting by . . ." He's a real original.
                    —Gogol, *The Inspector General*

An asterisk in the text marks a word or phrase that is discussed in the editor's notes, pp. 149–175. The numbered footnotes are by Sinyavsky.

Despite all our love for Pushkin, a love that borders on worship, we for some reason find it difficult to explain why we consider him such a genius and why Pushkin and no one else always comes in first in Russian literature. Aside from the grandeur that makes us want to shower him with honorific titles, behind which his face melts into one big familiar blur with sidewhiskers,* the difficulty lies in the fact that he is absolutely accessible and at the same time inscrutable, enigmatic in the obvious accessibility of the truths he enunciated, truths that don't contain, it would seem, anything so special (a gesture of uncertainty: "What can I say . . . I'm getting by"). We have the right to ask, to express our doubts (and many have doubted): is your Pushkin really so great, what's he so famous for anyway, once you take away a dozen or so skillfully cut-out pieces, about which you can't say anything except that they are skillfully stitched together?

> . . . Nothing more
> Will you squeeze out of my story*

—that's how Pushkin himself summed up the absence in his works of anything more than amusing anecdotes, elegantly and tastefully told. And perhaps we will find Pushkin easier to understand if we approach him not through the front hall, which is crammed with wreaths and busts that have an expression of uncompromising nobility on their brows, but rather with the help of the anecdotal caricatures of Pushkin that were sent back to the poet by the street, apparently in response to and in revenge for his great fame.

Let's throw away the heavy-handed bawdiness of these creations of the street—which make up for deficiencies in grace and wit with unsophisticated plebeian obscenity. It has nothing to do either with Pushkin or with the matter at hand. Let's also leave aside for the time being frivolity of the storylines of these jokes, to which Pushkin does have a certain indirect relationship. What then will be left of the caricature double fond of jokes and pranks and therefore more or less suited to accompany us on our excursions through the sacred verses of the poet— to keep them from immediately transposing us into an exalted key and leading us by a direct route to the Pushkin Academy of Sciences and Arts* with the aforementioned wreaths and busts on every paragraph? What will be left of the generally known jokes about Pushkin if we clean them up a bit, getting rid of the scabrous trash? What will remain are those same indestructible sidewhiskers (he'll never get away from them), a walking stick, a hat, flying coat tails, sociability, light-mindedness, a talent for getting into scrapes, and a ready tongue for parrying right and left with the dexterity of a magician—in flickering flashes, like the frames of a silent film, the sidewhiskers, the walking stick, the frockcoat . . . What will be left is Pushkin's fidgetiness and a kind of omnipresence along with his ability to evaporate and suddenly reappear, buttoning himself up on the run, taking on himself the roles of recipient and dispenser of impromptu kicks, the mission of scapegoat, of everybody's solicitor and well-wisher, who pokes his nose into everything, of the elusive and ubiquitous universal No Man, whom everyone knows, who'll put up with anything, who settles up for everyone.

"Who'll pay?" "Pushkin!"

"Who do you take me for—Pushkin—that I'm supposed to be responsible for everything?"

"Pushkinspieler! Pushkinstein!"*

He's our Charlie Chaplin, a contemporary ersatz Petrushka, who spiffed himself up and got the hang of strutting his stuff in rhyme . . .

"Well, how's it going, Pushkin my friend? . . ."

Does this rough-hewn popular image have anything in common with the beautiful original we're seeking, the one we're trying to get to know more intimately through contact with his sprightly and obliging executor? Probably, it does. Probably, there was something in Pushkin, in the real Pushkin, that encouraged the later familiarity, and that something tossed his name out for the amusement of the crowd, transforming the solitary genius into a darling of the public, a habitué of dances, restaurants, and sporting matches.

Lightness is the first thing—the most general and immediate feeling—we get out of his works. Lightness in relation to life was the basis of Pushkin's worldview, a trait of his character and his biography. Lightness in verse became a condition of his creativity from his very first steps. He had barely started out when the critics began to speak of the "extraordinary lightness and facility" of his verses: "It seems they cost [the poet] no effort at all," "it seems as if they flowed out of him of their own accord" (*Neva Spectator,** 1820, no. 7; *Son of the Fatherland,** 1820, sec. 64, no. 36).

Before Pushkin there was almost no light verse. Well—there was Batyushkov, there was Zhukovsky.* But even with them we stumble. And suddenly, out of the blue, there appeared curtsies and turns comparable to nothing and no one, speed, onslaught, bounciness, the ability to prance, to gallop, to take hurdles, to do splits and then to draw in or to stretch out the line of verse as needed to emulate those curvets, about which he writes immersing himself so thoroughly in the role, that the stanza-ballerina along with Istomina's art of the dance becomes a letter of introduction for the author:

> She
> Touching the floor with one foot,
> Slowly turns the other,
> And suddenly a leap, and suddenly she soars,
> She soars, like down from the lips of Aeolus;
> Turning her torso right and left,
> One swift foot beating against the other.*

But before learning to dance like that Pushkin had to go through the training of the lycée—to get used to undue familiarity, to develop flexibility in deliberately unserious speech, which committed him to nothing and was entertaining primarily because of the spontaneity of the tone with which conversation curled around insignificant and empty subjects. He didn't begin with verses—but with verselets. Instead of striving for poetic mastery as it was understood at the time, he learned to write badly, any old way, worrying not about perfecting his "winged epistles" but only about writing them on air—thoughtlessly and fast, without exerting himself. His concentration on *unpolished* verse was a consequence of this "careless" and "frisky" (favorite epithets of Pushkin at the time) manner of speech, attained by means of an open disregard for the status and authority of the poet. At the time when he was making his debut, the first adherent of pure poetry in Russian literature (as it later turned out) couldn't have cared less about art and demonstratively preferred the perishable gifts of life.

> Summon me no longer
> To toils left forever,
> Nor to the thrall of poetry
> Or polished verses.
> So what if I sometimes sing
> Weakly and with mistakes?
> Let Ninette enflame and calm
> My carefree love
> With but a smile!
> Work is cold and empty:
> No poem could ever be worth as much
> As a smile on lustful lips!*

Taking such liberties with verse, freed from all possible fetters and obligations, from the binding necessity—even!—to be called *poetry*, to dream of eternity, to strive for fame ("the fruits of merry leisure are not born for immortality,"* insisted the young author, not so much out of modesty, as out of the desire to preserve his independence from the weighty tasks that were being pressed on him from all sides), presupposed relaxed conditions of creation. Bed became his favored place of composition, disposing not to work, but to rest, to lazy idleness and drowsiness, in which state the poet now and then scribbled bits and snippets willy-nilly, without tiring himself out with unnecessary mental strain.

Bed for Pushkin was not only a cherished habit, but the creative environment that corresponded most closely to his spirit, the workshop where his style and method were formed. While others crawled up the steps of lofty tradition onto a pedestal and never thought of taking up the pen without mentally arraying themselves in full-dress coats or togas, Pushkin, without stopping to think, tumbled down on his bed and there—"in pleasant oblivion, his head inclining toward the pillow," "with a slightly drowsy hand"—jotted down something or other that demanded neither concentration nor effort. That's how his manner, so striking in its freedom of thought and language, was worked out, and with it came a freedom of the word hitherto unprecedented in our literature. It turned out that it was easier for him to become Pushkin when he was lying on his side, and he rejoiced in his discovery:

> When I'm in this lazy pose,
> Verses flow this way, that way, and the other.*

At that stage his poetry was immersed and dissolved into everyday life. Shunning grand programs and majestic goals, it lowered itself to the level of after dinner toasts, love notes and the other stuff and nonsense of the prose of daily life. Instead of laboriously hatching a *Rossiad*,* Pushkin's poetry squandered its talents on trifles and was dispensed cheaply in his circle of friends—in albums and witticisms. The adherents of LEF would later call these forms of poetic displacement into everyday life "art in production." Without following any theory, Pushkin began where Mayakovsky ended.*

> Nowadays I dash off after my own fashion
> Verses for namedays.*

For instance, it cost him nothing to compose a bit of verse inviting someone to a cup of tea. There was no lack of occasions or requests. "I hear that you've written verses for a lot of people, but you still haven't written anything for me," Ya. N. Tolstoy begged him, also in verse, in the pleasant manner of the time. "How long are you going to begrudge your words: Is it so hard to write a trifle?" And he received some stanzas as a gift.*

Pushkin was generous with trifles. The genre of the poetic bagatelle had attracted him from infancy. Mastering lack of discipline and the instantaneous resolution of a theme, he completely excluded any suspicion of serious intent, diligence, or constancy. In literature, as in life, Pushkin jealously guarded his reputation as an idler, a flighty person, and a scapegrace, unacquainted with the torments of creation.

> Don't think, my gloomy censor,
> That I rage all night in agitation
> Engulfed by poetic thought,
> That I sacrifice my laziness to poetry.*

All the same, there are those who have thought just that. Later biographers, with the polite smile of police augurs accustomed to turning a blind eye to the escapades of the big bosses, explain to readers that of course Pushkin was not nearly the loafer he is for some reason considered to be. Informers turned up who had peeped through the keyhole while Pushkin panted for long hours over drafts.

We aren't interested in such gossip. We're not concerned with evidence—whether it be the truth or the invention of learned pedants— that lies beyond the boundaries of the truth as the poet presented it, even more so that contradicts the version adhering to which he managed to endow us with a whole universe. If Pushkin (let's assume!) was only pretending to loaf, it means that he needed that pretense to free his tongue, that it suited him as the plot motivation for the unfolding of his destiny, and without it he couldn't have written anything good. No, it was not the coquettishness of the successful artist alone that turned lolling about into a matter of principle, but a necessity for his work and an understanding, growing stronger with every passing hour, of his place and lot in life. He didn't play, but lived, joking and playing, and when he died, having pushed the game too far, Baratynsky,* they say, together with the other commissars who sorted through the papers of the deceased, among which, for example, intruded *The Bronze Horseman*, exclaimed, "Can you imagine what astonishes me about these poems more than anything else? The abundance of thought! Pushkin was a profound thinker! Who would have expected it?" (I am citing from Ivan Turgenev's speech at the unveiling of the monument to Pushkin in Moscow.)*

The readers of today, who have been taught since childhood that Pushkin was a profound thinker (although, speaking frankly, he really wasn't much of a thinker!), are amazed at Baratynsky for not having noticed the obvious profundity. Without cudgeling our brains over these profundities, let us rather wonder together, in concert, at the power of suggestion that Pushkin exerted to the grave in the role of a carefree youth. His contemporaries attest almost unanimously, "Pushkin's youth lasted his whole life, and at thirty he seemed, though less a little boy than he had been before, all the same a little boy, a lycée student. . . . Flightiness was the main, the fundamental trait of Pushkin's character" (*Russian Antiquity*,* 1874, no. 8).

Naturally this flightiness could not get along without women. The weaker sex probably never played such an important role in the formation of anyone's style, in winding up the verse as it did in Pushkin's case. Trifles dedicated to lovely women found their justification in feminine weakness and went up in price, were filled with the air of pleasant and profitable circulation. The young poet was becoming a professional at playing the role of Lovelace. In the company of ladies, he was apparently on the job.

Meanwhile his carefree, careless speech earned him approval: who after all can remain serious with young ladies, whose every sound prompts you to smile and sets all the members of your body vibrating? The object of glorification itself disposed to light-mindedness and endowed the poetry with a profusion of motion. In converse with women his poetry practiced the art of cajoling and, skimming across the surface, touched on forbidden topics and secret subjects with a free and easy grace, as if it were nothing special, and our lady trembles all over and grabs at her sides as if she were being tickled and, shaking, slaps the fingers of the rogue with her fan. (See the epistle "To the Beauty Who Was Sniffing Tobacco," which, I remember, fell right into her bodice, where the fifteen-year-old rascal displays such energy and agility that we gape in envy: Oh, why am I not that tobacco! Oh, why am I not Pushkin!)*

Pushkin ran into great poetry on thin erotic legs and created a commotion. Erotica was his school—above all a schooling in nimbleness—and we are, as a result, indebted to it for the flexibility of the *Onegin* stanza as well as for other tricks about which it was said, not without bragging:

> At times I turn a verse sharply,
> It's obvious it's not the first time I've wound one up.*

The ability to wind up a line of verse was acquired in collisions that demanded an extraordinary ability to maneuver, like the one in which, for example, Don Juan once found himself, when he took it upon himself to court two parallel girls at the same time. In a situation like that you have to get a move on whether you want to or not.

Or sometimes Pushkin throws out a phrase, the decisiveness of which puzzles us: "I almost came to hate my native land" (?!). Don't worry: it goes on—alley-oop!—and the honor of the fatherland is restored:

> I almost came to hate my native land—
> But yesterday I caught sight of Princess Golitsyna
> And I was reconciled with my native land.*

And the maestro, smiling, takes his leave.

*　*
*

But what is this? Fidgety jumps and grimaces, openly motivated by a youthful fascination with women, suddenly sprout the wings of a soaring angel . . . As if the substance of one passion were transformed in flight into another, chaste and translucent, in order, however, to be immediately reincarnated in its previous form. The erotic element in Pushkin's verses is free to dissipate, to grow thin, reaching the distant pinnacles of the spirit as a quivering echo (continuing on its way to produce and nurture ribald creatures of the lower order). The heavenly creation, once it has resurrected for the bard "divinity, and inspiration, and life, and tears, and love,"* can turn into a floozie whose bounties are trumpeted abroad with the poet's usual mischievous garrulity, but even she should not lose hope that once again given the appropriate opportunity she might pass for a madonna.

Isn't that why no one takes offense at Pushkin and why the ladies willingly forgive him his immodest hints at their reputations: they are flattering, they are prayer-like . . .

Pushkin succeeded in subjecting to a poetic striptease the very substance of the female sex in all its plaintive and seductive holiness, a substance that glows with a subterranean—so as not to say celestial—phosphorescence (which more closely resembles the invisible currents, the spiritualist rays that are emitted by a revolving table, than it does material flesh). It is not flesh, but the ethereal body of flesh, its Psyche, its tender aura that Pushkin caught, putting into circulation all those rosy and lily-white little feet,* cheeks, bosoms, shoulders, detached from their mistresses and waltzing off independently, "like a fleeting apparition, like the genius of pure beauty."

Pushkin's amorousness—precisely because of the breadth and inflammability of the feeling—takes on the dimensions of a life devoted solely to a single occupation practiced around the clock, an eternal circulation among feminine charms. But the size of the collection and the abundance of the hero's love do not allow him to concentrate exclusively on a single object nor to go farther than simple flirtation, which in essence exhausts his relations with these enchantresses. His readiness to chase after every skirt endows the ventures of the womanizer with traits of disinterestedness, selflessness, renunciation of personal needs, satisfied in his spare moments, on the run, constantly digressing from the goal and letting his attention wander. It was as if Pushkin had made up his mind to indulge and humor all women, bypassing in his bustling nary a single fleeting beauty, and he was dazzled, and he didn't have enough hands to go around, and there was neither the time nor the money to take care of himself. Contemplating so many perspectives, captivated by impressions that made his head spin and plunged him into prostration, he ceases to be a lover and becomes an admirer, an erudite of the science of love, and as usual the best dishes go to others.

When you read Pushkin, you get the feeling that he has some bond with women, that he is at home with women—moreover as a specialist,

one of those people you let into your house at all hours, someone in-
dispensable, like a tailor, a hairdresser, a masseuse (she, after all, is a
procuress, she, after all, is good at reading the cards), like a fashionable
neurologist, a jeweler or a pet lapdog (so perky, with little curls . . .).
You don't have to stand on ceremony with a person like that, and every
now and then you have to take him down a peg (You bastard! You up-
start!), but you don't kick him out, you don't show him the door, you
value him, you ask him for advice behind your mother-in-law's back
and sometimes you even suck up to him.

Well and, naturally—you never say no to him. How could you? It's
Pushkin who's asking!

He found his way into women's bedrooms and was in his element
there, just like the uhlan, disguised as a cook, who made himself at
home in the little house in Kolomna, but with less success than Pushkin, who in the poem was unquestionably describing in a playful style
his own experiences, his adventures in the world of the beautiful. In
his writing career he also worked on the sly masquerading as a woman
and managed to please women by scurrying around the riddle of their
charm. "She, like a spirit, passes by,"* Pushkin uttered, and we quail
as if touched by a mystery . . .[1]

Let's pause to think: why do women fall in love with flirts? What
do they have to offer—nothing but upsets, promissory notes, betray-
als, and disappearances, but that's the way it is, can you believe it?—
women love them, no matter how they weep and wail, they love them.
It must be that flirts are somehow akin to women's aery composition,
because of which they unconsciously want everything both within and
around them to fly and flutter (isn't that, by the way, the origin of the
skirt and other muslin and gauzy zephyrs of the feminine toilette?). It's
easy for a woman to find a common language, to strike the right tone
with a flirt. In short, women involuntarily sniff out in the flirt a brother
in spirit.

1. *The Fountain of Bakhchisarai.* The harem (one so wants to get into). Byron.
Byron's Juan, who got there by dressing up as a maiden. The caped uhlan, who followed
in his footsteps (rereading *The Little House in Kolomna*, I for some reason did not find
in it the above-mentioned uhlan, who was shaving disguised as a female cook, but all
the same it seems that there was an uhlan). So the uhlan, in imitation of Byron,* stole
his way to Parasha's side—just as Pushkin, by the same Byronic path, in *The Fountain
of Bakhchisarai* stole into the harem, dressed in feminine stanzas. "She is enchanting
and capricious, like a southern beauty," A. Bestuzhev (Marlinsky) wrote of the poem in a
review of contemporary literature (*Polar Star*,* 1825), without pausing to think, however, of the resemblance between Pushkin's fountain and a woman. But we will think
about it . . .

Moreover, flights on broomsticks have as their scientific basis the same volatility of the feminine nature, which Pushkin extolled in the unforgettable "Hussar," which, like *The Little House in Kolomna*, is largely autobiographical. Let us remember how the landlady stripped herself naked and slipped away into a chimney, setting an example for her cohabitant:

> What the devil! I thought: now
> We'll try it too! and in one gulp
> I drank the whole bottle; believe it or not—
> But I suddenly soared upwards like eiderdown.
>
> Headlong I soared, soared, soared,
> Whither, I neither remember nor know;
> I only shouted to the stars I met:
> Keep to the right!*

What do you mean a hussar!—it's not a hussar but Pushkin who flew up like eiderdown after women and earned the honor of being the first aviator in Russian poetry!

Feast your eyes: *Ruslan and Lyudmila*,* which was the first offshoot of Pushkin's erotic lyrics in the epic, is thoroughly scribbled over with figures of trick flying. Barely visible at first, the little speck of a bird sent from afar ("there in the clouds before the people across forests, across seas the wizard carries the bogatyr"), drawing closer, bobs up and down like merry-go-rounds of flight routes. The heroes hang about in space like inflated balloons and transform the text into a series of picturesque monograms. There are lots of flourishes that grab our attention in the poem. But, take note, this whole pretty kettle of fish—no!—Christmas tree, decorated with golden gewgaws (its prototype appeared in the prologue,* by the curved seashore, where Pushkin of course depicted not an oak tree, but our good, winter fir tree, decorated with wood demons and mermaids, covered with all the knickknacks in the world, and Pushkin with his *Ruslan* stuck it in the place of the legendary oak, where it stands to this very day—by our common cradle, by the curved seashore of our new literature, and how fitting and fairytale-like it is that Pushkin and no one else gave us this fir tree decked in toys for New Year's in his very first large creation), so this Christmas tree, this palm tree, this deliberate deshabille of romanticism, fancifully tangled, sent into a tailspin—tournaments in tournures, cocottes in kokoshniks, sugar-coated berries, gingerbread knights, bears on a bicycle, hunters at rest*—they all have their source in the same passion, which snatches up all this wonderful, barbaric hodgepodge of the poem and sends it soaring into the air, like fireworks.

That source is scoffed at and ridiculed in the retelling of Ruslan's plot, temporarily transplanted—in one of the songs—into the soil of indecent farce. In this inserted novella-scene, which serves simultaneously as both a parody of and a commentary on *Ruslan and Lyudmila,* the action is transferred from the chambers of the palace to a country henhouse. (It must be that hens—in the poultry, court, courtly, and adventure senses of the word—corresponded to the ideological intentions of the author and to the style chosen for the poem—the Old Slavic rococo.) Here, in cordial and hospitable shamelessness, Pushkin's equivocations and the double play of erotic images find their beginning or take their end, when Pushkin identifies Lyudmila, the tender Lyudmila breathed out by Zhukovsky,* with the banal hen that the rooster Ruslan chases through the yard, until the appearance of the rival hawk interrupts this foolishness at the most interesting moment.

> When in pursuit of the cowardly hen
> The arrogant sultan of the henhouse,
> My rooster, had run around the yard
> And with passionate wings
> Was about to embrace his girlfriend . . .

Lasting impressions from his childhood sojourns at the family's summer home are reflected in this frank treatment of the relations between the sexes. Pushkin thumbs his nose at his hero-lovers like a little boy. But what a bright chord, what an infinite dreaminess resolves this scene, as soon as the event is lifted into the air together with the rival—on the wind of heartfelt melancholy, inspiration!

> In vain in his sadness
> And stricken by the chill of fear,
> The rooster calls to his beloved . . .
> He sees only flying down,
> Carried off by the speeding wind.

An assonance is suggested in the last lines—how pure and elevated they are—"The ephemeral range of clouds grows thin . . ."* It grows thin, and the border between eroticism and flight, between clouds and feminine forms, between frivolity and freedom disappears—because all of them are not so much equivalents in Pushkin's works as connected, communicating vessels. Inclined to make indecent gestures in public, he manages to retain a genuine chasteness in what are at times the most risqué episodes—not because at those moments something holds him back or embarrasses him; on the contrary, he recognizes no taboos and is ready for the sake of piquancy to encroach on the heavens; but it is the very readiness of Pushkin's restless eroticism to touch everything on the face of the earth, sometimes eclipsing this world and sometimes returning its light, that deprives this very eroticism of distinct boundaries and helps it pour itself out into thoughts that at first glance have no relation to it and seem uncharacteristic of it, but which in fact demonstrate its force and tensile strength.

As in the joke where the rooster didn't catch up with the hen, but at least got warm,* Pushkin knows how to transmute one energy into another, providing unbridled sensuality with an outlet into all spheres of life's work. "Blessed is he who knows the lust of lofty thoughts and poetry," he says in a moment of relaxation from immoderate skirt-chasing. What is he talking about? "Lust of *thoughts*" and to top it off "*lofty*"?! It's very simple! Everything is lust to him: dances with rhymes, and galloping under fire, and a quiet morning walk. "Love of poetry, love of my freedom . . ."* Do you hear? Not love of Ninette or Temira or even Parasha,* but of *freedom* (and *my* to boot!). Extremely vague, objectless, but nevertheless your heart misses a beat: love!

Pushkin's eroticism, when it wants, is capable of taking a fancy to traveling, of setting off into history, dabbling in politics. His youthful radicalism was in no small measure indebted to it for its tender outlines, which perceived freethinking as a type of intellectual frivolity. Under his speedy pen the newest ideas of the age often took the form of that instinctual agitation of the blood experienced only by those in love. "We await the moment of sacred freedom in a languor of hope, just as a young lover awaits the moment of faithful meeting."* That's the analogy Pushkin proposes. Poetry, love, and freedom united in his head into a single whole—a free, winged state of the spirit, which manifested itself in the guise of diverse words and moods, but nonetheless signified approximately one and the same ardor. The main thing lay not in the words, but in their inclinations and pirouettes.

Poetry understandably occupied first place in this triumvirate. But if only a hundredth part of this dubious theory—that artistic talent feeds on the emanations of eros—is true, then Pushkin is the most straightforward and the most concise illustration of it. He scampered up to the subject to be depicted like an impatient admirer, whispering to the figure who had touched his strings: "By you, by you alone . . ."* And he knew how to be persuasive. "Elle me trouble comme une passion," he wrote of Marina Mnishek.* "She disturbs me like a passion."

The amorous mimicry that accompanied his growing love for art led to the long-standing and close association of Pushkin's Muse with a pretty gentlewoman, who gave rise to naughty thoughts, if not deeper feelings, as was the case with his Tatyana. She, as is well known, besides being Onegin's ill-starred partner and the cold and distant wife of the general, was Pushkin's personal Muse and fulfilled that role better than any other woman.* I even think that's the reason why she didn't get hitched up with Onegin and remained true to her unloved husband, so she'd have more free time to read and reread Pushkin and to languish over him. Pushkin, so to speak, kept her for himself. `

The gaps in her character, in which (so much space!) the ends don't meet—Russian tastes and French habits, common sense and hazy dreaminess, social brilliance and provincialism preserved as a pledge of loyalty to something higher and eternal—allow us to speculate that in portraying Tatyana Pushkin copied certain features from the portrait of his own poetry, combining them with other virtues dear to his heart, just as he assigned to her his old nanny and his own loneliness in his family as a child. Perhaps Pushkin incarnated himself personally in Tatyana more accurately and more fully than anywhere else—in this all-comprehending woman's soul, which hovered over him, which alone could understand and help, and, tell me, what in the world would we do if women didn't hover over us? . . .

Perhaps that's why he, jealous man, didn't let the poor girl go, deprived her of all pleasures and forced her to love hopelessly not so much Onegin, who was unworthy of her, stuffed as he was with caustic contemporaneity (Tatyana got the eternal part), as the earlier triumvirate love-freedom-poetry, which through their union had brightened her maidenhood. Feeling nothing for her elderly spouse but respect, which insured her against the temptation of yielding to Onegin, in the first place, and, in the second place, having given Onegin nothing but bitter admissions, thrown in his face as a challenge to test his strength against hers, she finds in this steadfast bifurcation a guarantee of remaining herself—of betraying with no one the vocation reserved for her by Pushkin in calling her forever *his*.

Lonely since childhood, among relatives, among her friends, lonely in high society, which was prostrated at her feet, lonely on strolls, at the window, with her beloved books, she is the chosen one, and that's why Pushkin takes her by the hand and leads her between the Scylla of spent feelings (if Tatyana had belonged to Onegin) and the Charybdis of domestic banality (if her marriage to the general had been happy). What then do we see? Scylla and Charybdis met and devoured one another, leaving her—the chosen one—unharmed, virginal, like a nun, given neither to the one, nor to the other, but to a third, to Pushkin alone, she who managed to save herself like a vessel from which not a single drop has spilled, nor evaporated, nor grown old, nor turned sour, and so she, the chosen one, offers this cup of pure femininity to *her* chosen one and nursling.

> All my life was a pledge
> Of true meeting with you;
> I know that you were sent to me by God,
> To the grave you will be my keeper . . .
> You appeared to me in dreams,
> Before I saw you, you were already dear to me,
> Your wondrous gaze made me languid,
> Your voice has echoed in my soul
> For a long time . . .*

Lord, how the waves crash, how the sea rocks, and we lick the tears from our cheeks with our tongues as we listen to the feverish ravings, the omnipotent babble of Tatyana's letter to Onegin, or is Tatyana writing to Pushkin or Pushkin to Tatyana, or to the black sky, to the whole wide world . . .*

> I'm writing to you—what more is there to say?
> What can I add to that?

She can't say anything, in one surge laying herself open in inconsistent lamentations, the idea of which—if we approach them with the literal measure of her fruitless romance with Onegin—can be roughly reduced to two rather typical and trivial ideas:

(1) "now you will despise me" and
(2) "but all the same you didn't learn the secret of my soul." But how they are expressed!

Having opened Tatyana's letter, we fall. We fall into the person as if we were falling into a river that carries us along in its freely churning current, washing clean the contours of the soul that is completely expressed in the flow of speech. Though from the first word we recognize Tatyana, true blue Tatyana splashing ahead, behind, and around us, we nonetheless understand nothing of her words, which function exclusively as the spontaneous movement of what is said.

> Who imbued her with this tenderness
> And with the lovable carelessness of her words?*

Pushkin asks in wonderment, Pushkin, who himself imbued her with all of this in the call of duty (in conformity with his own taste and his ear for the tender carelessness of speech). But that doesn't stop him from experiencing what has happened as something like confusion, fright . . . Wait! Who after all imbued whom? There is obviously some sort of mixup here, a forgery. Pushkin himself assures us that Tatyana couldn't have written it herself, for "she expressed herself with difficulty in her native language" and wrote the letter in French,* which the author took upon himself to translate to the best of his poor abilities.

> Here is
> An incomplete and weak translation,
> A pale copy of the living picture . . .*

But if this is only a pale copy, then what is the beautiful original like and what could be more complete or more original than the document we have here?! . . . The reader is given the right to think what he wants, filling in the empty spaces that have been formed with surmises and groping his way among the incongruities. Pushkin obstinately insists that his "translation" is inspired by Tatyana's "foreign words" and assigns them a place above his own creation. The letter cooling down in front of us is only a weak imprint of a previous relationship between the poet and Tatyana, which remains outside the boundaries of the text— where Pushkin keeps the inaccessible original of her letter, which he reads eternally without ever tiring of it.

So we may well ask if it wasn't perhaps Tatyana who had appeared to him while wandering alone in the woods.

> From morning till evening in the mute silence of the oaks
> I diligently attended to the lessons of the mysterious maiden;
> And, gladdening me with a chance reward,
> Tossing the curls from her dear brow,
> She herself took the reed pipe from my hands:
> Her divine breath brought the reed to life
> And my heart was filled with sacred enchantment.*

Like Tatyana, Pushkin believed in dreams and portents. They say he had his reasons for that. We needn't go into them. It's enough to refer to his works, in which unexpected opportunities that allow glimpses into the future recur with the persistence of an idée fixe. One after the other Ruslan,[2] Aleko,[3] Tatyana,[4] the Pretender,[5] and Grinyov[6] have prophetic dreams. And that's without taking into account other sorts of portents and predictions—in "The Song of Oleg the Seer," *Mozart and Salieri,* "The Queen of Spades" . . .* With inexhaustible curiosity Pushkin again and again probes the slippery theme of fate predicted in several isolated links and predetermined as a whole.

He was possessed to an inordinate degree by a sense of fate. Only for a brief moment in adolescence did the illusion that he might hide from it in lyrical seclusion flash through his mind. Fate answered him in rhyme, despite the field ten years wide that lay between these lines; as if the author were discarding an unsuccessful sketch and writing a clean copy over it.

> 1815:
> All earthly joys are in our dreams!
> The poet is much more powerful than fate.*

> 1824:
> And fatal passions are everywhere,
> And there is no defense against the fates.*

But even without this he already sensed that he could not get away from fate. "We are not the masters of our fate,"* was Pushkin's eternal refrain. Remember the hermit Finn who relates to Ruslan the parable of his life: for the sake of a heartless beauty, disregarding the disposition of providence, the poor man wasted fifty years on heroic exploits, on exercises in sorcery, and received nothing for his pains but a broken trough.*

> Now, Naina, you are mine!
> We are victorious, I thought.
> But in fact the victor
> Was destiny, my stubborn persecutor.*

2. "And the hero had a prophetic dream . . ."
3. "I had awful dreams! . . ."
4. "And Tatyana had a wonderful dream . . ."
5. "Always the same dream! Is it possible? For the third time!"
6. "I had a dream, which I could never forget and in which to this day I see something prophetic, when I think of the strange circumstances of my life in relation to it."

Meanwhile, there is a way out. All you have to do is give up, pin your hopes on the will of fate, and—oh miracle!—yesterday's oppressor will take you under his protection. Fate loves the obedient and indulges them on the sly, and how lighthearted are they who remember this.

> He to whom irresistible fate
> Has allotted a maiden's heart,
> Will be loved despite the universe;
> It is foolish and sinful to quarrel.*

Pushkin professed trust in fate—a banal bit of wisdom—with as much conviction as if it were a guiding star that shone for him alone. In its light trust flares into a symbol of faith. From its height the ordinary laziness and carefreeness of the scapegrace, which he extolled in his student verses, acquire the sovereign authority of a moral law.

> Only I, subservient to fate in everything,
> The faithful son of happy laziness,
> Ever carefree, ever indifferent . . .*

To be lazy meant to be trusting and unimportunate. The lazy man is inexplicably lucky. The lazy man in Pushkin's works is the same thing as the fool in a fairy tale: shrewder than everyone else, more agile than everyone else, the hardest worker. There is a certain logic in fate's protection of the carefree man: after all, who else would worry about someone like him? And there is a method: the last shall be first! And so Cinderella finds herself in gold. Trust is rewarded.

The lazy genius of Pushkin-Mozart is incapable of villainy, because villainy, the hallmark and weapon of the untalented failure, originates in vain attempts to correct fate arbitrarily, to impose the principle of envy on fate through blood and deception.* Laziness, on the other hand, is a type of humility, the grateful receptivity of the genius to whatever happens to fall into his mouth (with the concomitant danger of drinking poison given to him by an untalented villain).

The calculating man in Pushkin's works is a despot, a rebel, Aleko. The usurper Boris Godunov. The petty thief Hermann.* The calculating man, having calculated everything, stumbles and falls, never understanding why, because he is always dissatisfied (grumbles at fate). Pushkin relates in dozens of variations how opponents of fate are brought to their knees, how despite all ruses and intrigues fate triumphs over man, mixing up his cards or surreptitiously throwing in a surprise. His plots are governed by decisive twists and turns and sudden coincidences that wind the story tight and round it off at the end. Pushkin's "The Snowstorm," which misplaces the bridegroom and the bride just so that they, having lost their way once and for all, can find one another and fall in love not where they expected to and not as they wished, stuns us with the artistry with which fate, disconnecting and connecting, autocratically cuts out of the darkness of the storm of human passions and intentions the spiral of its own whimsically created being.* It's hard to say what many of Pushkin's works are for or what they are about—to such an extent are they about nothing and to no end but the roundedness of fate and the plot.

The figure of the circle with its intricate family including all sorts of ellipses and lemniscates best corresponds to Pushkin's spirit, in particular to his method of hunting down his heroes by tossing the line of fate, like a lasso, which manages in the course of the story to roll itself up into a pretzel, a noose ("like a black ribbon, it wound itself around his leg, and the prince suddenly bitten uttered a shriek").* The roundest writer in Russian literature, Pushkin everywhere exhibits a tendency to close the circle, whether it be the contour of events or the sharp outline of a stanza strung like ring-shaped rolls into rhymed garlands. There is something providential in Pushkin's consonances: his discourse, which has scattered in different directions without a backward glance, suddenly notices in amazement that it is surrounded, locked up by an agreement between fate and freedom.

In his poetry, however, the idea of fate, which acts with the speed of lightning, has none of the rigidity or purity of a religious doctrine. The chance occurrence is the point that places this idea into a position of faceless and unstable indefiniteness, which nonetheless retains the right to judge us. Chance in serving fate conceals it under a veil of sporadic coincidences, which, although they occur with suspicious precision, are sufficiently trivial and capricious, if we try to explain them without resorting to metaphysics, to be taken for an innocent conjunction of circumstances.

> "Pure chance!" said one of the guests.
> "A fairy tale!" remarked Hermann.

That's how the public reacts in "The Queen of Spades" to Tomsky's information from the realm of the supernatural:* that which for some has lost its reality—the "fairy tale"—is still allowed by others in the humble attire of the chance occurrence, which totters on the boundary between the impossible and the probable. The chance occurrence both cuts fate off at the root and reconstructs it on a new, scientific basis. Chance is a concession that was made to black magic on the part of precise mechanics, when it discovered the origin of things in the flickerings of atoms and managed under the very nose of the perplexed church to explain the world order as disorder out of which, as from out of the top hat of a magician, through a sudden collision of little balls, civilization was formed without needing a creator.

Under the influence of this news, as a result of the rotation of invisible forces, man got into a muddle of mathematics and palmistry and began to experience a certain melancholy.

> Futile gift, gift of chance,
> Life, why were you given to me?[*][7]

Homelessness, orphanhood, loss of purpose and direction—despite all this, blind chance, raised to a law, suited Pushkin. In it the enlightened century preserved untouched, for the time being, a taste of mystery and chicanery that was dear to the poet's heart. There was something in it of the card games that Pushkin so loved. Chance signified freedom—both the freedom of fate, transformed by a lapse of logic into arbitrariness, and the freedom of the precariousness of man, lacerated by drunken torment. It was an emptiness fraught with catastrophes, which held the promise of adventure and taught how to live by bluffing, running risks and competing in those risks with the blows of fate, striking as they fell, heads or tails,[*] by perceiving in these outbursts the sole chance, foreseen by no one, of rising in the world, of coming face to face with the unknown, of losing one's sight, of demanding an answer, of being noted and of knowing as you fall that you haven't been killed but have been found, singled out by the finger of fate as material proof of the chance occurrence, which is no longer a trifle, but the signal of a meeting, of eternity—"perhaps, a pledge of immortality."[*]

. . . With the accession of freedom everything became possible. The horizon swarmed with changes, and every object strove to stand upright, threatening at that very minute to turn world development in a different direction not as yet experienced by humanity. Conjectures of the sort "and what if Bonaparte had not caught a cold at the right

7. "Not in vain, not accidentally,/Was life given to me by God," the hairsplitting Metropolitan Filaret[*] corrected Pushkin's mistakes. Pushkin sighed in contrition, repented, hesitated, and held his ground. The circles of poetry and religion did not coincide at the time.

time?"* came into fashion. Pushkin, having the time of his life, played the solitaire of the so-called natural-historical process. If you drew the wrong queen,* the whole picture would change irreparably. He was amused by this easy reversibility of events, which gave him food for thought and style. Galloping in the toe shoes of fate over the flagstones of the international forum, history, it seemed, was ready—for show, by bluffing—to replay its scenes from the beginning, to renew and change everything. Pushkin's hands itched at the sight of such vacancies in the business of plot construction. In plain view, world-famous myths became overgrown with fresh stories, all ready to be set down on paper. Every louse aspired to become Napoleon. A little later and Raskolnikov would say: all is permitted!* Everything was shaking. Everything was tottering on the brink of a conceptual abyss: and what if?! . . . the excessive hypotheticalness of being took your breath away.

In remarks he made on *Count Nulin** in 1830 he shared his research:

At the end of 1825 I was in the country. Rereading *The Rape of Lucrece*, a rather weak poem by Shakespeare, I asked myself what would have happened if Lucrece had taken it into her head to slap Tarquin? Perhaps that would have dampened his ardor and he would have been forced to retreat in shame? Lucrece would not have stabbed herself, Publius would not have become enraged, Brutus would not have driven out the Caesars, both the world and the history of the world would have been different.

So, we owe the republic, the consuls, the dictators, the Catos, and Caesar to a seductive incident similar to one that occurred not long ago in my neighborhood, in Novorzhevsky District.

I had the idea of parodying history and Shakespeare, I couldn't resist the double temptation and wrote the story in two mornings.

Count Nulin has another analogue in history as well—the revolt of the Decembrists. It also could have come out either way. But the story contained a deeper lesson in that it promoted the anecdote and parody to the status of philosophy, making them universal weapons of thought and vision.

Is it necessary to say that Pushkin was at least half parodic? That his works are rife with such switches, which outrageously distort authoritative texts? The classic comparison of the poet with an echo dreamt up by Pushkin is right and not only in the sense of their mutual responsiveness. In responding to "every sound," the echo mimics us.*

Pushkin neither developed nor carried on tradition but rather teased

it, continually stumbling into parody and with its help diverging from
the main road in the history of literature. He went not forward but
sideways. Only later, through the efforts of the schools and the opera,
was he turned and brought back onto the main road. He himself had
chosen a side road.[8]

Pushkin's irrepressible passion for parody was warmed by the realization that if everything in the world is accidental, then it must also
be alterable, that from the sublime to the comic is but a single step.
In proof of this Pushkin strode from the *Iliad* to *The Gabrieliad*, from
Zhukovsky and Ariosto to *Ruslan and Lyudmila*, from Karamzin's
"Poor Liza" to "Mistress into Maid," from his own *Stone Guest* to a
ball at "The Undertaker" 's.* As a result of such oversteppings the hierarchy of genres was shattered, and avalanches and landslides ensued,
like *Evgeny Onegin*, which collapsed from a novel in verse into an
antinovel—a match for Sterne's *Tristram Shandy*.

The anecdote stoically withstood the collapse of form that had
already begun. Chance appeared in it not in its destructive, but in its
constructive, formative function, in the guise of the well-constructed
episode, which was full of merit and interesting in its own right and
held off for a brief second the overthrow of values through a pointed
punch line. "The unexpected event amazed all of us,"* Pushkin used
to say, admiring the anecdote's ability to focus on the quick-wittedness
of life and to heighten interest in it—to reveal the common sense in its
riddles and extraordinary occurrences.

Although the anecdote is somewhat lightweight, it is also solid and
local. It employs precise gestures: there and suddenly. Through the
eccentricities of the anecdote the table of ranks* inadvertently emerges
victorious, and objects by the slash of a sword reestablish name and
rank. The anecdote announces to us once again that reality is rational.
It gives reality back its prestige. In it the chance occurrence stands up
from its seat and pronounces a coronation speech: "Quiet, hold your
tongue," answered the teacher in excellent Russian, "hold your tongue
or you are lost. I am Dubrovsky."*

The anecdote is the opposite of parody. The anecdote is noble. It
gives spice to history, which has become bland after so many parodies,
and inspires us anew with the certainty that the world is our dwelling

8. He wrote to Vyazemsky of Zhukovsky (May 25, 1825): "I am not his heir but his
pupil, and I have only that advantage that I don't intrude on his road but wander along
a side road."

place. "In history I love only anecdotes," Pushkin could have repeated after Mérimée, "Among anecdotes I prefer those in which, it seems to me, there is an authentic depiction of the customs and characters of a given epoch."*

Still, what a sense of peace and sober-minded domestic harmony there is in this, a sense of being at home in the universe, where all objects stand on their proper shelves! . . . Let us cite an anecdote that served as an epigraph in "The Queen of Spades"—sustained in the character of Pushkin, in the spirit of Mérimée:

> The deceased Baroness von V—— appeared to me that night. She was all in white and said to me: "Hello, Mr. Counsellor!"—*Swedenborg*.

Still, what a sense of coziness! . . .

In his partiality for the anecdote Pushkin remains true to the tastes of the eighteenth century. It is from there that he adopted the old-fashioned elegance he deploys in the exposition of entertaining parables of the sort that satisfied the curiosity of the century about everything phenomenal. Read Ivan Khmelnitsky's *The Light Seen through Personifications*,* and you will see that at that time the Crocodile and even the Hurricane and Snow belonged to the category of anecdotal situations.

The anecdote minimizes the essential and cannot bear abstract concepts. It describes not a person, but a birthmark (but it's Madame de Pompadour's birthmark), not *The History of the Pugachov Rebellion*, but *The Captain's Daughter*, in which everything turns on a chance occurrence, on a rabbitskin coat.* But the anecdote evinces great respect for the person who has been chosen; bourgeois equality in relation to the facts is alien to it; it has a weakness for the particular, the strange, the extraordinary, it presents us with trivialities as if they were a sign of our initiation into the realm of rarities. Therein lies the whole trick, Grinyov's life and his bride are saved not by force, not by valor, not by cunning, not by the purse, but by a rabbitskin coat. That unforgettable coat must be made of rabbitskin: only a *rabbitskin* coat can save you. *C'est la vie.*

Pushkin was like a fish in water in the vicissitudes of fortune. Chance spurred him on, excited him, rejuvenated him and brought him back to the fold. He was akin to it. He played with fire every chance he got and went looking for trouble. But even at the height of rage, he never tried to out-argue fate: he longed to experience its handshake.*

That was the verification of his lot. He would go to a duel just as he

threw himself under the fire of inspiration: impromptu, at every opportunity. He tempted fate in his thirst to be convinced that it remembered
him. He was lucky. "But luck toys with me maliciously,"* he noted,
secretly flattered at this certification of his primogeniture. The lot of
the poet was repaid by adversities in everyday life. The sum was large
and required compensation. The ancients called this the "jealousy of
the gods," and he numbered among their favorites, and the position
carried obligations.

No one squandered life as foolishly as Pushkin did. But who else
entered literature in such an absurd way? He himself did not notice
how he became a writer, the match was made by his uncle* in a
drunken stupor.

> At first I was just playing,
> Daubing verses in jest,
> And then I recopied them,
> And then I published them,
> And what happened? Like it or not,
> Now I'm a brother
> To this one, that one, and the other,
> What's to be done? It's my own fault!*

Nonetheless this lot, which had all the earmarks of a passing whim,
of child's play, was dearer to him than all other gifts, earthly and heavenly, taken together. It was easy for him to begin the match, but once
it was begun, he had to play for high stakes, for the whole wad. "Generals and privy counsellors left their games of whist to watch such an
unusual game. Young officers gathered in the drawing room. . . . It
resembled a duel. A profound silence reigned all around."*

Baratynsky was shocked by his death. "Why did it happen that way
and no other?" he asked in tears of bewilderment and hurt. "Is it natural for a great man of mature years to die in a duel like a careless boy?"
(Letter to P. A. Vyazemsky,* February 5, 1837).

To this we answer: it is natural. Pushkin died in accordance with
the program of his life and could have said: we're quits. The chance
gift was sacrificed to chance. His end resembled his beginning: he was
a boy and died boyishly, surrounded by an aura of scandal and heroic
exploit, like Don Quixote. The tone of the anecdote was sustained to the
end, and was it not perhaps to improve the joke that Pushkin somehow
managed to hit d'Anthès' button?* Fate has a sense of humor.

Death in a duel so suited him that it looked like a passage from one of Pushkin's works. The passage, it's true, came out as something of a parody, but after all that was also in his style.

In his carefree youth, when he was rounding off *The Gabrieliad*, the poet threw down the gauntlet to the archangel and jokingly suggested that they would square accounts at the end of his life's road:

> But the days are flying, and time with gray
> Quietly silvers my hair,
> And a grand marriage before an altar
> Will unite me with an amiable wife.
> Beautiful consoler of Joseph!
> I beg you on bended knee,
> Oh, defender and preserver of cuckolds,
> I pray—then bless me,
> Grant me carefreeness and humility,
> Grant me patience again and again,
> Peaceful sleep, trust in my spouse,
> Peace in the family and love for my neighbor!*

His neighbor turned out to be d'Anthès. Everything came out almost exactly as written. The proposition was evidently accepted: Fate had the last shot, and it made it with a small correction on its own fantasy: Pushkin was denied contentment and quiet. Didn't he have a presentiment of this concluding stunt in *The Stone Guest*, in "The Shot," in "The Queen of Spades"? Or do we see in action here the ancient literary convention according to which fate mysteriously makes short work of an author, using the texts of his works as a blueprint—to the greater glory and confirmation of their amazing insight? . . .

> At that moment it seemed to him that the queen of spades screwed up her eyes and grinned. He was struck by the extraordinary resemblance . . .
> "The old woman!" he cried out in horror.

An old camp inmate told me that Pushkin, anticipating his article of the criminal code, kept two revolvers on him at all times. Those who like to take risks are very prudent: reckless in life, they are superstitious in fate.

Despite dissensions and preventative measures, Pushkin had a sense of fellowship with fate, which liberated him from fear, suffering, and vanity. *Volya* (freedom) and *dolya* (fate) are synonymous rhymes in his works. The more we trust in Providence, the more freely we live, and complete submission is as happy as a lark. Of the many Russian proverbs, the one closest to him is perhaps the refrain, "Sleep! Morning is wiser than evening."

Beyond Pushkin's submission to fate can be heard a sigh of relief—regardless of whether it brought him success or failure. Thus, thanks to the author's good offices, we enthusiastically accept Oleg's foreordained death. The horse's move is justified: the prince is checkmated: fate comes out on top: the game's over—sound the fanfare!*

> The warriors remember bygone days
> And battles they fought together.*

Through communion with providence a higher point of view—characteristic of Pushkin—is attained on any subject, in the light of which we endure misfortunes almost with pleasure, as long as they aid and abet fate. A state of freedom and peace comes,* prompted by the realization of one's own helplessness. It is as if we have thrown off a heavy load: now lettest thou thy servant depart.*

> "It's time to ride our separate ways!" they said,
> "We'll entrust ourselves to unknown fate."
> And each steed, not heeding the bit,
> Chose a road according to its will.*

Despite the common opinion that freedom is proud and recalcitrant, in *The Gypsies** Pushkin clothed it in robes of humility. Humility and freedom are one when fate becomes our home and trust in it spreads out like the steppe into the summer night. In this case ethnography coincided felicitously with the predilections of the author, who, being Russian and being Pushkin, was not indifferent to the gypsy way of life. To the wretched nomad tents of the gypsies—"those humble adherents of pristine freedom," "the children of humble freedom"—Pushkin harnessed his nomadic soul, filled with laziness, carefreeness, passions, idle reverie, vast horizons, wanderings—and all this under the care of fate, not weighted down by rebellion and grumbling, under the light of the moon, soaring up in the clouds.

Here the moon is the main character. Of course, this is romanticism, but not only that. Pushkin is more deeply implicated in this poem than in the others. He floats in *The Gypsies* like the moon in oil* and passes to it the reigns of government over his poetry.

> Look: beneath the distant firmament
> The free moon strolls;
> It pours equal light
> On all nature in passing.
> It stops at a cloud,
> Luxuriantly lights it up—
> And lo—it has passed on to another;
> Nor will it tarry there for long.
> Who will point to a place in the sky,
> And utter: stop there!
> Who to the heart of a young maiden will say:
> Love one only, don't betray?[9]

The moon and fate as well, which stroll about the universe filling everything they encounter with their radiance, are both the pledge and the nature of Pushkin's universalism, of Pushkin's adaptability and imitativeness. Humility in the face of the inscrutability of providence and an identification with it opened up the way to a broad mental outlook. Pushkin's gift for understanding and penetrating everything owed much to this inclination to shift obligations onto fate, assuming that it knew better. From its position you really can see farther.

In *The Gypsies* Pushkin looked at reality from the height of the soaring moon and saw the field (*polye*)—which rhymed with "will" (*volya*) and "fate" (*dolya*)—over which, like the moon in the sky, the gypsy camp was wandering, gently rocked by an easygoing love and the most easygoing betrayal in love. These intersections of meanings, inherent in the nomadic way of life, characteristic of the female heart as well, and of the moon, and of fate, and of the camp, and of the author—endow the poem with an exceptional organicism. Everything in it seems to rotate in a single patch of light which, however, embraces the entire universe.

Perhaps only the noisy ball, which occupies just as honorable a place in his poetry, can compete with the gypsy camp as a symbol of the collected works of Pushkin. The image of lightly and freely intersected space filled with a motley confusion of figures, clothing, dialects, and fortunes over which the condescending gaze of the poet glides, waltzing, lighting up with momentary attention now one, now another tableau—those are the general outlines of his creation.

---

9. See the fragment "Why does the wind whirl in the ravine," in which a similar series of associations—between winds, maidens, moons, etc.—ends in the poet.

> Friends! Does it make any difference:
> Whether you lose yourself in idleness
> In a brilliant hall, a modish loge,
> Or in a nomad tent?*

Clearly—it makes no difference. Pushkin's good breeding is akin to his passion for the nomadic life. He gave a memorable description of this idea in *Onegin*. "There there will be a ball, and there a children's party. Whither will my prankster gallop?" Our scamp has a finger in every pie—we can make bold to vouch for Pushkin. Not for nothing did he take up geography at an early age. After the Russian Ruslan we hear nothing but: the Caucasus, the Balkans, "and the Finn, and now the savage Tungus, and the Kalmyk, friend of the steppes,"* before becoming future admirers of Pushkin, were collected by him into one band in *The Robber Brothers.** That was a mandate for world literature.

Pushkin's mobility, his life on wheels allowed him to clear the most difficult national and historical hurdles without delays. Light-mindedness became a means of communication with other peoples, the traveler accepted the relay baton from the ballroom show-off. There was a war going on, he was dispatched into exile, sent on missions on the bloody trails of Paskevich, Ermolov,* Pugachov, Peter, and the ball got bigger and bigger and the number of guests, attires, and of tribes and fortresses smashed to dust grew.

> So my Muse, lighthearted friend of Reverie,
> Soared to the boundaries of Asia
> And gathered herself a garland
> Of wild Caucasian flowers.
> She was captivated by the fierce attire
> Of tribes nurtured on war,
> And often the enchantress
> Appeared to me in this new clothing . . .*

Pushkin loved to dress up in foreign costumes both on the street and in his verses. "Just look—Pushkin is a Serb or a Moldavian, women of his acquaintance gave him the clothing. . . . Look again—and Pushkin is a Turk, Pushkin is a Jew, he talks just like a Jew." These girlhood reminiscences about the poet's escapades in Kishinyov could pass for literary scholarship. "Adaptable and sociable in its relations with foreign languages"—that's what the Russian language was like according to Pushkin, and that's what Pushkin himself was like, for he knew how to make himself at home in any idea or language. Sociable, on a first-name basis with the whole world, tolerant "sometimes even to a fault," he, according to the testimony of his acquaintances, chatted with equal willingness with fools and clever people, with scoundrels and vulgarians. Pushkin's ability to communicate knew no bounds. "Everyone has a mind," insisted Pushkin, "I find no one boring, from the policeman on duty right up to the tsar." "He sometimes conversed with lackeys," A. O. Smirnova-Rosset* adds respectfully in her old age.

> . . . and the underwater movement of sea snakes,
> And the growing of vines in the dales.*

All themes, like women, were accessible to him, and running through them he marked out roads for Russian letters for centuries to come. No matter where we poke our noses—Pushkin is everywhere, which can be explained not so much by the influence of his genius on other talents, as by the fact that there isn't a motif in the world he didn't touch upon. Pushkin simply managed to write about everything for everyone.

As a result he became the Russian Virgil, and in this role of teacher-guide he accompanies us in no matter which direction of history, culture, or life we go. When you go strolling today with Pushkin, you meet yourself as well.

> Holding my nose, I turned away my face.
> But the wise guide drew me ever farther, farther—
> And, having lifted up a stone by a bronze ring,
>
> We descended—and I found myself in a cellar.*

Pushkin valued benevolence in people above all else. He talked about this a few days before his death. Along with the theme of fate, which was so dear to him, he wrote about this in a review of Silvio Pellico's book* *On the Obligations of Man* (1836). "Silvio Pellico spent ten years in various dungeons and, after he had been given back his freedom, published his notes. There was general amazement: people expected complaints, filled with bitterness—instead they read touching meditations filled with serene calm, love, and goodwill." In this "inviolate benevolence toward everyone and everything," the reviewer discerned the "mystery of a beautiful soul, the mystery of a Christian man" and numbered his author among those elect souls "who were greeted by the Angel of the Lord with the name *men of goodwill.*"

Was Pushkin one of the elect? Probably he was—in a different manner.

When we come in contact with Pushkin's language, we are enveloped by an atmosphere of benevolence, which seems to be quietly exuded by the words and which compels objects to open themselves up and exclaim: "Here I am!" Pushkin more often than not likes what he's writing about, and since he wrote about everything, it would be impossible to find a more benevolent writer in the world. His sociability and responsiveness, his trust in providence and his confluence with it are either called forth by goodwill, or they draw this feeling up out of the depths of the soul out into the open with the same sacred simplicity with which light is sent to the earth—onto the righteous and sinners alike. Therefore he is welcome everywhere, and his love is reciprocated. He is amiable to whatever he is depicting, and it clings to him.

Let's take some very popular lines and see wherein lies the punch.

> Winter! . . . The peasant, rejoicing,
> Takes to the road again on his sled . . .*

(What triumph on such an insignificant pretext!)

> Why are you neighing, my valiant steed? . . .*

(How could the horse not answer and not start to speak in a human voice?!)

> My uncle, the most high-minded of men . . .*

(Under the influence of this uncle—whose requiem reads in the tone of a toast to one's health—the ever melancholy Lermontov wrote his only upbeat lyric, "Borodino":* "Tell me, uncle, is it not in vain . . . ?")

> The Ukrainian night is quiet . . .*

(And it sounds like an exclamation—but why? Because Pushkin regards this as a merit on its part and bestows the medal "quiet" on it with the same cordial solemnity with which he admires the comfortable circumstances of his hero—"Kochubei is rich and famous"*—as if all other nights were bad, but the Ukrainian one is—quiet, do you hear, I'm announcing it to the whole world: "The Ukrainian night is quiet!")

> The children ran to the cottage,
> Hastily they called their father . . .*

(They danced to this refrain, forgetting about the drowned man. In general in Pushkin's works everything begins with the festive ringing of a bell, and ends on the quiet . . .)

> Godspeed on your long journey!
> You'll find your way, God willing.
> The moon is shining; the night is clear;
> The cup has been drunk to the dregs.*

(Not bad for a "funeral dirge"! He tries to propose a toast about what is saddest and most awful . . .)—

> So—praise to you, Plague!*

Pushkin lost no love on the official ode, but even after he had switched gears, in some part of his soul he remained a writer of odes. Only now he was writing odes in honor of an inkwell or to greet the coming of autumn.* Even if his odes were facetious and prone to laughter, they were still filled with praise. "I sing of a young acquaintance and the multitude of his whims," he said, playing the fool in *Onegin*, letting us know that he wasn't so backward while at the same time immortalizing both his pal and every petty detail of his toilette. More firmly than many of his contemporaries Pushkin kept for himself the entourage and the title of the poet, standing guard over the interests of the privileged subject. He celebrated these privileges, however, not in magniloquent bombast, eclipsing the subject of discourse with his poetical eloquence, but by manifesting a tender susceptibility toward the personal characteristics of the adored object, so that it, even while being bathed in praise, did not lose its real features, but only became more distinct and, that means, more attractive. In Pushkin's works every object looks like a golden apple on a silver plate. As if he were saying to each and every one of them:

> Frost and sun; what a wonderful day!
> You are still sleeping, my charming friend—
> It's time to wake up, my beauty:
> Open up your eyes closed by sweet bliss
> To meet the northern Aurora,
> Appear like a star of the north!*

And they appear.

"There is no truth where there is no love"—on Pushkin's lips this rule meant, among other things, that true objectivity is attained through the partialities of our hearts and minds, that in loving we are transported into the beloved being and, imbued with it, more truly comprehend its nature. Morality, without suspecting it, plays into the hands of the artist. But as a result it must sometimes love scoundrels.

Under the sway of Pushkin we become so immersed in Salieri's torments that we are ready, like Salieri, to doubt Mozart's merits, and only an unprecedented act of villainy committed before our very eyes restores justice and forces us to be horrified by him who, by his casuistry, had almost inveigled us into becoming his accomplices. In the interests of complete equilibrium (not worrying too much about Mozart, who was a kindred spirit) the author with the generosity of the true creator gives Salieri a head start and, having spotted him enough points to put him in the lead, openly favors the murderer and reveals the workings of his heart with sympathy and compassion.

The dramatic poet—Pushkin demanded—must be impartial, like fate. But that's true only within the boundaries of the whole work (put in parentheses); but while the action is going on, he is partial at every step and takes care by turns now of one, now of the other side, so that we don't always know whom we are supposed to prefer: with Pushkin's assent we manage to become friendly with both warring sides. The tsar and Evgeny in *The Bronze Horseman*, the father and the son in *The Covetous Knight*, the father and the daughter in "The Stationmaster," the count and Silvio in "The Shot"*—and we get confused and exert ourselves trying to figure out whom the obliging author favors. But he favors everyone:

> An exchange of fire beyond the hills;
> Both our camp and theirs look on;
> On the hill before the Cossacks
> A red banner waves.*

But from which vantage point is Pushkin looking? From both sides at the same time, from their camp and ours? Or perhaps from above, from the side, from some third point of view, equally distant from "them" and from "us"? In any case he plays up to both sides with relish ("Heh, Cossack! Don't rush into battle." "Standard-bearer! Stay clear of the attack"), as if setting them on each other to test their equal forces in action as fast as possible. Well of course the bold men can't wait any longer and rush at one another.

They've rushed, collided with a common cry . . .
Look! How are they?
The banner is already on the enemy's lance,
And the Cossack is without a head.

No, what an author! It's as if he's chuckling to cleanse his conscience—after all I warned them!—and he enjoys the fun and rubs his hands together in glee: I can work with this.

How would Silvio Pellico have conducted himself in these circumstances? Probably he would have prayed for both sides—don't kill—and if they killed, then for their bloodstained souls. Pushkin also prays—for both opponents to win. If Pellico's prayer were to be answered—reality in its current form would disappear, history would grind to a halt, the fighters would embrace one another and everything would come to an end. Pushkin's prayer is for the good of the world—as it is, and it consists in wishing it long life, good health, successes in battle, and personal happiness. Let soldiers fight, tsars rule, women love, monks fast, and Pushkin, let Pushkin watch it all and write about it all, helping and inspiring all of them.

God help you, my friends,
In the cares of life, of service to the tsar,
And at feasts of riotous friendship,
And in the sweet mysteries of love!

God help you, my friends,
In storms and in domestic sorrows,
In distant lands, on the deserted sea
And in the gloomy chasms of the earth!*

Probably, never has so much sympathy for people found expression all at once in a single poem—and such a little one at that. You want to weep—Pushkin is so good. But let's imagine for a minute both the "gloomy chasms of the earth" and the "cares of service to the tsar" in a less Aesopian aspect. As everyone knows, it was the Decembrists* who were suffering afflictions in chasms at the time. And service to the tsar included standing guard over those chasms. It turns out that Pushkin is wishing both of them the swiftest success. To the prisoner—mercy, to the fugitive—the forest, to the tsar's servant—to capture and punish. Is that the way it is?! Yes (with a sigh)—that's the way it is.

Was it not we who galloped here yesterday,
Was it not we who trampled in rage,

> Burning with zealous vengeance,
> The evil betrayers of the tsar?*

This was written on the day after the 14th of December—at the same time as an encouraging epistle to Siberia.* Portraying a young oprichnik, Pushkin in passing sympathized with him as well, along with his unfortunate victims. After all, the oprichnik was very nice—it would have been a pity to send him away empty-handed . . .*

"What a strange mixture this magnificent creature is!" Pushkin's friend Pushchin complained about him.* He was always too broad for his friends. Rubbing elbows with everyone, obliging everyone, Pushkin seemed to everyone alternately intimate and remote. They enticed him, pestered him, tried to teach him how to live, tried to take him at his word, tried to make him into a Jacobin, a courtier, a Mason, but he, following the example of beautiful Spanish women, managed "touchingly to combine piety with love, to give the prearranged sign from under a mantilla"* and slipped away, just as Kolobok slipped away from the old man and woman.*

Was there anyone whose appearance Pushkin couldn't adopt? Was there anyone with whom he couldn't find a common language? "God, don't let me go out of my mind"*—he disavowed madness the better to imagine himself in the position of a madman. He, who in the guise of Grinyov managed to wage war against and be friends with Pugachov at the same time, was able to enter on tiptoe into the conscience of the hangman, which had not been cleansed for years, and came away with a good word in his bosom.

"They dragged me to the foot of the gallows. 'Don't fret, don't fret,'—my executioners repeated over and over again, perhaps truly wanting to cheer me up."*

How much bashfulness, tact, irony, hope, and brutal vigor there is in that terse "Don't fret!" You can't make that up. You can only experience it, eavesdrop on the fateful moment, or capture it, as Pushkin did, with the help of inspiration. By the way, inspiration, according to Pushkin, is above all "a disposition of the soul to the liveliest receptiveness to impressions."*

A disposition to receptiveness. Friendliness, pleasantness. A disposition to the first person you happen to meet. To whatever the Lord grants. He grants—the disposition—benevolence—peace—and the calm that makes you feel at home—inspiration . . .

E. A. Engelhardt, the director of the lycée, had worse to say about

Pushkin than anyone else did. Worse than anyone else—because his opinion was not without insight, despite the professional obtuseness usual in such judgments. But if, let's assume, his words to the effect that the most important thing in life for Pushkin was to "shine," that he had a "completely superficial French mind," can be put down to the narrow-mindedness of the pedagogue, all the same in places his characterization of the famous graduate is striking in its piercing sadness and a certain timorous perplexity in the face of this unique and puzzling anomaly. About Pushkin, about our Pushkin, he said: "His heart is cold and empty; there is neither love nor religion in it; perhaps it is as empty as ever a youthful heart has been" (1816).

Nothing would be easier than to brush aside the frightened director with a laugh: an old fogy, a Salieri who failed to recognize the new Mozart, a liberal and an Engelhardt. But perhaps Engelhardt's confusion in the face of that "as ever has been" is worthy of serving as a prologue to the enormity of Pushkin, who himself was quite willing to sigh over the inadequacy of his heart and gobbled up distances as if he wanted to sate his empty belly, which demanded nothing less than— the whole world, lacking the strength to stop, having no reason to linger for long on any one thing.

Emptiness was Pushkin's content. Without it he wouldn't have been full, he couldn't have existed, just as there can be no fire without air, no inhalation without exhalation. It more than anything else ensured the poet's receptivity, which yielded to the fascination of every caprice and to the colors of pictures that he hastily devoured and let fly like glossy postcards: How natural! Absolutely true to life! Let us remember Gogol, restlessly, nightmarishly preoccupied with himself, painting everything in the perverse light of his own crooked nose.* Pushkin had nothing to worry about, Pushkin was sufficiently empty to see things as they were, without foisting himself off on us as a willful daydreamer, but filling himself up with things to the brim and reacting almost mechanically, "Is a beast howling in the remotest depths of the forest, is a horn blowing, is thunder thundering, is a maiden singing beyond the hill"*—benevolent and indifferent.

Loving everyone, he loved no one, and this "no one" gave him the freedom to nod to all and sundry—every nod an oath of loyalty, an intoxicating rendezvous. He winds the spring of these obeisances tight in Don Juan,* who puts all of himself (not much is needed when there's nothing to put!) into each new passion—ever ready to be transfigured into the image of the person being seduced, so that at any given moment our betrayer is truthful and sincere, in accordance with the astonishing change that has taken place in him. He all the more industriously and truthfully devours the souls of others because he doesn't have enough stuffing of his own, because for him impersonation is a way of life and subsistence. Here before our very eyes the profligate blossoms into a lily of innocence—he's sucked out the blood of the virtuous Doña Anna, has drunk his fill, is soaked with it and, inspired, says:

> Thus for a long time was I
> An obedient disciple of depravity,
> But from the time I first saw you,
> It seems to me, I was completely reborn.
> In loving you, I love virtue
> And for the first time I meekly bow before it
> On trembling knees.

Verily, verily—in fact passion transformed Juan into an angel and Pushkin into Pushkin's creation. But don't get too carried away: what we see before us is a vampire.

Something of the vampire was hidden in so heightened a susceptibility. That's why Pushkin's images have such a luster of eternal youth, of fresh blood, high color, that's why the present manifests itself in his works with such unprecedented force: the whole fullness of existence is crammed into the moment when blood is transfused from random victims into the empty vessel of the one who in essence is no one, remembers nothing, does not love, but only declares to the moment: "You're beautiful! (You're full of blood!) stop!"*—guzzling until he slides off.

When Doña Anna tries to grill Juan about how many check marks there are on his list, he objects with dignity: "To this day I never loved a single one of them"—and he's not lying at all: everything vanished in the moment of the hunt, except the fullness and truth of the moment being experienced, it is all that exists, it sucks in, it suffices unto itself, absorbing the cherished image, it will pass and someone will say, stretching and summing it all up with an empty yawn:

> Having reveled in pleasure,
> I view the victim of my caprice
> With insurmountable disgust:
> Thus the heedless fool,
> Having committed an evil act in vain,
> Having slit the throat of a beggar in the forest,
> Curses the flayed corpse . . . *

On his way again as fast as possible, to a new meeting, to new food for mind and heart—"The clouds rush, the clouds whirl" (unseen the moon).*

Isn't it strange that so much space is devoted in Pushkin's works to unburied bodies smuggled in between the lines? At first you don't attach any significance to this fact: so someone died—who doesn't, what author hasn't killed off a hero or two? But that's not the point . . . In *The Gypsies*, for example, toward the end of the poem, two characters are killed and buried, and there's nothing peculiar in that. The peculiar begins when the dead body is moved to the center of the work and breaks up the plot with its unnatural intrusion, and suddenly it turns out that, strictly speaking, the action as a whole unfolds in the presence of a corpse, which, as in "The Queen of Spades," wanders through the whole story or lies about through the entire length of *Boris Godunov:* * "I saw the slashed tsarevich lying . . ."

And although they seem to bury him, he will lie that way throughout the play ("We saw their dead bodies," they will say in the apotheosis) in the guise of frequent mentions of the body of the murdered boy, of whom False Dmitry is but a pale echo, the Pretender who is so horrifying to Tsar Boris precisely because while *this* tsarevich grows, *that* tsarevich lies about, and his image is doubled.

Boris's fears make it evident that he is tormented by the suspicion that perhaps the lawful heir has survived, he is crushed by the burden of his sin, worried by the success of the Pretender, but besides all that, together with it, there is his main fear, the assumption that strikes him to the marrow, that he, the tsar—despite the fact that common sense would dictate that he rejoice at such idleness—has for his rival a *dead* tsarevich, whose protracted condition of being slaughtered threatens to become an ulcer capable of undermining Boris's dynasty. The clever Shuisky* hammers away at precisely this point, reassuring and terrifying the tsar with the fact that Dmitry is dead, yes, so dead that Boris is not the only one who feels sick from the prolonged deadness that has been put out on display.

> For three days
> I have visited his corpse in the cathedral,
> Accompanied there by all the people of Uglich.
> Thirteen bodies lay around him,
> Torn to pieces by the people, and they
> Had already begun to decay,

> But the childish countenance of the tsarevich
> Was clear and fresh and peaceful . . .

The ambiguous pronouncement "He is sleeping" does not return the dead boy to life but slows down and galvanizes the corpse in a fixed position, endowed with the capability of moving and directing events, pulling up strata of historical existence by the roots. It—existence—is set in motion by a greedy, unclean languor of the spirit, which scavenges not far from the enticing cadaver and sends the huge tsardom the way of the corpse—from the face of the earth into the crater of the grave. The relics of the tsarevich know no peace. The signs of death are inflamed in them to the eerie, supernatural rawness of a wound that has not healed for years, bleeding drop by drop, until at last blood spurts out of the mouth and ears of the overgorged Boris and drowns the country in a flood of strife.

The boy bleeding in Uglich leaves a trail through Pushkin's works— first to the gate of Marko Yakubovich, whose son, after the death of the unknown guest, begins to exhibit similar symptoms:

> The healer came to Yakubovich,
> Looked at the child and said:
> "Your son is dangerously ill;
> Look at his white neck:
> Do you see the bloody wound?
> It's from the tooth of a vampire, believe me."

> Immediately the whole village set off
> For the cemetery after the old healer;
> There they dug up the grave of the traveler,
> And saw that the corpse was rosy and fresh—
> Its nails had grown as long as the claws of a raven,
> And the face had grown over with a beard,
> The lips were besmeared with crimson blood—
> The deep grave was full of blood.
> Poor Marko brandished a stake,
> But the corpse began to squeal and nimbly leaped
> Out of the grave and ran into the forest . . .*

Now let's glance back: look, there's a corpse, and there, and there, and there . . . The traveler leaves gifts in one home after another. But—miraculously—the appearance of these corpses energizes Pushkin's text, just as if an armload of birchwood had been thrown into a burning stove. "Wait . . . in the presence of a corpse! . . . what should we do with him?"—Laura asks Juan, who, as soon as he arrives, stabs his rival by her bed and, right after he stabs him, falls at the feet of the woman, who is somewhat taken aback by the change. How—what to do?! Let it lie there, let it be present: in the presence of a corpse everything is merrier, more frantic, more interesting. In the presence of a corpse Juan caresses Laura, in the presence of a corpse he ventures to begin an intrigue with the unapproachable Doña Anna, who, if there hadn't been a grave there, might have remained unintrigued. The dearly departed in Pushkin's works serve, if not always as the source of the action, then as its catalyst, in the vicinity of which the action swiftly gathers force and speed. Thus the body of Lensky, slain by his friend, stimulates the process of transformation, in the course of which Onegin and Tatyana radically switch roles, and the whole dynamics of life gains much in this death.

> Zaretsky carefully laid
> The frozen corpse upon the sleigh;
> He drove the awful treasure home.
> Scenting the corpses, the horses
> Snorted and struggled,
> Wet the steel bit with white foam,
> And flew as swiftly as an arrow.*

Reasoning hypothetically, we come to the conclusion that corpses in Pushkinian usage represent the prototype of the inexhaustible spiritual vacuum, which pushed the author into making more and more pictures and served as a photonegative in the creative process of the genius. Therefore, more specifically, his corpses are not at all phantasmal, not sepulchral, but are repulsively corporeal, being the empty casing of someone who is in essence absent. Their gestures look automatic, mechanical, robot-like.

> And having recognized the naked guest,
> The peasant slammed the window shut:
> He suddenly froze: "Blast you!"
> He whispered, shuddering.*

Out of fear, one might think that it is the importunate critic Pisarev (prematurely drowned) who has come to knock at Pushkin's door with the suggestion that he occupy himself with something more useful than poetry.* But the facts suggest otherwise. The naked guest, doomed to wander "beyond the grave and the cross," is closer to him who was his whole life obsessed with aimlessly sliding over an immense plain, which he had to traverse and describe in its entirety, at times awakening an inexplicable loathing in sensitive people with chaste dispositions. Pisarev, who like Engelhardt was horrified by Pushkin's scandalous lack of content, nakedness, and empty-belliedness, used textbooks of chemistry, physiology, and other useful sciences pulled up by the ears to justify his childishly direct impression. But it seems that the basic reason for Pisarev's outrageous enmity was rooted in the irrational fear that Pushkin at times inspires by vacillating unlike any other poet in the reader's perception—between being a giant of the first order and a complete nonentity.

As a result, to the childish question, Who really does periodically knock "under the window and at the gate"? the most correct answer is: Pushkin . . .

If one were to construct a model of the universe according to Pushkin (as it was drawn according to Ptolemy or Kepler), it would be absolutely necessary to envisage this perpetuum mobile at the center of the earth:

> There is a high mountain,
> In it is a deep lair;
> In that lair, in mournful darkness,
> A crystal coffin sways . . .
> And in that crystal coffin
> The tsarevna sleeps an eternal sleep.*

All of them—the imperishable Dmitry, the water-soaked victim of drowning, the red-lipped vampire, the tsarevna swaying like a carpenter's plumb—despite differences in coloring represent variations on one guiding idea: the inexhaustible corpse, condensed death. Here something of Pushkin's own philosophical hindsight creeps in, although as always it takes the form of a modest, copybook morality. Pushkin's slogan, "Let young life play at the entrance to the grave," contains by the law of contrast not only a notion, pleasing to all, of the whirl of life that promises an abundance of pleasures, but also the ruinous condition under which the game of cat and mouse attains supreme artistry. "The entrance to the grave"* (or "exit") assumes the shape of an orifice, from which (to which) the whirlwind of reality rushes with mad force, and the closer it comes to us, the larger looms the gloomy pole of nonexistence, the more furiously, fully, and artistically we pass the hours entitled: *The Feast in Time of Plague.**

The plague is the reason for the feast, and the wagon loaded up to the top with corpses, driving past the feasters with a black Negro on the coachman's seat, puts a damper on the orgy only for a moment in order that it, having died down, might blaze up with redoubled passion (the analogy with a furnace into which firewood is thrown suggests itself once again). That's why deadness in Pushkin's works is not so terrifying and usually does not even attract our attention: the impression is trumped by the positive result. As the Chairman explains, melancholy is necessary

> So that afterwards we can return to enjoyment
> More recklessly, like one who is torn
> From the earth by a vision . . .

Feast in time of plague!—that's Pushkin's formula for life, served up in the best possible way and crowned with its flowering before death: poetry. No other work of Pushkin exudes as much art as this tiny mystery play, which, although devoted to another subject, seems woven entirely out of the fluid of pure artistry. It is precisely here, sitting in state at the very edge of the plague-infested pit, that the poet is filled with the greatest potential for flights of his fantasy, which rushes from madness to illumination. For the way of life in *The Feast* is ecstatic, the bacchanalia inspired. On the threshold of destruction all the forces of instinct for existence produce this upsurge, which is marked by a creative act that resembles an outpouring in prayer. We hear a breach open up in the heavens through which currents of air pass between the sky and the earth, and the effect is heightened by the composition of a fresco executed according to medieval canons, in which the souls of the beloved women—Matilda and Jenny—are placed in the heavens, raised above the netherworld on both sides of the picture, at the beginning and at the end of the tragedy.

> Oh, if only it were possible to hide
> This spectacle from her deathless eyes!
> . . . .
> . . . .
> . . . Holy child of the light! I see
> You there, whither my fallen spirit
> Can no longer attain . . .

Yes, fallen. Yes, cannot attain. But gazes, sounds, rays to and from—intersect; airiness of thought is achieved thanks to fall, shame, disgrace; he who has condemned himself to art can no longer escape them.

To the priest's speech demanding that he abandon the path of depravity the Chairman responds with a refusal. Pay attention: through his words art begs forgiveness from religion. He presents an extensive list of causes and symptoms, which hold sin in place—in that same form and composition in which that other dissolute Chairman cultivated it, and threw it into a pit with the corpses, and professed it as his faith (calling it art for art's sake):

> I cannot, I must not
> Go after you: I am held here
> By despair, by the terrible memory,
> The realization of my lawlessness,
> And by the horror of that dead emptiness,
> Which I find in my home—
> And by the newness of these mad gaieties,
> And by the beneficial poison of this cup,
> And by the caresses (forgive me, Lord)
> Of this creature damned, but dear . . .

Judging by Pushkin's standards, art clings to life through death, sin, lawlessness. Art itself is complete lawlessness, called forth by the emptiness of the dead house, of the walking corpse: "This creature damned but dear . . ."

To console the artist, who has been condemned and damned, let us cite Michael Psellus,* a medieval scholastic: "Brilliant speeches wash the dirt from the soul and impart to it a pure and ethereal nature." [10]

> For a long time I have been planning to visit you
> In the German city whose praises you sang,
> To drink with you, as poets drink,
> The wine you praised in verse.
> Kiselyov, whom you glorified,
> Has already asked me to go with him . . .*

That's how Pushkin greeted Yazykov in one of his letters. Reality was measured by the lists of things whose praises he sang. The colo-

10.   But Jenny will not abandon
             Edmund even in the heavens!

nization of countries by means of belles-lettres was beginning, and literature seemed to plunge headlong, having suddenly caught fire with the hope of being able to represent everything that is. No one had a clear idea why this was necessary—least of all Pushkin, who understood better than others the need for putting the life around him into verse. He acted just like a savage Tungus,* singing without pausing to think about any tree he happened upon along the way—"Look, there stands a tree!"—or a hare—"Look, there runs a hare!"—et cetera, about all and sundry that happened to catch his eye, integrating the passing landscape into the flow of his song. In his texts pulses the primeval joy of the simple naming of things, which are transformed into poetry simply by a magical summons alone. Isn't that why many of his stanzas resemble catalogs of the articles and rubrics most popular at the time? The idea was that a fashionable word found in a line of poetry would provoke amazement: how authentic!

> Having donned a wide-brimmed bolivar,
> Onegin rode to the boulevard . . .
>
> . . . .
> He rushed to Talon certain
> That Kaverin was already waiting for him there.
>
> . . . .
> Bloody roast beef lay before him,
> And truffles, the luxury of youth,
> The finest flowering of French cuisine.
> And an imperishable Strasbourg paté
> Between a runny Limburger cheese
> And a golden pineapple.*

The passion for quantity in the registration of the world by names made Pushkin's compositions resemble an address book or the telephone directory of our day, which moved Belinsky to conclude that *Evgeny Onegin* was a whole encyclopedia.* His brilliant and superficial education at Tsarskoe Selo, his wide circle of acquaintances and human interests, helped Pushkin to compile a universal index that included everything he had ever seen or read. The absence of a strict system, a clear worldview, and mental discipline, and the author's omnivorousness and irresponsibility with regard to the fundamental doctrines of his day, assisted no little in this. If Pushkin had been more learned and methodical in his eagerness to enumerate all the details of existence, we would have gotten stuck with him on the very first letter of the alphabet. Fortunately, "we've all studied something a little bit somewhere,"* which in combination with his easy-going character gave his lists an air of careless sketchiness and superficiality. The inventory of his property was made according to the specifications of a picture glimpsed through the window of a rushing carriage. The impression created is as cursory as it is exhaustive:

> The closed sleigh rushed over ruts and bumps.
> Stalls, old ladies, little boys,
> Shops, streetlights,
> Palaces, gardens, monasteries,
> Bukharans, sleighs, gardens,
> Merchants, huts, peasants,
> Boulevards, towers, Cossacks,
> Apothecaries, milliner's shops,
> Balconies, lions on gates
> And flocks of crows on crosses flashed by.*

He loved to cover paper with such batches of attributes. He had something of Peter's managerial mettle in him. Instead of describing life, he made a head count. Read his reports, familiar to every preschooler, on the characteristics of the Russian climate, on the round of customs. With Humboldt's simplicity of spirit Pushkin relates to us that it's hot in the summer and cold in the winter, and that when winter comes the days become shorter, people sit at home, ride around in sleighs, et cetera. He does not shy away from making lists of bits of information that before him were considered too banal to be admitted into literature without being properly cleaned up. For all the versatility of his vision, Pushkin had a weakness for what was lying around underfoot.

His universal sweep did not prevent him from showing his preference for every insect he happened upon near at hand. While shying away from caricature and hyperbole, Pushkin is trivial to the point of caricature and hyperbole—like Plyushkin,* who squandered his estate collecting junk. For the first time in our literature the hair-splitting art of the detail swelled to the dimensions of the epic. What poet before him had noticed what jacket a man was wearing, what kind of nail file, toothbrush, toilet water he used?* Pushkin introduced the tradition of linking the concept of realism primarily with low and trivial matter. He invented the wheel that Chekhov had ridden into the ground. He even selected a pseudonym in Chekhov's style: Belkin.*

On the other hand, this meticulousness about insignificant details

served as a garnish to Pushkin's grand scale. If every little smell of
Onegin's luncheon menu has been so thoroughly sniffed out, then it
must mean that the epoch is truthfully reflected in the novel. But it
doesn't mean that at all. The novel's encyclopedicity is to a large extent illusory. The illusion of totality is achieved through the minute-
ness of the finishing touches applied only to some inessential details
of the surroundings. There are a lot of dishes, weather conditions, and
dancing feet, and consequently it seems as if there's nothing that isn't
there. In fact, the most important thing is arrogantly absent from the
novel, and the text amounts to almost nothing but incidental moments.
Bestuzhev-Marlinsky, who was unable to see the forest everyone had
expected for the trees, was offended by *Onegin*'s pointlessness. "Why
are you trying to shoot a butterfly with a cannon? . . . What is the point
of carving figures out of apple seeds, like the Indian Brahmins, when
you have Praxiteles' chisel in your hands?" (Letter to Pushkin, March 9,
1825.)

But Pushkin was deliberately writing a novel about nothing. In
Evgeny Onegin he could think of nothing but shirking his responsi-
bilities as narrator. The novel is made up of poor excuses that draw
our attention away to the margins of the verse page and hinder the
development of the plot line selected by the writer. The action is just
barely held together by the two letters and two monologues of amorous quid pro quo, which lead to absolutely nothing, and by a nonentity
elevated to the status of hero, and almost every sentence comes close
to drowning in distracting secondary material. No less than three balls
are held in it, and, taking advantage of the attendant fuss, the author
loses the thread of his narration, wanders off, marks time, beats around
the bush and sits it out in the underbrush, in the background of his own
story. For example, Onegin's quarrel with Lensky, which should play
first fiddle in the conflict, almost comes to nothing, crowded out by the
pies baked for the heroine's nameday party. You literally have to force
your way through to it through towering verbal delays, beginning with
the crowd in the entryway—"the barking of pekineses, the kissing of
maidens, the noise, the laughter, the crush on the threshold," contrived
so as to draw our eyes away from the center to the periphery of events,
whither, like a tarantas into a ditch, the narration skids:

> Of course, Evgeny was not the only one
> Who could see Tatyana's confusion,
> But at the time all thoughts and eyes

Were focused on the rich meat pie
(Unfortunately oversalted);
And then they were already bringing in
Tsimlyanskoe champagne in bottles sealed with tar
Between the stew and the blancmange;
Then came a column of wine glasses
Thin and elongated as your waist,
Zizi, crystal of my soul,
The object of my innocent verses,
Enticing vial of love,
You, who so often made me drunk!*

But now the guests have finally finished their meal, have wiped off their mouths, and are waiting for something to happen at last. Nothing doing. In the Onegin stanza thoughts don't move in a straight line, but slantwise in relation to the course charted, thanks to which, as we read, we slip down along a diagonal to the side of what is happening. Observe how one direction is successively replaced by a second, a third, a fifth, a tenth, so that by the end of the stanza we have forgotten what was being talked about at the beginning.

As a result we are periodically carried beyond the frame of the story—into the expanse of an unimportant, unnecessary discourse that has nothing to do with the matter at hand but is the only thing that is important to the poet, whose agenda is—without really saying anything and wandering round and about the proposed plot—to create an atmosphere of spontaneous, boundless existence, in which all of our attention is swallowed up by nameday parties and teas, visits from the neighbors and maidens' dreams—the vegetative breath of life. The novel slips through our fingers, and even in decisive situations, in portrayals of the main characters, where pride of place is assigned not to human beings but to interiors, it becomes elusive, like air, threatening to melt into no more than a thinly painted preparatory sketch and, blurring, to come to naught—mere calligraphy on paper. That's why he left room on his pages for so many empty spaces, blank spots, which, to heighten the absurdity, he covered with sieves of ellipsis points,* at which the public in its time had a good laugh, encountering the art of graphic abstractionism for the first time. You can bet that there was nothing concealed behind this indication of omitted stanzas but the same air that circulates through the space of the book, which extends its borders into the infinity of the subject, to the point of losing track of what strictly speaking the scatter-brained author intended to tell us.

He constantly faults himself for yet again spouting nonsense, he accuses himself of forgetfulness, pulls himself up short—"Where in the world is my incoherent story?"—hypocritically appealing to his muse, "Don't let me wander every which way," which only makes us feel more keenly the boundlessness of the confusion and transforms his chatter into a conscious stylistic principle. Here's where he put to use the habits of seductive dandyism worked out through the lessons of the erotic lyric. The idle chatter of the salon freed Pushkin's hands, and he dropped the reins and allowed himself to be carried along.

Barely having begun *Onegin*, he informed Delvig: "I am now writing a new poem in which I babble beyond all measure" (November 1823). And soon in the same vein he concocted the theory: "The novel demands idle chatter: tell it all!" (Letter to A. Bestuzhev, April 1825).

Idle chatter defined the genre of Pushkin's "novel in verse," where the line of verse becomes a means of eroding the novel and finds in the chatter a valid reason for its own limitlessness and restlessness. In the chatter lack of content was combined with a superabundance of ideas and the maximum number of direct hits per minute on objects scattered any old way and linked by a network of gesticulation monkey-like in its tenacity and nimbleness. Later Pushkin's talkativeness came to be considered the height of realism. He defined it differently.

> My tongue is my enemy: everything is accessible to it,
> It has gotten into the habit of chattering about everything!*

For all its generally sophisticated tone idle chatter presupposed a deliberate lowering of speech into the sphere of private life, which was thus dragged out into the light of day with all sorts of household junk and domestic trash. That's where the *realism* came from. But this same idle chatter excluded the possibility of any serious or prolonged acquaintance with reality, which the author dismissed with his compliments, and blowing kisses on his way, he dashed off to swat flies. There's no point in asking Pushkin's realism, But where is the representation of serfdom? And what did you do with the famous tenth chapter* of *Evgeny Onegin?* He always manages to get himself off the hook: I was just kidding.

What was most important to him was to cover space not already occupied by verses and, having covered it, to pay his respects. It's striking how often his inspiration got along on ready-made clichés—just so he could spread himself thinner, rattle things off faster and be done with them. Had he wanted to, he probably could have gotten along without them, but with them he could go faster and the verses glided as if on skates, without touching the consciousness too deeply. Pushkin's stanzas fly in one ear and out the other: despite all their refinement, they are quite ordinary and spin like the devil, not being too squeamish to resort to common plagiarism and rhymes beloved of poetasters for the sake of tempo.

> And in order to open up a broad, free way
> I will provide them with Words . . .*

He made it a rule never to refuse cheap tips and was only too happy to employ the services of colleagues he despised.

> Devout Shikhmatov used to write that way;
> And I, for the most part, write that way too.*

Without considering the consequences, Pushkin elevated into a generally accepted cult that smoothness of poetically literate writing that prompts every schoolboy to scribble verses à la Pushkin.

People laugh at his cleverness at exposing worn-out clichés:

> O, dreams, my dreams! Where is your truth?
> And where is its constant rhyme: sweet *youth?*

Or:

> Ta-tá ta-tá ta-tá reposes,
> Ta-tá ta-tá ta-tá the past . . .
> (The rhyme you now expect is *roses;*
> So here it is! Now take it fast!)*

You can laugh, but meanwhile he palms off on the reader the same old stale goods, and to everyone's delight—Faster, faster!—gets it off his hands. Pushkin's truisms resemble a game of go-fish: You're waiting for roses? Then you get roses! Love? Above! Passion? Fashion! Take them and be quick about it, and that's the last you'll see of him.

He had good reason to hurry on: progress in literature began with Pushkin.

Later Chekhov, as a writing lesson, advised, "Describe an ash tray!" —as if art had no more fitting objects. Oh, this frenzied descriptiveness of the nineteenth century, which lacked character and forgot hierarchy; this deadly desire to log every speck of existence as it slipped away in nets of typographical signs, which along with the railroad offices of that century transformed the land into a patchwork of official documents with dull headings: *Poor Folk, Dead Souls, An Ordinary Story, A Boring Story** (if it's so boring, then why do you have to tell it?), until there wasn't a single undescribed nook or cranny left in the world!

One artist dared to call his novel *Life*. Another wrote: *War and Peace* (all war and all peace at the same time!).* Pushkin was no match for them: he composed "The Shot." Pushkin had to make even Nulin a count, even the miser a knight.* And although in Russia the custom of *depicting reality* began with him, Pushkin was still ashamed of flaunting his realism, and in order to avoid a misalliance, he shoved his provincial tales off onto the meek Belkin (who couldn't be held responsible) so that he personally—God forbid!—wouldn't be compromised by vile prose.

Although he discovered progress and sometimes even outdistanced it (he was, after all, editor of the *Contemporary*),* Pushkin both in gesture and in word still retained his aristocratic habits and believed in the hierarchy of genres. And that is precisely why he violated that hierarchy. He never would have written *Evgeny Onegin* if he hadn't known that you weren't supposed to write like that. His prosaisms, his descriptions of everyday life, his trivialities and colloquialisms were to a large extent conceived as deliberately unacceptable devices calculated to shock the public. In his works, reality appeared like the devil through a trap door, in the form of a frivolous joke, an audacious exception, which proved the rule that you shouldn't talk about things like that in polite society. The "moralistic and decorous" novel* of the old type still reigned there, and Pushkin took off from it and used it as his point of reference while parodying literature with the voice of life. The latter—life—sounded like an aside, which on occasion turned the whole panorama upside down without radically altering the noble tone appropriate to poetry, only underscoring by the very coarseness of certain expressions the imprint of presumption and elegance it bore. As a result, what came out was the same pastoral turned inside out, a "moralistic and decorous" burlesque novel.

> Natalya Pavlovna at first
> Read it attentively,
> But soon somehow grew distracted
> By a fight beneath her window
> Between a billygoat and a dog
> And quietly devoted her attention to it . . .
> Three ducks were splashing in a puddle;

> An old woman was crossing the dirty yard
> To hang her laundry on the fence;
> It was beginning to look like rain . . .*

Later all this irony came to be deployed in all seriousness. *Anton Goremyko* sailed out of the puddle formed from the tears of Pushkin's stationmaster . . .*

Pushkin is the golden mean of Russian literature. Having given it a swift kick into the future, he himself swung backwards and came to play in it more the role of an eternally flowering past to which it returns in order to be rejuvenated. Every time a new talent appears, Pushkin is right there prompting and supplying crib notes, and successive generations, decades later, will again discover Pushkin standing behind their backs. If we transport ourselves back in thought to days long past, to the sources of our native language, he'll turn up behind us even there—before and on the eve of the first chronicles and songs. An archaic smile plays on his lips.

In the literary development of the nineteenth century as well, Pushkin remains a child who is at one and the same time younger and older than everyone else. His mobility, his inconsistency in pursuit of the phantom of life, in roaming the seas and the waves—today he's here, tomorrow there*—were tempered in him by a craving for order, peace, and equilibrium. Like a conscientious classic, he considered peace "a necessary condition for the beautiful" and had a knack for combining recklessness with enviable good sense. The most fashionable garments fit him as if they had been tailored to a somewhat old-fashioned pattern, which lent him an appearance of unshakable stability and solid conservatism despite certain risqué poses. With Pushkin you won't end up with your face in the mud, you won't perish like a Swede at Poltava.* You can depend on him. Even when raving he retains his sense of measure, which is called taste and which he acquired in the well-run boarding-house of nature: "One-sidedness is the death of thought," "Love of measure and concord is an inherent property of the human mind."

For all occasions he provided justifications that reconciled the words with the circumstances. Every whimsy that came out of his mouth acquired a legitimate sanction just because it was pertinent and well timed. He always managed to keep the beat.

> When youth sweeps away
> The gaiety of youthful days in a light smoke

> Then we'll wrest from old age everything
> That can be wrested from it.*

In anticipation of old age, he let soar a winged phrase (which in turn served as a prelude to Tolstoy's exploration of the family) "[She] would be a faithful wife and a virtuous mother."* And from such a Lovelace!

> For everything there is a time, everything has its moment;
> Ridiculous are the frivolous old man
> And the staid youth alike.*

How reasonable Pushkin is! Despite all the flaws and outbursts of his temperament, he seems to us the epitome of a normal person. Undoubtedly, this perception of him is reinforced by the fact that he neatly packaged his passions and intentions and sorted them onto predetermined shelves according to age, place of residence, origin, historical juncture, et cetera. The universe, as he understands it, is proportional and periodic and is based on the correct alternation of stresses. "Sleep comes in its turn, hunger comes in its."* Pushkin had a partiality for depicting the most common life cycles—day and night, lunch and dinner, winter and summer, war and peace—all those "habits of existence" whose roots stretch back to time immemorial, and only in their intimate circle did he feel completely at home. That's why he liked to describe the weather so much. In essence, he did nothing in his works but retell the rhythm of the world order.

Here's where fate once again took a hand in his cards and in his plans. In counting out its blows, it imparted sequence and periodicity to the undifferentiated process. Fate transformed life into a well-balanced composition. It made the transience of phenomena a stable means for the just distribution of goods. The mutability of existence enforced the supreme law of recompense: everyone gets their fair share. In Pushkin's view, the past does not mean only disappearance but is equivalent to a prize awarded, property earned; if something existed, it was bestowed (whether it be the title of count or the executioner's block).

> Joy is granted to everyone in turn;
> What was will not be again.*

It was—will not be—will not be repeated—we bear this unrepeatability of a personality or an event like a shield or a title. In expiation of our guilt we'll say: we *were* . . .

To the standardizing tendencies of his age Pushkin opposed the aristocratic principle of evaluating history and biography that made provision for the participation of fate in human affairs. History, like the universe, is divided into classes, is hierarchical, and is formed out of heraldic signs, etched into our memory to the glory of passing shadows. "I never shared anyone's democratic hatred for the aristocracy. It has always seemed to me a necessary and natural estate of a great educated people. . . . The Kalmyks have neither a nobility nor a history. Savagery, meanness, and ignorance do not respect the past, groveling before the present alone" ("Refutation of Criticism," 1830). "Ignorant disdain for everything past, weak-minded astonishment before one's own age, blind passion for novelty"—all these features of *semi-Enlightenment,* which he so hated, separated Pushkin from contemporary life, despite the swiftness with which he adopted its new beliefs.

Pushkin's aristocratic manners had, besides everything else, one and the same emotional source. Pushkin was a nobleman twice over, because he was historical. But he fussed over his nobility more than others did also because he was Pushkin by the grace of God. Thomas Mann comments on these feelings (with regard to Goethe):

> Characterizing the basis of his individuality, Goethe speaks with gratitude and humility of "the charity of destiny." But the notion of "charity" or "grace" is more aristocratic than it is generally thought to be; in essence, it expresses the indissoluble bond between luck and merit, the synthesis of freedom and necessity, and signifies "inborn merit"; while gratitude and humility at the same time contain in them-selves a *metaphysical consciousness* that, under any circumstances, no matter how things turn out, they are assured of the charity of destiny. ("Goethe and Tolstoy: Sketches on the Problem of Humanism")

We can add that Pushkin had a personal score to settle with history. By inserting two Pushkins—Gavrila and Afanasy*—into the action of *Godunov,* he seems to hint that he was there as well. Pushkin's passion for his ancestral roots was reinforced by the anticipation since ancient times of the birth of the foremost, the most unique member of the clan. Aristocratic means ancient, blessed, promised. The one! Loyalty to the honor of his grandfathers meant, in particular, that the genius was a legitimate child of the national family and that he had grown up, not in the street, but in the ancestral cradle—in history. Pushkin had to defend often and unsuccessfully this right of foreordained birth, pri-mogeniture, and, whether he had to or not, he presented crumbling birth records as a pass to his estate (just as later Mayakovsky in his poem *At the Top of My Voice* presented a similar ticket to gain entrance into history).*

But Pushkin had already torn himself away from the solid genealogy of his ancestors. He treated their real and imagined accomplishments without the necessary seriousness and understood their merits quite loosely. Fate rewarded his kinsmen with memorable drubbings, and all to Pushkin's greater delight.

> My forefather did not get on with Peter,
> And so was hanged for this by him.*

Pushkin derived no less profit from the forefather who had been hung than from the forefather who had had a hand in the ruling dynasty. What was more important to him was that time had baptized and marked his ancestors, but how and what for wasn't all that important. What he valued was not honor in the precise sense of the word, but the trace a man left on history, and the fateful traces it, history, left on the narrow path of the man. He extolled the stratification of society into classes as the basis for personal freedom and as a sign of his own independent and unusual fate. Nurtured by the natural juices of historical invention, Pushkin's genealogical tree raises its broad, rustling summit into the ephemeral sky of poetry.

. . . So, aristocracy. Hierarchy. But translated into the language of literature, this becomes a sense of genre. And of rhythm. And of composition. A sense of boundaries. From point A to point B. There are no upheavals, subterfuges, mixups, scrapes capable of getting to Pushkin and shaking him out of this stable sense of the weight, measure, and place of all things under the sun. While Gogol tossed everything into a single heap ("What a motley heap!" he said in amazement of *Dead Souls*, which tumbled down like the Tower of Babel, like an unfinished *Iliad* that had tried to clamber up to the heavens and elevate petty gentry prose to a heroic epic, to a poem about the resurrection of the dead),* Pushkin thought mainly in fragments. That was his style. Many of Pushkin's works (some of his best, by the way) were in fact designated as such: "a fragment." Or "scenes from . . ."—from Faust, from the times of chivalry.* Other works in their essence manifested traits of the fragment. The fragmentariness of *Onegin*—which breaks off in mid-sentence—is obvious, as is that of the "little tragedies" and *Godunov . . .**

His works resemble a collection of antiques: mostly torsos and busts, this one without a head, that one without a nose. Yet strangely enough these losses don't spoil them, but seem to impart to the images a true completeness and look like necessary strokes dictated by the very nature of the object. The fragmentariness here, we suspect, is called forth above all by a penetrating awareness of the whole that has no need for the complete shape but is inherent in each separate piece. These are pieces in which, despite their incompleteness, everything is there and everything is arranged in a free and easy order, in balance, where characters stroll in pairs or are seated vis-à-vis and life is accompanied by death, joy by grief, and vice versa; where the fatal love triangle teaches a lesson in how to arrange harmoniously the happiness of others and one's own peace: "I loved you so honestly, so tenderly as, God willing, you'll be loved by another"* (how she must have eaten her heart out when she read this, forced, like Buridan's ass, to try to split herself in half between two equally distant and attractive suitors); and wonderful sounds are tossed in a grand gesture onto a scale where "a" corresponds to "o" as "fight" corresponds to "feast," and the scales swayed and froze in a beautiful accord from which we can deduce that harmony and composition are means of restoring forgotten justice to the world as Peter the First had done with the conquered enemy—

> That is why in this joyous hour
> The tsar's cup is full,
> And the Neva is shaken far into the distance
> By heavy salvoes.*

It is precisely this fullness of being, which is achieved primarily by the skillful arrangement of figures and the self-containedness of the fragment, that allows us to feel more keenly the material boundary marking off this chipped piece which has fallen here from another world, like a meteorite, and transforms it into a self-contained work, into a microcosm with its own special nucleus, which has the same order as the universe and which therefore competes with it almost on equal footing. Thanks to the well-constructed plan that permeates the entire structure of the tiny island, an illusion of the free breadth and voluminousness of the sovereign state situated on it is suggested to us.

We see from Pushkin's drafts how he first knocks together on a blank piece of paper a compositional grid, which, through a system of pulleys and ties, holds in place the likeness of a habitable space where you'd already like to run about, and which, if so desired, could pass for a completed house. Two gestures exchanged by strangers placed in opposite corners suffice to produce out of this meeting of crossed glances and movements a scene requiring no further development:

She paused for a moment
And went into the house. He unmoving
Gazed at the door through which,
Like a dream, his beauty had disappeared.*

What is most essential here is that he follows her with his eyes just as long as she is walking away from him, and freezes just as instantaneously when she looks back. This tent of interchanged turns and glances is already fit to live in and what happens later, what kind of love will start up between them or who will ruin whom, can be left to the imagination . . .[11]

The statues at Tsarskoe Selo influenced Pushkin greatly. He grew up among them and revered them as his true teachers to the end of his days.

I loved the sound of clear water and leaves,
And the idols white in the shade of trees
And the imprint of motionless thoughts on their countenances.

All this—the marble compasses and lyres,
The swords and scrolls in their marble hands,
The laurels on their heads, and the purple mantles on their shoulders—

---

11. We sometimes discover a similar layout in lines which are integrated into a broader context and pitched like a tent with the help of opposing vectors:

> . . . the magician makes a great effort, wheezes
> And suddenly soars away with Ruslan . . .
> His ardent steed follows them with its eyes;
> The magician is already under the clouds;
> The hero is hanging by his beard . . .

Follow the angle of the horse's gaze: the magician ascended along it; but in order to keep this cartwheel, launched in a triple rotation into the sky, from disappearing from view, the author adds Ruslan, as a parodical weight:

> They fly over gloomy forests,
> They fly over wild mountains,
> They fly over the gulf of the sea;
> Growing numb from the strain,
> Ruslan holds on with tenacious hand
> To the villain's beard.

All this filled my heart with a certain sweet fear;
At the sight tears of inspiration
Welled up in my eyes.

. . . .

The whole day long I wandered gloomily in silence
Among the youths—the idols of the garden all the while
Cast their shadow on my soul.*

This shadow lies over his works. Pushkin more and more often and concertedly set about depicting statues. But the point is apparently not that his works are sculpturesque in the ordinary sense of the word. He was conceivably drawn to statues by his spiritual kinship and conceptual correspondence to them—the wish to halt the fleeting moment by recasting it into a permanent, eternally prolonged gesture. "The maiden sits eternally sad beside an eternal stream."*

This is the hallmark of the representational quality of his work. You want to look at Pushkin's pictures for a long time. You follow them with your eyes and involuntarily return to them, carried by a reverse or repeat current back to the point of departure. They are like smoke from a chimney which both rises and stands like a pillar. Like a river that flows without flowing away. It is apropos to remember here once again the analogy Pushkin draws between the poet and the echo. The echo prolongs and reproduces what has passed. The echo erects a monument in the air to fleeting sounds.

Sculptural images properly speaking do not come immediately to mind, probably because they far from exhaust Pushkin's variety, but appear in his works rather sporadically to express a constant and all-embracing tendency of his poetry in its most extreme and purest aspect: the Bronze Horseman, the Stone Guest. A statue comes to life, and a human being freezes into a statue, which again comes to life and flutters and flies and stands still in mobile immobility. Statues are one of the forms of existence of Pushkin's spirit. The eternally outstretched arm of the Bronze Horseman is nothing other than Peter's gaze cast at the beginning of the poem intensified and extended: "And [he] looked into the distance." Reproduced many times, seconded by the paws of the marble lions, this gesture begets a whole pantomime, which culminates near the finale of the poem in the reciprocal movement of Evgeny's hand, which he, martyr-like, meekly presses to his heart.*

This same tendency, however, can be discerned even where Pushkin has no sculptures. Our conceptions of his characters are often accompanied by a vague feeling that they seem to repose even now in a somnambulistic state of activity assigned to them by the poet. Thus, Pimen* is still writing. Boris Godunov to this day feels nauseated, and his head is spinning, and the blood-covered boys are before his eyes. Kochubei, awaiting his execution, is still sitting and looking glumly at the sky. The Covetous Knight endlessly feasts his eyes on the sight of his treasures.

But perhaps this tendency to prolong and sustain the image is a characteristic common to all art? If so, Pushkin elevated this generic trait to an individual degree of particular partiality. His Covetous Knight intends even in death, reciting his monologue, "to sit on his trunk like a vigilant shade." Pushkin's friends laughed at the petrified gesture of Girei, who "raised his saber in fateful combat and, with all his might, suddenly remained motionless." And this really does seem ridiculous if we view his characters as living people. But what if, in addition to everything else, they are just a little bit statues as well?

His heroes do not so much live as sort through their past. They linger, fall into meditation. They do not simply speak or act once and for all, but—sunken in reverie, slumbering in their poses—they seem to be reproducing fragments that have already been performed or uttered earlier. They are drawn to the bottom, into the depths of a picture that has already passed away and which they are now beginning to remember as it passes before our eyes as well—again, for the umpteenth time. Everything is lit by the glow of afterthoughts: Now what was I doing? When and where did it happen? "The chairman remains, sunken in profound meditation."* "I am involuntarily drawn by an unknown force toward these sad shores. Everything here reminds me of the past . . ."* "Memory silently unfolds its long scroll before me . . ."* Pushkin's poetry very closely resembles that scroll, which, as it unfolds, leads us again and again to traces of the past and uses them to reconstruct life in its lasting sojourn. "But I can't wash away these sad lines."* He couldn't have washed them away, for therein lay his vocation.

The act of remembering defined the way he constructed his phrases and cut out his plots. "I gaze like a madman at the black shawl, and sadness torments my soul."* Objects in Pushkin's poetry exist as tokens of memory ("A withered and scentless flower . . .").* They are talismans and souvenirs. He sometimes turned to a friend or acquaintance merely as an excuse for remembering something: "Chaadaev, do you remember the old days?"* The consummate "Once again I visited . . ."* is executed entirely as a landscape immersed in reminiscences of, among other things, how something long past and receding ever further into the past was remembered in the distant past—"other shores, other waves." It is here that Pushkin passes on his legacy—remember!—to posterity.

Pushkin's mania and magic lie in the act of remembering—in recognizing the world through its image, which had receded into the past and flickered only dimly in the memory and is now suddenly awakened, resurrected. This is that same cherished "crystal ball." His best love poems are devoted not to love in the strict sense, but rather to memories occasioned by love. "I recall a wondrous moment." The secret of this famous text is that it guides us into the depths of a soul muddied on the surface by the drone of everyday cares and plucks from oblivion the "thou!" that breaks over us with the force of a stunning revelation. Following the poet's lead we experience the joy of a meeting with our own image, resurrected and recognized over the span of ages and oceans. Like the One Who sent him, he says "behold" and "arise" * and creates the poetic image as a mystery of the *appearance* of things that have long passed, become cluttered over and lost in time (love, woman, nature—whomever and whatever you like) and have been re-stored from head to toe, anew, from scratch. The creatures reanimated in his art no longer exist in reality. You won't find them there: they're gone. But to make up for it they now repose with one foot in eternity.

The poem "To ———" (1825) has a literary prototype, following the rhythm and the meaning of which it was most probably written. The earlier text is not perhaps as perfect as its successor, which ended up a masterpiece, and of course it's not as famous, but it allows us to peer a bit further into that ill-defined region whence the poet proceeded in his renowned "wondrous moment," certainly having more in mind here than just a meeting with a woman who was visiting him for the second time.

RESURRECTION (1819)

An artist-barbarian, with somnolent brush,
Blackens the work of a genius
And senselessly scribbles
His own lawless drawing over it.

But with the years the alien paints
Fall away like decrepit scales;
The creation of the genius appears before us
In its former beauty.

> Thus delusions vanish
> From my tormented soul,
> And in it visions appear
> Of days primordial and innocent.

The past resurrected in Pushkin's poetic reminiscences is not just events that once were and then were no more, and then emerged once again—this time in verse. Although it should be noted that this reciprocal process of appearance-recognition of realia that at one time vanished and suddenly in the course of time emerged out of the darkness (necessarily out of darkness: "Your eyes gleam before me in the gloom,"* and a grandson will remember Pushkin "in the dark of the night,"* overcoming all darkness, all the horror of nonbeing through an inspired burst of consciousness), so, as I was saying, this process is itself essential and is saturated with meaning, creating the confused atmosphere of a text wandering in vague remembrances, as if it were composed (as in the poem "To ———") out of several currents of dark air that flow into one another and in which the beloved features now grow dim, now glimmer faintly.

You can't call Pushkin a poet with a good memory. He is rather forgetful, absent-minded. Because before he could remember someone, that person had to disappear completely, dissolve in his memory, and only then could his memory set to work, turning everything upside-down and rescuing the desired image from the grave: "Appear, beloved shade . . ."* But along with events that took place and were timed to coincide with certain meetings and dates, his agitated memory, brought to the point of fermentation, sometimes—and this is what is most important—like a wave in the sea, casts up from the depths some other, who knows what kind of "visions of days primordial and innocent."* Are they of childhood, or perhaps even earlier, of some disembodied pre-human existence beyond infancy?

They are rarely mentioned, but they nonetheless color and bathe the whole past in a heavenly flame, because of which his images seem brighter than the impressions surrounding them and, I'd say, exude a sweet fragrance and smile in the childlike trustfulness of primal bliss that knows nothing of good and evil.

It's quite possible that the poet practiced his constant, obtrusive backward glances into the past in order to remember, along with all the other old stuff, something more important, by scooping a handful of the water of life out of a distant well. Why else, the question arises, would he have stirred the wretched stuff so persistently and pointlessly, why would he have lost himself in meditation and looked back if not for a vague hope of immersing himself in the original source out of which, he knew, his meaninglessly sonorous stanzas flowed as well?

Poetry, as Pushkin understands it, is based on the recollection of sounds he once heard and dreams he dreamed earlier, which subsequently, in the course of his work, are liberated from under the weight of the barbarian's scribblings, the husk of time is peeled away, revealing the work of genius. That work exists ahead of time, before all creation, independently of the artist whose task is to rediscover it, by remembering what has been forgotten, and to clean it off. That is why he bustles about, wrinkles his brow, stretches out his hand to his beloved: "Your heavenly features . . ." Is this really addressed to the woman he loves? Or wouldn't it be truer to say that it refers to the infant's candle lamp that glows ahead of us in the mist like some inaccessible distance?

> And reveal the bright distance
> Of cherished life beyond the mist!*

"Reveal"! and he reveals—sometimes in a trivial verse, rarely calling it by name (in any case it is given to no one to pronounce its real, full name), and sometimes confusing the coordinates he terms it grandiloquently "the star of captivating happiness" or something even more absurd, but it's no longer important.

> The profound darkness dissipated in the sky,
> Day was falling on the dark valley,
> Dawn broke. Along a distant path,
> The freed prisoner was walking;
> And in front of him in the mist
> Russian bayonets were already gleaming,
> And Cossack guards
> Called back and forth in the hills.*

This is the "bright distance" shining in the mist. Only it, this bright distance, as he approaches it, is for some reason already mysteriously shining behind him. Earlier and behind him. Like the homeland. All songs can pass for its echo.

> They remind me
> Of another life and a distant shore.*

Well, all right, all right—go to sleep. Father, reveal to us that we are Thy children.

. . . .

Pushkin had one other, slightly cold and solemn word: perfection. Self-contented, full to overflowing equilibrium. The poet was supposed to uplift all his creations (a paltry deception) to the level of perfection. And he uplifted.

But in order for Pushkinian features to appear, something had to be added to the perfection. A bright distance. A wondrous moment. Or something else.

> Your voice, my darling, carols the sounds
> Of native songs with savage perfection . . .*

The moment he said this, all existing compositions, which had remained immovable for centuries, listed and began to sway. On the verge of collapse. Can you believe it—with savage perfection! Like throwing a match into a barrel loaded with gunpowder. "The folk are silent."* And we thought: a fragment, balanced, calm. The calm at the brink of a wild abyss. "And was not the creator of the Vatican a murderer?"* We stagger. The austere marble is exposed to the winds. What did you expect? That's what a fragment is for—to expose. To expose what was concealed. To let incompleteness into perfection? What nonsense. "And was not the creator of the Vatican a murderer?" Back-wards! We are drawn backwards to plug up the hole, to reread, to check: Was he or wasn't he? What were the folk silent about? . . . To the edge—it's frightening just to think about it. "Your voice, my darling, carols the sounds . . ." Boundaries are collapsing. A fragment is not the park at Tsarskoe Selo, not a piece of marble, but the sea. The masts list. Don't be afraid. It's too late. We are in boundlessness.

> And the sails swelled, full of wind;
> The huge mass began to move, cutting the waves.
> It sails. Whither should we sail? . . . .
>   . . . .
>   . . . .*

And instead of a rudder, there's a half page, a whole ocean—of nothing but dots. . . . .
. . . .
. . . .
. . . .

Pushkin's name is always associated—and this, to everyone's surprise, makes him new, fresh, up-to-date, and interesting—with the sense of physical presence, of unmediated closeness, that he produces under the pretense of being a good fellow, one of us, our kind of guy, accessible to everyone, acquainted with everyone, the one who was casting his pearls here just yesterday. His appearance as a private person who depended on no one and represented no one but simply strolled along on his own, striking up conversations with his readers right there on the boulevard—"Hello, I'm Pushkin!"—was like a bolt from the blue after all the circumlocutions, ranks, and official posts of the eighteenth century. Pushkin was the first civilian to attract attention to himself in Russian literature. A civilian in the fullest sense of the word, not a diplomat, not a secretary, a nobody. A goldbricker. A deadbeat. But he made more noise than any military man. He was the first poet who had a biography instead of a service record.

The biographies of poets before Pushkin were almost unknown and held no interest outside of affairs of state. Even Batyushkov for a time held forth while wearing officer's epaulettes. Even the modest Zhukovsky was a senior tutor at the court.* While greatly admiring Derzhavin, Bestuzhev (in his article "On N. Polevoi's Novel *The Oath at the Tomb of Our Lord,* 1833) maintained that the fame of the Russian Horatio was not due to his talent: "Everyone worshiped him because he was a favorite of Catherine, because he was a privy councillor. Everyone imitated him thinking they could use Parnassus as a jumping off point into a higher class, to get a signet ring or a place setting at the far end of some bigshot's table or at least permission to hang around in his reception room . . ."*

And suddenly—let there be rejoicing!

> To be a clerk or an uhlan is all the same to me,
> Laws and shakos are all the same too,
> I'm not busting my gut to become a captain
> And I won't crawl on my hands and knees to become an assessor.*

This was tantamount to throwing down the gauntlet to society—to decline a post, to renounce active service for the sake of poetry. It was desertion, treason. Even Lomonosov insisted: "You don't have to be a poet, but you must be a citizen!"* But Pushkin, who didn't give a damn about the civic rights and duties of his time, became a poet the way some people become tramps.

This all sounded particularly unseemly with regard to military prowess, which still made the voices of bards tremble. At the age when a youth was supposed to be dreaming of a hussar's pelisse and sword knot, Pushkin, the clod (we fed, nurtured, brought you up and educated you, and look how you repay us!), made himself out to be a hermit, whistling in his hut:

> Stillness is dear to my heart;
> I don't, I don't chase after glory.*

It was no trouble at all for him to depict a battle and mentally match swords in it to test his mettle. But it just wasn't the real thing—these weren't really brave deeds or heroism, but merely the psychological exercises of a person who had forgotten even to think of military service. War amused him as a source of keen sensations, a risky game. "I like war's bloody entertainments, and the thought of death is dear to my soul."* (Later Lermontov would touch these same nerves.)*

Bad examples are infectious, and ten years later, when Pushkin happened to travel to Erzerum, Bulgarin* was obliged to state with bitterness: "We thought that the author of *Ruslan and Lyudmila* had rushed over the Caucasus to nurture himself on lofty poetic sentiments, to enrich himself with new impressions, and to pass on to posterity in sweet songs the great deeds of contemporary Russian heroes. We thought that the great events in the East, which astounded the world and won Russia the respect of all enlightened peoples, would excite the genius of our poets—but we were wrong. The famous lyres remained silent, and only the pale, weak Onegin appeared once again in the desert of our poetry. Your heart aches to look at this colorless scene" (*Northern Bee*, March 22, 1830, no. 35).

Bulgarin made just one mistake: there is nothing heroic about *Ruslan and Lyudmila*. Even then its author preferred solitude under shady boughs to heroic deeds.

> My soul is bored with the empty
> And destructive phantom of glory in battle.
> Believe me, innocent pastimes,
> Love and peaceful oak groves are
> A hundred times dearer to my heart.*

And now this, to put it bluntly, parasite and renegade, who spent his whole life evading a service career, pounced on us with the full weight of his biography. And as if that were not enough, he dragged after him a whole gang of his acquaintances, buddies, enemies, and mistresses to whom he has brought greater fame than did Derzhavin to Felitsa. Didn't they become famous only because they palled around with Pushkin and quarreled with him, feasted and exchanged kisses with him and so ended up in textbooks and anthologies? How many people we remember and love only because they happened to live in Pushkin's vicinity. Even those who were quite well respected, who were some-bodies in their own right—Kyukhelbeker, for example, famous mainly because Pushkin once overate and felt "kyukhelbekerish."* No mat-ter what the poor guy did—went to Senate Square, wrote a tragedy—nothing helped: he was stuck forever with that "kyukhelbekerish."

Not fair, you say? And what about Delvig?* The Raevskys?* Benkendorf? As soon as we pronounce their amiable names, PUSHKIN lights up next to them and eclipses and warms them all with his prox-imity. It wasn't just his genius that was to blame—it was Pushkin's per-sonality, his animated physiognomy, which came into the world to pay an unofficial visit and let into history with him half of Russia together with the tsar, his ministers, the Decembrists, ballerinas, generals—as retinue to his person, which was distinguishable only by the face.

Having begun his literary démarche primarily with epistles to pri-vate persons on private occasions, Pushkin filled poetry with a great deal of personal material, which at first was intelligible only to a nar-row circle of his closest friends and acquaintances. With the help of memoirists, biographers, and textologists, we have put it all together and think that's as it should be and that we have to know everything: when, where, with whom, and about whom. Names, dates, hints, tid-bits of gossip, and squabbles, all gathered together to pay homage to one name—Pushkin. His entire corpus of works lies before us like a private letter that accidentally ended up among the official papers of our national literature. (What a contrast with Gogol, who managed to conduct a private correspondence with his friends and publish it as government legislation!)*

The lycée unquestionably served as a hothouse for his epistles and, in a broader sense, for all of Pushkin's easygoing intimacy and jovial impudence. The lycée was a family—which replaced for him the un-loved and inhospitable parental hearth—brought together by chance and by the community of his friends' individual interests, which taught him to think bypassing official channels, stewing everything in the same juice of slang expressions, dares, nicknames, puns, and jokes, understandable only to classmates, which Pushkin unloosed like a

storm cloud over the virgin soil of poetry. He remained forever grateful
to this milieu, which gave wings to his character and style and formed
a sort of alliance, a secret conspiracy of children who rallied together
in their schoolboy high jinks against the cold and punctilious society
of adults. In the huge and gloomy future, Pushkin saw himself as an
emissary of the lycée, a member of a free brotherhood, an affiliation he
maintained as a pledge of loyalty to his childhood. He considered the
lycée tradition a guarantee of his incorruptibility, and year in and year
out he delighted in celebrating a never-ending stag party as a sign that
neither misfortunes nor the years could efface his personality. Others
became senators, professors, writers; Pushkin all his life remained a
lycée student. It was an order of foundlings who had been cast by a
vagary of fate into the roles of after-dinner philosophers and peripatetic
rhymesters. The lycée—interpreted from an abstract, romantic point of
view—served as a haven for the Arts, and its fosterchild Pushkin observed the unwritten rituals of the lycée to the end of his days, enticing
young Russia into friendship with the Muses beneath the canopy of
its trees.

> We remain the same: the whole world is a foreign land to us;
> Our homeland is Tsarskoe Selo.*

Yet this native abode, which encouraged isolation from the world of
established rules and regulations inimical to poetry, in another sense
branched out and expanded to take in the whole wide world under the
green vaults of the lycée. The habits of friendship and skirt-chasing
leaped from school desks to literary gatherings and artistic circles, and
there, you'll see, Pushkin was now monkeying around with Lyudmila
and winking to Onegin and Pugachov as if they were his buddies. The
crowding of dormitories and classrooms disposed to familiarity and
friendship in a big way, on the scale of humanity at large, to neighborly
relations with life and fictional characters, whom he selected on the
basis of affability and familiarity.

> Why shouldn't I write about him?
> He's my neighbor and my friend.*

The form of epistles to friends became the content of Pushkin's
poetry as a whole, which unequivocally lets us into the private life of
the bard, who flaunted his accessibility—through his mimicry of true-
to-life features, through details that bore a resemblance to his day-to-
day life and his portraits. The reading public, little by little, learned

to be voyeurs spying on the author's adventures, trysts, banquets, misfortunes, and squabbles on the most private occasions—all of Russia looked on in admiration to see what trick Pushkin would come up with next.

He immediately found himself in the position of a movie star and, kicking up his heels, began to live in the public eye. "News of his every step was spread from one end of Russia to the other," P. P. Vyazemsky recalled. "Pushkin knew how to stage his escapades so skillfully that at first even his best friends were horrified and spread rumors under the influence of this first impression. There's no doubt that even in Pushkin's youth it wasn't just his talent that made an impression on all of Russia. His escapades greatly increased his popularity, and the very enigma of his character attracted attention to the man from whom you could always expect the unexpected."

This somewhat dubious notoriety could not but—on the rebound—have an effect on Pushkin's personality. He felt the curious looks directed at him and tried his best to cut a dash, although, according to his own words, he was none too proud of the fact

> That the ardent agitation,
> And tempests of my soul,
> My thirst for freedom, and persecution
> Made me famous among men.*

Nevertheless, he was pleased and wanted to live up to expectation. He ran the risk of falling prey to the growing fashion for the Pushkin who had taken to cultivating extravagant sidewhiskers and fingernails. "There was much in his very appearance," his fellow countrymen noticed, "that was quite unique: at times he let his hair grow down to his shoulders, at other times he left his curly hair disheveled; he sported big and tousled sidewhiskers; dressed carelessly; walked briskly, twirling his cane or whip, whistling or humming a tune. Many in their time imitated him, and those people were called à la Pushkin" (*Russian Antiquity*, 1874, no. 8).

He could have gained repute as a demonic figure and, playing himself up in a triumphant scandal, gone the route of staging the legend of his own unique, mysterious, and horrible destiny. History provided precedents for this, and Pushkin knew whom to imitate. Two brilliant stars shone on the horizon: Napoleon and Byron. When both were extinguished, one right after the other, Pushkin heaved a sigh: "The world's grown empty . . . Now whither would you carry me, ocean?" *

So it would seem that he was quite taken with the spectacle of the proud genius whose death threatened to leave humanity in a desert and leave Pushkin in the shadow of Lermontov, which hung over him and fell under his feet, emanating from him and taking his place.

In the seventeenth year of his life Lermontov snarled, "I was born for the whole world to bear witness to either my triumph or my destruction." This phrase almost escaped Pushkin's lips. If it had, then he would have ended up as Lermontov and would have gone even further, mercilessly whipping up his biography, which had grown inflated with fights and lightning bolts. But Pushkin came to his senses in time, bit his tongue, and returned to the domestic chores that were more in character for him, to his indulgent objectivity and devout fellowship with the world family, while Lermontov pursued the plot of the solitary and lawless comet immersed in the gloomy spectacle of its own triumph and fall. To spice up the plot, transforming his biography into the myth of the persecuted poet Lermontov, he began to make up a lot of nonsense about himself, in the romantic spirit, claiming he was a villain, a genius, Byron, the Demon,* and even Napoleon Bonaparte . . .

Now from a distance it is difficult for us to imagine what the figure of Napoleon meant for the new Europe. The century was obsessed with him, the superman who came out of nowhere and had no one to thank but himself for his rise to world rule. Goethe called Bonaparte nothing less than a demigod. In the shadow of a statuette of the titan, Balzac fervently swore to devour Paris. In the eyes of bystanders, Napoleon overshadowed Julius Caesar and Alexander the Great, two of the highest rollers in the ancient world: they had acted with sanction, whereas he was a parvenu, which increased Bonaparte's charm and inspired dreams of greatness.

In his article "On Mr. Olin's Tragedy *The Corsair*" (1827) Pushkin unmasked Bonaparte in Byron (which sheds new light on the closeness of these figures in his poem "To the Sea"): "*The Corsair*'s incredible success was due to the character of its protagonist, who for some mysterious reason calls to mind the man whose fateful will at that time ruled one half of Europe and threatened the other. . . . The poet never spelled out his motive: it flattered his vanity to identify himself with Napoleon."

Having paid his respects to Napoleon, Pushkin withdrew, perhaps out of a fear of becoming like his tempter Byron, whose one-sided power prompted Pushkin to tune himself all the more fundamentally in his own key. He managed, for the most part, to escape more subtle temptations as well, such as exploiting the privilege of genius to put the real-life person on show or imputing to himself, the man, the imposing bearing of the Poet. That's just what romantics of the Byron-Lermontov type did. They always had ready to hand among their stage props the mask and script for the role of the Poet, which became so deeply engrained in their personalities that when they walked out onstage and successfully played themselves, they might just as well have been standing in for the Corsair, Napoleon, and the Demon. All they had to do in any situation was to maintain the natural but at the same time effective pose—the authoritative bearing of the Bard—which they had received with life itself. Poetry is, after all, by its very nature extraordinary, and it is predestined to awe and amaze. Poetry in and of itself is an uncommon spectacle.

But Pushkin took a different path—an even more interesting one. He split the single whole of man-poet in two, into Poet and man, and, giving all the advantages to the former he left the man with nothing, without even a ghost of his elegant profession but in all his petty and undemanding simplicity. He turned them into his right and left hands and with them he embraced reality from all sides as if they were tentacles; he worked them together and separately, like a juggler— for example, while the right hand was writing poetry, the left might be picking his nose—like Indian sculptures, in a storm of gestures, a many-handed idol running, *figaro-figaro-figaro*, raging along two keyboards. He knocked their heads together: while the Poet majestically sauntered, the man was forced to squeal and weep. But let's proceed in order:

> When the poet is not called
> To the sacred sacrifice by Apollo,
> He is faintheartedly immersed
> In the cares of the vain world;
> His holy lyre is silent;
> His soul savors a cold sleep;
> And among the insignificant children of the world,
> He, perhaps, is the most insignificant.*

It hurts to hear this sort of thing. Pushkin, the genius, and all of a sudden—he's worse than everyone else.

"Not worse than everyone else, but better . . ." It sounds absurd. "It's just the perfectionism of a great poet, a genius . . ." "He wanted to leave himself an escape route. To women, to the glitter of high society.

He liked to enjoy life . . ." "Even he had his little faults: who doesn't? After all, he was a genius! The creative nature. It's forgivable, he more than paid for it . . ." "What kind of example is that to set for others! No, it's unacceptable, indecent. All the more disgraceful for a genius . . ." "You can't equate him with other people. A genius can indulge himself. After all, he's superior . . ." (And so on, and once again from the beginning.)

These are more or less the lines of reasoning adopted by those people who seek either to reproach Pushkin or exonerate him for this strange tirade, trying to get around it somehow, to invalidate it by placing the stress on those qualities of genius that obligate the man to conduct himself differently from what the author depicts and to live his life in a manner better befitting his position as a poet.

No, gentlemen. Pushkin is following a completely different (not ours) type of logic here. The Poet is insignificant from the human point of view precisely because he is a genius from the poetic point of view. If he weren't a genius, he wouldn't be more insignificant than everyone else. Insignificance, mediocrity on the plane of everyday life, is an attribute of genius. Obfuscating this conception by adopting apologetic or accusatory tones of voice (there's not much difference between them), trying to bring the man up to par with the Poet, means violating Pushkin's will in this cardinal issue. For this poem—written not to the human specifications by which we judge it, but from the heights of poetry—exudes not the naggings of conscience, not self-depreciation or self-justification, but an unprecedented arrogance. Such arrogance was beyond even the wildest dreams of Lermontov's Demon, who for all his theatrical costumes was nevertheless a man, while Pushkin's Poet is not human at all but something so wild and inexplicable that people don't know what to make of him, and they, together with his empty shell, swarm in the world below like ants, and looking at them you understand both the degree of separation and the height to which the Poet ascended when he shed his human appearance.

> But as soon as the divine word
> Reaches his keen ear,
> The poet's soul starts up
> Like an awakened eagle.
> He languishes among the amusements of the world,
> Shuns human talk,
> Does not bow his proud head

> At the feet of the popular idol.
> And full of sounds and confusion
> He runs wild and stern
> To the shores by deserted waves,
> Into the broad, rustling oaks.*

He is not even talking here about a transformation of the one into the other, but about a complete, uncompromising replacement of the man by the Poet. A similar story is set forth in Pushkin's "Prophet," * where the man is struck down and dissected like a corpse so that when he arises as a Poet, he can no longer find anything of *himself* left in him. Conceived as an advance on Pushkin's, Lermontov's "Prophet" * cannot breathe in this lofty air and in essence returns the Poet to his human image, forcing him to experience feelings of rejection and insulted self-esteem which he doesn't even remember at Pushkin's higher level. "... As souls gaze from on high at the bodies they have abandoned ..."

Pushkin had predecessors who had tried to establish the basis for the rights and duties of the Poet by demanding from writers many things they had not even dreamed of earlier, sincerely believing that their whole task consisted in writing in hours left free from their other pursuits poems that were useful and pleasant to people. At the beginning of the century, poetry was emancipated and claimed first autonomy and then hegemony over the lives of its authors, who not long before had enjoyed the favors of the Muses somewhere between duty and leisure. Suddenly it became clear that art wanted more.

"It is necessary," warned Batyushkov, "that all his life, all his secret thoughts, all his predilections incline to one object, and that object must be Art. Poetry, I dare to say, demands the *whole* man.

"I wish (let them call my wish strange!), I wish that a special way of life, a poetical *dietics* could be prescribed for the Poet, in a word, that the life of the Poet could be made into a science.

"The first rule of this science would have to be—live as you write and write as you live" ("A Few Words on Poets and Poetry," 1815).

Pushkin shared this new view of the artist, but apparently not completely. The first part (the demand for the whole person) couldn't have bothered him. The mature Pushkin was completely taken up by his poetry, devoured by it like Richard Wagner, who said that the "artist" in him had swallowed up the "man," and like thousands of other famous and nameless artists who gave themselves up to art without holding anything back. We've all heard the axiom, reminiscent of Batyushkov's declaration, that escaped from Pushkin's lips: "Poetry is exclusively the passion of the few who are born poets. It encompasses and absorbs *all* the observations, *all* the efforts, *all* the impressions of their lives" ("On the Introduction to Mr. Lemonte's Translation of I. A. Krylov's Fables," 1825).

In this sense—on the lower level—there is nothing in Pushkin that did not either openly or secretly serve poetry. Even the most insignificant "cares of the vain world," in which he was immersed when no Apollo was demanding some sacrifice from him, are invisibly tied to art, forming what can be called Pushkin's poetic personality, which was inseparable from the elemental forces of balls and amusement. This *is* a "dietics," to use Batyushkov's term. Pushkin eats, drinks, hangs around in drawing rooms, and flirts with the ladies, if not directly in poetic form, then with the unconscious aim of transforming all this bustle into that treasure whose brilliance and elegance so delights us. Even in this he is not, strictly speaking, completely human, but Pushkin to the marrow of his bones.

And all the same—what persistence!—he wouldn't have subscribed to the formula that you have to live as you write and write as you live. On the contrary, according to Pushkin (here there are several levels of consciousness in the relationship between man and Poet, and we are now ascending to a new level), the Poet lives not at all as he writes and writes not at all as he lives. So it's not just the balls and intrigues, his vanity and faint-heartedness that are insignificant, but his whole being—for as long as it exists, including the most noble thoughts and the very poems themselves in their empirical existence—has no meaning and runs counter to the higher power that bears the name Poet. "He runs wild and stern . . ." What kind of dietics is this—asceticism, razing to the ground everything still fettered to human flesh. Pushkin (it's frightening to say!) reproduces the self-appraisal of a saint. The saint in his heart's contrition proclaims himself the worst of sinners— "and among the insignificant children of the world, he, perhaps, is the most insignificant." Or even more direct—without the "perhaps." This is neither modesty nor hyperbole, but a real touch of sanctity, which no longer belongs to the man, who has realized the insignificance of the vessel into which it has been poured.

Pushkin's Poet (in his most extreme and, I repeat, loftiest manifestation) has no face—and this is very important. What happened to all the grimaces, the fidgetiness, and the chatter to which we've grown so accustomed? Where has all trace of Pushkin gone, leaving behind this figure that can't even be called a personality, to such an extent has all personality been trampled out of it along with everything human? If *this* is a state, then what we see before us is some sort of idol; if *this* is movement, then we are observing a tempest, a flood, madness. Just try to approach the Poet—Hello, Aleksandr Sergeevich!—he won't answer, he won't even understand that you are talking to him—to him, to this effigy that sees no one, hears nothing, holding a stone lyre in his hands.

> The poet strummed his inspired lyre
> With his vacant hand.*

Allegories and cold conventionalities are necessary to mark, even if only through ellipsis, this sojourn in the spirit of Poetry, which is inaccessible to language. We have reached the highest point we can attain in describing it; here all life ends, and only muted symbols try to convey the message that it is better to remain silent at these heights.

"For what reason was he given to the world, and what did he prove by his presence?" Gogol asked about Pushkin, with his characteristic meticulousness in posing metaphysical questions. And he answered himself: "Pushkin was given to the world in order to prove by his presence what the poet as such is and nothing more—what the poet is when considered not under the influence of any specific time or circumstances, nor as conditioned by his own personal character, but as a man, independently of everything; so that, if some higher anatomist of the soul wished someday to dissect and explain to himself what the essence of a poet is . . . , then he could satisfy himself by looking at Pushkin" ("What Is, Finally, the Essence of Russian Poetry, and Wherein Lies Its Uniqueness," 1846).

"Independently of everything . . ." Yes, Pushkin showed us the Poet in manifold and exhaustive variations, including independently of everything, of the world, of life, of himself. Reaching this point we stop, deafened by the silence that suddenly falls, powerless in any way to express and restate in words the pure essence of Art, which barely allows a cloak of phenomena to be thrown over it.

> Like a deity, it does not need
> The outpourings of earthly raptures.*

In the meantime, however, on the earth the completely normal author lives and languishes, wandering about with nothing to do, only occasionally going insane or falling into a stupor of a higher order. He fidgets and fusses and suffers and knows the beautiful and frightening secret of his connection with the Poet, and he wants to name it in human language, to find an approximate synonym. He recalls various peculiarities of his biography, among which his attention is attracted by a blood line that is for some reason especially dear to his heart—the Negro branch,* which was grafted onto the genealogical tree of the Pushkin family.

Negro is good. Negro is No. Negro is the sky. "Under the sky of my Africa."* Africa *is* the sky. An exile from the heavens. More likely a demon. Not of this world. A priest. Like his second, celestial homeland, only more accessible, flowing in his veins, subterranean, hot, boiling up like the netherworld, and bursting out in his face and in his character.

This is now the absolutely real, immediately recognizable Pushkin (not the Poet), only slightly exaggerated, combining in himself human and poetic features in that very thick mixture that gives birth to a new quality, the indissoluble unity of marvelous exotica, of spiritual ardor and attractive ugliness, which is more appropriate to the rank of the artist than the standard mask of the singer with a reed pipe. Pushkin's irreproachable taste chose a Negro for a co-author, having figured out that the black, monkey-like physiognomy would suit him better than the angelic face of Lensky, that it really was his true face of which he could be proud and which enhanced him in the same way as lameness did Byron, ugliness—Socrates, more than could all the Raphaels in the world. And besides, goddammit, there was a huge amount of irony in that face! . . .

Oh, how Pushkin seized upon his negroid appearance and his African past, which he loved perhaps more dearly than he did his aristocratic ancestry. Because besides the blood kinship, here was a spiritual kinship as well. A kinship in fantasy. There were many noblemen, but there was only one Negro. In all of immense, pale mankind there was only one poet, bright as an ember. Othello. A poetic negative of a man. Italics. Graphite. Special, unlike anyone else. Such a one didn't even need a Demon. He was himself a Negro.

In those days children probably didn't read Mayne Reid* and Jules Verne and didn't play games in which they pretended to be in exotic countries with hot climates. But Pushkin already had his own personal (you can't have it!) Africa. He played at Africa just as a boy of today, while playing cowboys and Indians, might suddenly realize that he himself is a real Indian,* and he finds it funny, and for some reason he feels sorry for himself, and everything quivers inside from a bittersweet feeling of happiness—he has to bump along with his quite ordinary mama on a summer carriage ride through Razuvaevka* (on the Moscow-Tashkent line) while he is an Indian and won't forget it to the end of his days. Like being carried on the wings of fate, evidence of a past life lost in time, a premonition that, though you are a legitimate son, all the same you're a foundling, an abandoned child, an uninvited guest, a prisoner of the Caucasus in this vale of tears, and God knows how you got here, and nobody knows or remembers about you, but you have your own ideas. You are stronger, you are older; you're closer to the animals, to savage tribes and forests. A wild genius. A steaming, blood-soaked piece of poetry with an opening into chaos. And you look out from under your brow, like a Moor on the prowl, remaining calm until the hour strikes for you to take on any city that comes your way. "Give 'em hell!"—you'll bare your teeth, just try me, the crowd will part, and calmly and quietly, all keyed up, you will bear your inscrutable face through the parted crowd. "At the sight of Ibrahim,* they all began to whisper: 'The Moor! The tsar's Moor!' He hurriedly led Korsakov through this motley crowd of servants." "He felt that to them he was a kind of rare beast, a peculiar, alien creature, who had accidentally been transplanted into a world that had nothing in common with him. He even envied people whom no one noticed, and considered their insignificance a blessing."

Pushkin wrote this when he had already grown tired of the spectacle, fame, and slander that swirled in his wake and secretly yearned for happiness "on the common path." Since youth he had regarded his black otherness in society, inherited from his grandfather Ibrahim, with great enthusiasm, rightly viewing his wild pranks as a sign of the elemental force raging within him. Whereas the white bones of his aristocratic kin gave Pushkin legitimacy in the national family, in history, his Negro blood took him back to the primordial sources of art, to nature and myth. The black race, the experts tell us, is more ancient than the white one, and inspired by it the poet plunged into Dionysian games, wedding in a single guise Africa and Hellas, art and animal instinct.

> And I, the eternally idle scapegrace,
> The ugly descendant of Negroes,
> Nurtured in savage simplicity,
> Not knowing the sufferings of love,
> I, through the shameless frenzy of my desires
> Find favor with young beauties;

> With an involuntary flame in her cheeks,
> A young nymph, herself not understanding why,
> From time to time sneaks a glance at the faun.*

And here again his black grandfather, Ibrahim, came in handy. How convenient that he happened to be called Hannibal! A whole geyser of visions spouted forth from this name. The path that the Negro boy Pushkin took to come to us led there, there—back to prehistoric antiquity, to goat-legged gods and maenads. Pushing the pudgy boyars to the far end of the table, "My black grandfather, Hannibal" became the central hero of his genealogy—the poet's first and most important ancestor.

Besides the famous name and black face, he bequeathed to Pushkin one more treasure: Hannibal was Tsar Peter's favorite and godson, standing at the beginning of the new, European, Pushkinian Russia. *The Blackamoor of Peter the Great* relates in detail how the tsar arbitrarily married the Moor off into the boyar aristocracy, grafting him to a good Russian stalk (probably hoping to get a rare plant—Pushkin). What was immeasurably more important, however, was that, thanks to Hannibal, the dark-complected physiognomy of the grandson unexpectedly radiated a striking resemblance to Peter. Since being Peter's godson was as good as being Peter's son, through his black grandfather the poet managed to become related to tsars and advance into the ranks of proud firstborns, the successors of the great skipper.

> This skipper was that famous skipper
> Who moved our land,
> Who powerfully set a stately
> Course with the rudder of our native ship.

> And he was Hannibal's father . . .*

Having secured such relatives, he could boldly say to himself: "You are a tsar, live alone . . ."* The path from the Negro led to the sovereign. Pushkin solved the vital problem of the relationship between the poet and the tsar, which tormented him for so long, with the equation: the poet is a tsar.

Pushkin reigned under the sign of Peter, many traits of whose character—the diversity of his interests and intentions, the audacity of his innovations, his benevolence and simple-heartedness—as we all know, corresponded to the ideals and personal qualities of the poet, who, with a regal nod of his head, fitted out his poems as if they were flotillas and mustered them into a toy army ("I recruit an army out of worthless scum"),* and so on. These analogies with Peter were dictated by the scope of the reforms that Pushkin, trying to keep pace with Peter's decrees, undertook in Russian literature.

"Only a revolutionary thinker like Mirabeau or Peter could love Russia the way a writer loves its language," Pushkin swore. "Everything in Russia and in the Russian language is creative."*

Already back then, the idea that there might be an interconnection and similarity between Peter and Pushkin was conceived in the minds of the admirers of Russia's foremost poet. Baratynsky wrote to him (December 1825): "You, in whom genius resides, go, finish what has been started! Raise Russian poetry to that station among the poetries of all peoples to which Peter the Great raised Russia among states. Accomplish alone what he accomplished alone; and we will give you our gratitude and wonderment."

Pushkin, of course, took all of this into consideration. Yet it wasn't just historico-cultural parallels and interests that drew him to Peter as to an important relative, his godlike double, but also a more lasting, inner yearning. Pushkin discovered in Peter and made public what he had not found in Napoleon—an embodiment of his own personal and superpersonal power, an exemplar and image of the Poet independent of absolutely anyone's laws or decrees. The wild genius and autocratic will of Peter, who had built the fabulous city on an empty swamp, captivated Pushkin, and, although he had not intended to identify himself with his characters and created, so to speak, objectively, remaining faithful to diverse colorings of time and space, the parallels that came of themselves were too obvious. Pasternak sensed this when he wrote so brilliantly of Pushkin:

> On the bank by deserted waves
> He stood, full of great thoughts . . .*

In this respect, both *The Bronze Horseman* and *Poltava* contain, aside from the obvious events, the theme of the Tsar treated so as to resemble the destiny of the poet. "In my changeful fate," he remarked in the Dedication to *Poltava* and tried to place this changefulness into the broader scheme of the ordeals that had befallen Russia and Peter in the painful and beneficial "changes in earthly lot" that had seasoned them and thrown them both onto the crest of a great wave, while the arrogant Charles, going the route traversed by all of Pushkin's antipodes, tried to order destiny according to his own caprice and therefore, as always, lost ("He wants to make destiny wheel like a regiment marching to a drumbeat"). When the waves of history had washed away and leveled everything, only one, no, two in one person—the Poet and the Tsar—remained on earth.

> Only you, Poltava's hero, have erected
> A huge monument to yourself.*

Do you hear? "I have erected a monument to myself not made by hands . . ."*

The monument to the tsar becomes the hero of *The Bronze Horseman*. For some reason, the many interpreters of the poem have not paid sufficient attention to the fact that this tale recounts a very personal psychological conflict, that Peter and Evgeny bear the same relationship to one another in it as do the Poet and the man in the poem "When the poet is not called," that Petersburg and the elemental forces that inundate it are not enemies but allies, two sides of the same idea, which bears the name of Art, Poetry, . . . , which stands in opposition to the man who, in his fussy insignificance, fears and hates it.

It has been noted that Evgeny, astride the lion, staring into the distance, into the nearby distance of his personal happiness ("And, like a poet, set to musing"), which was later washed away by the flood, paraphrases the contours of the monument to Peter. But all his poses and movements invert those of the monument, and the egocentric twitchings of Evgeny's arms convulsively waving around his frail body echo the hand stretched upward—Pushkin's miracle-working hand, which summons the storm and subdues it, transforming the chaos of nature into the harmonious cosmos of the City. This is the human being—pitiful and touching in his thirst for happiness—who imagined in his blindness that the Horseman was chasing him (some people have believed this and have become indignant with the Horseman—such a big bully chasing that poor little man!): as if the Horseman just kept chasing him, going after him, doing everything on account of this half-wit who landed by accident in the churn of Poetry just because he happened to be at hand.

Evgeny! What an important name that was to Pushkin, always denoting roughly the same plot of a person who is deaf to poetry, remote from it, but for whom nevertheless the author somehow feels a certain attachment. Evgeny . . . Come on! Isn't it the secular, lay name of the one who in his holy orders is known as Aleksandr Pushkin?! We all know his parodical thoughts ("My ideal now is a spouse, all I need is peace and a pot of soup, and I'll be okay"),* which are close to Evgeny's small, run-of-the-mill happiness, giving rise to talk of Push-kin's solidarity with Evgeny's soup pot dreams and his, the author's, hostility toward the monument that shattered all pots. Especially since in the poem the monument is invariably called an idol or, even worse, a graven image. That is to say, an unfeeling idol, a Baal of the state . . . But what does Baal have to do with it? It's a completely different kind of an idol. And after all, for Pushkin "idol" wasn't such a bad word. In any case, in the clash between the pot and the idol there's no doubt which one the poet chooses. The poet says to the mob:

> You have to find a use in everything,
> You value the idol of Belvedere by its weight,
> You see no use, no use at all in it,
> But this piece of marble is a god! . . . So what?
> A soup pot is more valuable to you:
> You cook your food in it.*

The whole problem is that we don't believe in Apollo. We consider him a fiction, a poetic allegory. But for Pushkin Apollo wasn't just an empty sound, but a real god, to whose summons he harkened and whose image he depicted.

> His eyes
> Shine. His countenance is terrifying.
> His movements are swift. He is beautiful,
> He is like the wrath of God.*

What an extraordinary, mind-boggling combination: terrible-beautiful! How did Pushkin guess that that's just the way it is, that the beautiful is terrifying, that the Delphic sovereign, in whose image we unexpectedly glimpse something African, savage, and at the same time sublime—a striking, thunder-bearing face that blinds us like the sun—excites mixed feelings of ecstasy and terror. He was himself to the fullest degree Tsar—Apollo—Hannibal—Poet.

Among the marble statues at Tsarskoe Selo that struck the boy's imagination, two graven images stood out; Pushkin ascribed to them the leading role in his spiritual development.

> They were representations of two demons.

> One young face (the Delphic idol)
> Was wrathful, full of terrible pride,
> And exuded an unearthly power.

> The other, a feminine, voluptuous,
> Dubious and false ideal was
> An enchanting demon, deceitful, but beautiful.
>
> In front of them I used to forget myself;
> My young heart would beat in my breast—cold
> Would run over me and set my hair on end.*

Evgeny at the foot of the Monument borrowed something of the vague terror experienced by the boy Pushkin standing before the statues in the Tsarskoe Selo garden. Both this idol and the others enchain, enchant, rule the soul of a man. But having transposed his adolescent feelings and walks around Apollo into *The Bronze Horseman*, Pushkin cut himself in two and winnowed himself into the images of Peter and Evgeny. Poetic terror and divine madness, torn away from Poetry, became in their human incarnation mortal fear and dark insanity. Chaos unillumined by genius swallowed up the unfortunate man. But Pushkin stepped over his own lowly nature and over the split between man and genius (which was the theme of *The Bronze Horseman*), and then rejoiced and raised himself up together with the Monument. For the latter he found a pose unique in its perfection:

> And with his back to him,
> In the unshakable height,
> Above the mutinous Neva,
> The idol on the bronze horse
> Stood with outstretched hand.

His back turned to man, his whole being in the graceful harmony of the spheres, flouting chasms and subjugating the very madness of the raging elements with a menacing sweep of his hand extended upward into the firmament, the hand with which he orchestrates destiny—such is Apollo, the destroyer and healer, the master of the friendly instruments—the bow and the lyre, the thunderer, filled with inhuman pride and unearthly greatness. Those lucky enough to see Apollo face to face have found him precisely as Pushkin portrayed him.

"I made an attempt to step beyond the limits of the human and to ascend to the height of the god Apollo.

"I beheld him full of wrath, in golden bronze, absorbed by thoughts and battle. This is my first attempt to rise above people" (From a letter of Antoine Bourdelle to André Suares, December 31, 1926).

Unfortunately, at the moment I have no way of finding out more precisely who was depicted in the second statue at Tsarskoe Selo, which made the young Pushkin tremble so. It is quite possible that it was Bacchus-Dionysus. I seem to remember that the ancients imagined him in feminine form. But whoever it was, it's not that essential to an understanding of *The Bronze Horseman*, the text of which belongs to Apollo, and Dionysus has no independent face here and is represented with his elemental forces as the flip side of Apollo, the sun-bearing god of Poetry, as its, Poetry's, so to speak, creative lining. Graven images and madness—these, as we have seen, are the guises in which the Poet appears in Pushkin's works in his purest and most exalted sense, independent of everything else. He either stands as still as a post, paying no attention to anyone, or rushes around like a madman "full of sounds and confusion." In *The Bronze Horseman* we are given both variants: the graven image–monument of Peter, who built the City, and the madness-flood, which threatens to drown them but was in fact summoned and sanctioned by them and is in league with them.

Through some dark intuition, Evgeny realizes that Peter is to blame for the tempest that fell upon St. Petersburg, that in the recurring flood tides of the elements the hand and design of the founder of the city can be discerned. In fact the waves and the Horseman act in concert, he is their leader, the general who sends them to attack his own strongholds. Let us not forget here Peter's passion for war and seafaring, which has a hand in the scene of the catastrophe, which is gloomy in spirit but joyous in intonation, and which is written with the same élan as, "We press upon the Swedes, one legion after another,"* and is lit up by the advance of inspiration audible in the howling and the whirlwind. The attack of the spirit, which rushed through the window that Peter cut* with a view on the sea, forces us to remember that it was customary for Dionysus to unleash passions, to let loose the elements, and to plunge the bacchante into a state of ecstasy—which is in fact the act of creation in its primordial, chaotic form—until such time as her frenzy passes over into its luminous derivative and madness is transformed into harmony. The ancients used to say of such transitions: "Dionysus fled to the Muses," suspecting, perhaps, the union between the two demons—Apollo and Dionysus—who were opposite in their qualities but equal in their prophetic powers and seemingly rivaled one another in the mysteries of art. Remember what Pushkin said about inspiration: "It sails. Whither should we sail? . . ." And so we set sail:

> The weather was growing ever fiercer,
> The Neva swelled and roared,
> Boiling up and steaming like a cauldron,
> And suddenly, in a frenzy, like a wild beast,
> It rushed upon the city . . .*

But this explosion of unbounded, indomitable, primeval energy is nevertheless held back at the very brink by the hand of that same Peter. No matter how the waves seethe, the summit remains unshakable, and the Idol resides there, galloping all over the place without even budging a finger, with fiery blood in his bronze body.

Notice that Peter rides over the Neva without going anywhere; the flood has the fiery nature of Peter and his steed; and the steed is all of Russia, Poetry itself, bolting in a frenzy toward the sky and at the same time frozen in a vortex of water, fire, and metal merged into one:

> But, filled with the triumph of victory,
> The waves still boiled maliciously,
> As if a fire smoldered under them,
> Foam still covered them,
> And the Neva breathed heavily,
> Like a horse come running from battle.
> . . . .
> How terrible he is in the surrounding gloom!
> What thoughts are on his brow!
> What power is concealed in him!
> And in this steed what fire!
> Whither are you galloping, proud steed,
> And where will you set down your hooves!
> O mighty lord of destiny!
> Did you not thus on the chasm's brink
> On high, with iron bridle
> Raise Russia rearing on its haunches?

In this soaring apotheosis—constructed of nothing but exclamations—skeptics have detected a note of dissatisfaction, almost a curse and a prediction of doom for the horseman who has ascended too high. As if "terrible" ("How terrible he is in the surrounding gloom!") did not suggest, as if it did not already contain in itself—"beautiful"! As if the abyss beneath the horse's hooves could discomfit the one who himself in dionysiac rapture exclaimed, "There is an ecstasy in battle, and at the edge of the gloomy abyss . . ."* As if this Russia rearing up on its haunches—of which it has been said that everything in this Russia and its language could only have been created by a visionary like Peter—or this storm, reined in at the edge of the chasm, which combined in itself the abyss of barbarism and the miracle of harmony, could stagger and collapse and not remain forever as a monument to the despot Poetry!

"Dionysus fled to the Muses . . ." The frenzied orgy of creativity is resolved in the harmonious concord and structure of the creation:

> I love you, creation of Peter,
> I love your profile's austere grace.*

And at every step there is stability and grace. "The heavy, sonorous galloping." Troops file past in "harmoniously rippling ranks." "Graceful structures crowd." The ponderousness of stone, the ductility of metal. "The smoke and thunder of your fortress." Pushkin's Petersburg appears as an offspring of the forces of nature tamed and cast into towers, palaces, fences. The granite is as strong as the storm is furious, and the harder the Neva beats against the fortress, "its noisy waves splashing at the edge of its graceful fence," the greater, it seems, is the durability it imparts to this fortress, while at the same time vitalizing it and nourishing it with its passion, not allowing it to cool off, expanding the bulk of the buildings and monuments. In this sense, the introduction holds the entire work in harmony, as if on a bridle; the poem is not washed away at the beginning of the flood but emerges out of the waves and the winds that inspired its structure and freezes into the crystals of the poem-city.

As a result, Petersburg the elemental force and Petersburg the capital, Pushkin's poetry in its two aspects—the wild genius and the marvelous city—are made manifest in a single image as something unified and whole. *The Bronze Horseman.* We can hear in the title the consonance of antagonistic principles—statics and dynamics, order and chaos, Apollo and Dionysus who passed from enmity to cooperation and peace. *The Bronze Horseman* is no longer merely the title, the hero, or the theme of Pushkin's tale, it has become an exhaustive definition of the poem which embraces everything that happens in it and everything there is in it, including the genre, style and verse form in which it is written. If we were to draw an outline around the poem with a pencil, we would get the Bronze Horseman. He grows out of it, rules over it, and, ultimately, coincides with it. That's why he appears in it so many times in one and the same form and gallops through the entire text, never for a single moment disappearing from view, growing in size, and there's no escape from him, no hiding because he encompasses the city

and the flood and the poet who is writing about him, sitting in his gar-
ret, looking out on the transparent streets, and Evgeny, who pitifully
mimics the poet, the Horseman, and the flood, deafened by "the noise
of inner disquiet," until finally he pronounces his own death sentence
with his "I'll show you!" and perishes under the hooves of the Idol,
who had no intention of trampling anyone and didn't even loosen the
reigns of the beast rearing over the abyss, but simply absorbed everything into himself and took command of the poem, crowding out the
man. Evgeny is gradually driven out of it as it assumes more completely
the outlines of the galloping Monument. He is expelled from it as a
body alien to poetry and is buried offhandedly in the final lines of the
poem—beyond the city limits.

The question arises, Does Pushkin sympathize with Evgeny? Of
course he does! After all, in Evgeny he careened over himself and
neutralized his own human dreams and triviality! Besides, he was
always more compassionate toward other people's misfortunes. But
even though he sympathized with Evgeny, he was merciless. Pushkin was generally cruel toward the man where the interests of poetry
were concerned. Despite his fondness for Byron, he wrote to Vyazemsky
(June 13–14, 1824): "You're grieving over Byron, but I'm so glad that
he died, because his death provides a lofty subject for poetry. Byron's
genius had faded with the passing of his youth. In his tragedies, including even *Cain*, he is no longer the fiery demon who created *The
Giaur* and *Childe Harold*. The first two parts of *Don Juan* are superior
to those that follow."

In short, you did what you had to do, so don't overstay your welcome, don't spoil the impression. The same attitude he had toward
himself.

Pushkin did not reject what was human in himself and did not sup-
press it; he gave it free rein and space and looked on indulgently at all
the man's pranks and escapades, giving himself up to them wholeheart-
edly. But he maintained a strict distance between himself and the man
and, while forgiving him much—perhaps too much—on the plane of
everyday life, he was severe and demanding when he allowed him into
his poetic chambers and constantly put him in his place as you would
a lackey: don't forget who you are. Pushkin didn't want him to get a
swelled head or make too much of himself and so wrote about himself impartially, watching with sympathy and scorn how that Evgeny
rushed about. Pushkin's detachment, his uncompromising position,
allowed him to watch over him with a clear-sightedness that would

have been impossible, unthinkable, for an author who identified himself too closely with the man; he soberly weighed all the pros and cons
and created a generally unflattering and unendearing portrait.

That's how he depicted Onegin, again Evgeny, again full of worldly
vanity, a mediocrity in which there is everything and nothing of Pushkin inasmuch as Onegin is a subject familiar to him right down to
the fingertips, his own, completely his own, taken apart bone by bone
by the poet, who has risen above the man. The epigraph to Pushkin's
novel (in French, "from a private letter") reveals how the portrait of
Onegin was made (bearing in mind as we read it that the "he" most
likely refers to the author): "Filled with vanity, he also possessed a
peculiar sort of pride that prompted him to own up with equal indif-
ference to both his good and bad actions—the result of a perhaps false
sense of superiority."

Where does he get this "peculiar sort of pride," this imagined ability
to look down his nose at his own ugliness and merits? Evidently, from
the poet Pushkin, who excreted Onegin as his human emanation and
calmly examined it—with a mixture of sympathy and malicious delight.

At a time when the romantics were busting their guts to become
Corsairs,* Pushkin took the opposite path and became a human being,
retreating into the shadow of the most ordinary, the most banal of men.
If we compare Onegin with Pushkin (and they are compared in the
novel), the first thing that jumps out at us is the "difference," seizing
on which the author muddles everything by giving us clues like, "I was
embittered, he was morose," or for a long time I couldn't get used to "his
caustic arguments, his jokes, mixed with equal parts of gall, and the
malice of his grim epigrams" (at least as far as epigrams are concerned,
Pushkin could have given Onegin a run for his money!).* All this covers
the traces of the true alignment of forces. Taken as a relatively whole
image (although in essence he really isn't), as he is seen from a distance,
as a literary type, Onegin bears no resemblance to Pushkin (what could
someone who hasn't a grain of poetry in him possibly have in common
with Pushkin?), while in specifics and trivial details he coincides with
Pushkin so closely that it seems as if the author had looked in a mirror
and copied himself feature by feature: superficiality, good breeding,
laziness, impiety, the attention he devotes to care of his fingernails, et
cetera. The result was a human parody of the poet, a zero without a 1 in
front of it (the 1 was the poet), and, having lost it all of Pushkin's natural qualities were transformed beyond recognition, turned so sour that

it was disgusting even to contemplate (thus the magnificent laziness of the poet became the ordinary idleness of an untalented good-for-nothing, the fullness of love was emasculated and became the sexless "science of the tender passion,"* and whereas the poet Pushkin was killed in a duel, the man Onegin himself had no qualms about killing a poet friend as trivial as himself). Everything loses its meaning and content, and perhaps only the outline of the respectable form of Nulin, who is clever enough by the standards of everyday life and who knows how to behave, remains.

No one at that time performed a more humiliating anatomy on the human organism, and in order to tone down the impression, to justify the expenses incurred on the psychological tissue that was disintegrating under his scalpel, the author endowed it with signs of the times and the milieu, with names of dishes he had sampled and books he had leafed through out of boredom, sometimes making Evgeny a man of the crowd, a regular guy, just like everyone else, and sometimes, contradicting himself, pulling out of the blue "an involuntary devotion to dreams, an inimitable strangeness"* (although Onegin dreams of nothing and is made up entirely of insipid imitations), so that ultimately you can make of him anything you want—a superfluous man, a petty demon, a Carbonaro, or simply a minor,* as a result of which his unstable character totally disintegrates, making room for the novel in verse. In short, once it had been dissected this way nothing remained of Pushkin's personality in Onegin; all that is left floating before our eyes is an indistinct gibberish, which teachers and schoolchildren have been beating their heads against for more than a century, trying to give it meaning and to fish the image bit by bit out of the rubbish Pushkin dumped out, gamely settling his scores with the devil that was sucking out his insides like a tapeworm, like some rented "I," borrowed from his human contemporaries because, after all, a poet had to live somehow, because, after all, he was still human . . .[12]

No, you can't throw a bridge to Pushkin over Onegin, with his blurred face and gaping lack of spirituality. A different sort of charac-

---

12. Tatyana caught a glimpse of Onegin's demonic past in her dream, where he was the leader of a hellish gang. The original nature of his image also shows through in "A Secluded House on Vasilevsky Island," from which we can draw the conclusion that in his final form Onegin is a transformed, disgraced demon who, once a tempter, ended up as a victim and was turned into a person with zero meaning. It must be noted that another path from that same "Secluded House" leads to Evgeny of *The Bronze Horseman.*

ter is what is needed here, someone who, even if he is bogged down in the masses, all the same elbows his way into history as a pretender to a higher post, someone who, even if he has been deprived of his rights or is marked by the shameful stigma of the scoundrel, is all the same a king (the king is naked!), vain, loud, aspiring to make his way out of the crowd into the ranks of the poets, someone with more bite than Onegin. What we need here is—Khlestakov! He was Gogol's discovery, but Pushkin suggested the image to him, made him a present of it along with the whole idea for *The Inspector General.* It's no accident that Khlestakov "is on friendly terms with Pushkin": like Pushkin, he mixes with the crowd and plays the Frenchie and, like Pushkin, he is nimble, talkative, free-and-easy, empty, universal, and sincere.* He lies and believes his own lies, as Gogol puts it, "aimlessly."

Isn't he the spitting image of Pushkin? "He presents himself as a private person" but is really a "damned incognito," "with secret instructions," "he is wearing civilian clothes and walks like this around the room and has such a serious expression on his face . . ."

"He isn't a general, but he's no worse than any general." "Once I was even taken for the commander in chief: soldiers leaped out of the guardhouse and presented arms." "When he went out for a stroll in his ordinary clothes, in his overcoat, he always wore it with one flap over his shoulder and the other dragging on the ground. 'Like a general,' he called it" (V. Yakovlev, "Remarks on Pushkin from the South of Russia," Odessa, 1887).

How slick he is! One moment it's Anna Andreevna, the next— Marya Antonovna. "Then you're in love with *her?*" "Love knows no distinctions."*

Of course, he's not a poet. Although "I confess that once in awhile I, too, like to lose myself in meditation—sometimes in prose, other times verses pop out. . . . My thoughts have an extraordinary lightness about them."*

But enough joking. There's obviously a profound, far-reaching similarity here. No matter how strange it might seem, if we don't go off to Africa, if we don't dredge back in history, but seek prototypes for Pushkin near at hand, in his contemporary milieu, we won't find a better candidate than Khlestakov—the human alter ego of the poet.

An impostor! But what is a poet if not an impostor? A tsar? A self-proclaimed tsar. He said it himself: "You're a tsar, live alone . . ." Since when do tsars live alone? Impostors are always alone, even when they're on top, when they're on the throne, because they themselves, on their own recognizance, have declared themselves tsars and know what no one else is supposed to suspect: they (voice dropping to a whisper) aren't tsars at all, it just seemed the right thing to say at the time, (still softer) first the throne, and then the gallows.

Pushkin knew just what to give Gogol. False Dmitry—Pugachov—Khlestakov. But if we look more closely, we'll see that Pushkin's impostors come in all ranks. Maybe it was in the air at the time, but his characters set off and dashed in all directions anywhere but to the station they were supposed to occupy: the lady became a peasant girl,* the uhlan—a cook, Aleko—a Gypsy, Dubrovsky—a bandit, the fugitive monk seated himself on the throne of the tsar. "I couldn't help wondering at the strange chain of events: my rabbitskin coat from childhood, given to a vagrant, saved me from hanging; and a drunk who once wandered from inn to inn lay siege to fortresses and shook the foundations of the state." *

It was the best of times for poets. They set out together with Khlestakov—to become Pushkins and Gogols. There was no holding them back. Each one thought he was a tsar. That's where all the trouble began. People were people just like everyone else, and then suddenly there was a poet. Who gave him the right? Where did he come from? From himself. Ha-ha! What do you mean from himself?!

Pushkin felt what it was to be an impostor more keenly than others did. Who else elevated the poet to such heights, who so desperately played out his destiny, was so deeply imbued with its spirit and savor? It's true that his poet is always from on high, a poet by the grace of God, not simply "I am a tsar," but the Lord's anointed. After all, impostors also—and Pushkin's impostors especially—know that they have been dealt a card, a providential ace, from on high. They do not simply proclaim themselves tsars, but believe that they had to proclaim themselves. They lie—and believe their own lies. "The shade of Ivan the Terrible adopted me!" *

Just look: Pushkin was adopted by the shade of Peter exactly the same way! His great-grand-godfather? We know all about godfathers like that! After all, Pugachov pulled exactly the same stunt,* before he had even thought of an uprising, long before, just for the sake of a good yarn, and Pushkin, obviously, didn't know anything about this interesting detail. He didn't know about it, but he duplicated it—in his own biography. While still in the army, Pugachov once happened to get drunk and, while under the influence, he bragged about his saber (good arms were awarded for distinguished service). "But since he had not at that time distinguished himself in any way, but had always wanted to gain repute, he said that the saber had been bestowed on him because he was a godson of Tsar Peter I. This was said, the villain swears, with no other intent than to make himself different from others. This rumor spread among the Cossacks and reached the ears of Colonel Efim Kuteinikov. However, these words were not held as a crime against him, and people simply laughed at him" (October 2–6, 1774, Interrogation Record, at Simbirsk).

For both Pushkin and Pugachov, the claim to be Peter's godson served as an internal trampoline catapulting them into Peter's ranks. Pushkin was always happy to draw distinctions between himself and others (it's a trait that poets and impostors have in common). But even more than in external signs, this exceptionalness was inherent in and confirmed by destiny: the man suddenly became suspiciously lucky. We all remember how it was with Pushkin—it went just the same way with Pugachov. "In regard to his undertakings to take possession of everything, he was himself surprised that at first he was so favored by chance, especially at the beginning as when he showed up at the town of Yaitsky having only a hundred men of his accomplices, but he was not captured. For this reason he firmly believes that it was God's will to bring misfortune on Russia" (Report to P. S. Potemkin by Lieutenant-Captain of the Guard S. Mavrin on the capture of Pugachov, September 15, 1774).

Luck like that, taken to be a sign of collusion, of assent from the highest quarters, spurs the impostor on to take decisive steps, which are to a certain extent justified in Pushkin's eyes by their very decisiveness. For him, False Dmitry was preferable to and in a sense more legitimate than Boris. The latter usurped someone else's throne through cunning and violence and then exerted massive efforts to retain it, whereas in the case of the Impostor the tsardom fell at his feet of itself, like a ripe apple. "Everything's on my side: both the people and destiny."

That's why the psychological type of Pushkin-Peter nevertheless shows through the rather bland character of the False Dmitry (he is too handsome, a short-lived plaything in the hands of Fortune): an ardent, generous heart; trustfulness toward the vagaries of fate; the ability to give himself up improvidently to first impressions. Like Mozart in the scene with the violin player from the tavern, he's ready to forsake his kingdom for the sake of a dying horse; like Peter, he has a good word for the enemy who has just beaten him, and he falls asleep like a baby after a crushing military defeat. Pushkin's False Dmitry is truly a born tsarevich: he bears the mark of miraculous grace.

> Sweet dreams, tsarevich!
> Utterly defeated, saving himself in flight,
> He is as unconcerned as a silly child;
> Providence of course watches over him;
> And we, friends, will not lose heart.

Pushkin's Pugachov is also blessed with regal manners. How after all did the young nobleman met in passing win his favor? Just by presenting him, in a manner worthy of a tsar, with a rabbitskin coat from off his own shoulders. It wasn't the coat that he valued but the shoulders. It was very much in the manner of Pugachov himself: "Whether you put to death or pardon, do it all the way." And he repaid Grinyov a hundredfold. Among other favors, he did not forget to reward him in a grand reciprocal gesture—with a sheepskin coat from his own shoulders.

But Pushkin's impostors are more than just tsars—they are artists as well, and he is particularly fond of that aspect of them. Dmitry is even portrayed as a patron of "the flowers of Parnassus," and Dmitry's patronage—"I believe the prophecies of poets"—betrays a lofty personal interest akin to that of Pushkin. For impostors also create deception by instinct and inspiration; they bear within themselves and enact their human fate as if it were a work of art. "Bored with the strictures of monastic life, beneath my cowl, I thought through my daring plan, I was making ready a miracle for the world."*

And his miracle came out of the Monastery of the Miracle.* Pimen's cell was Grigory-Dmitry's cradle. Despite differences in age and character, they are brothers in their craft, and Grigory continues the tale from the page where Pimen broke it off, he takes up the baton handed off to him by the elder: "I pass my labor on to you." Imposture has its source in poetry and unfolds according to its laws. Although its tales are written in blood and assume the form of historical events, their authors construct their plots like true artists. " 'Listen,' Pugachov said under the influence of some wild inspiration" (and the parable of his life and art* follows).

By the way, that's why they don't particularly insist on the literal authenticity of their royal origins. The story of the impostor is much more striking and entertaining from an artistic point of view. Dmitry assures Marina that he is offering her his hand and heart not as a tsarevich but as a fugitive monk. The personage and prestige of the artist are dearer to him than the high post—what a brilliant conception, what wonderful acting! What power of art!

This exciting plot, along with the task of the newly appeared tsar—to obtain control of the state and the throne primarily through special effects produced by his charismatic personality (his success depends in large measure on his artistic sense and talent)—transforms the destiny of the impostor into a theatrical spectacle. Everyone is looking at him, drawing comparisons, making suppositions; the crowd is both participant and spectator in the historical drama, applauding the lone actor.

Pugachov's very first appearance in public (not in royal regalia, but in his initial guise as a vagrant-guide) is staged as an uncommon spectacle. All attention is directed at the external appearance of the hero as he climbs down from a bunk; he is destined to take a central place in events that have not yet begun but have already been set to fermenting by means of the primarily visual impact. "His appearance seemed remarkable to me: he was about forty, of average height, thin, and broad-shouldered." The sentence sounds absurd—there is nothing at all remarkable as promised in his appearance. And Grinyov has no reason to stare at the muzhik he has just met, because he doesn't yet know who he's dealing with. But even though he doesn't know, he stares: this muzhik is a spectacle in himself and, moreover, one staged in such a way that the apparently absurd sentence will turn out to be prophetic. Pugachov will play not the tsar whose title he covets but the black-bearded muzhik, the impostor tsar, the tsar Emelyan whom Grinyov sees in his dream. This once again reveals the poetic nature of Pushkin's staging. In his works imposture lives, like art, not as a reflection of something else but by its own wits and ardor. It is willful and autocratic. Pugachov never overplays his role (which would seem to be inevitable in a play of this type), but instead he reveals his true face, his royal nature, which is why his rather ordinary appearance amazes everyone.

"An extraordinary scene presented itself to me: Pugachov and a dozen or so Cossack leaders were seated in their caps and colorful shirts, flushed with wine, their faces red, their eyes agleam at a table spread with a tablecloth and covered with bottles and glasses." Again "extraordinary"! Hadn't he ever seen drunken peasants before? No, what is extraordinary is the artistry with which they, in their drunken, brigand way, play poets and tsars. They play out their destined roles as convicts and gallows birds in a style worthy of tsars. "Their stern faces, harmonious voices, the gloomy intonation they imparted to their words, which were quite expressive enough without it—everything stunned me with a sort of poetic awe."

Walter Scottian forms of domestication of world history where great people appear as private persons (Catherine the Great in a nightcap and quilted jacket) alternate in *The Captain's Daughter* with blocking and stage sets executed in the style of popular street theater. Here the writer draws on his experience with *Boris Godunov*, taken together with the dynastic line of succession linking Emelka Pugachov to Grishka Otrepev, and develops it further, reaffirming the theatricality of popular theater and exploiting it in the drama of imposture. "Drama was born in the public square and was a popular form of entertainment. The folk, like children, demand amusement and action. Drama is for them an unusual, strange event. The folk demand strong sensations, for them, even an execution is a spectacle. Laughter, pity, and terror are the three chords of our imagination struck by the magic of drama" ("On Folk Drama and the Drama *Marfa the Mayoress*").

A performance of this kind is played out in *Poltava*, where the spectacle of the execution, with the scene of the executioner's block and the hyperbolic executioner in the leading roles, uninhibitedly strikes the above-mentioned chords with its rough-hewn aesthetic of blood and the ax, which induces a profound catharsis in thousands of spectators. We are left to wonder how Pushkin absorbed so organically these tastes of the folk carnival, which were alien to his epoch and milieu.

> The fatal scaffold stood in the middle of the field.
> On it, the executioner strolled, enjoying himself,
> And greedily awaiting his victim:
> At times he took the heavy ax
> Playfully in his white hands,
> At times he joked with the merry crowd . . .
> . . . .
> . . . . And then
> They came and ascended. Crossing himself,
> Kochubei lowered himself onto the block.
> The hosts of people were silent
> As the grave. The ax flashed as it swept down,
> And the head flew off.
> The whole field moaned. Another head
> Came rolling after it, winking.
> The grass grew red with blood—
> And, with his heart rejoicing in malice,
> The executioner caught both of them by the hair
> And with clenched hands
> Shook them both above the crowd.*

The Pugachov rebellion, as a phenomenon of folk theater that stepped down from the stage into the steppe and drew whole districts into a carnival of fires and executions, provided Pushkin with wonderful material for his directorial design. The palace-hut, pasted over with golden paper but preserving all of its original furniture: a hearth, an oven fork, and a washbasin suspended on a rope; a "heneral" Beloborodov in a heavy peasant coat with a blue ribbon across his chest; the scarred nostrils of a second "heneral," Khlopusha;* a gallows as decorative background (Grinyov bumps into it willy-nilly at every turn, underscoring the stereotypical effect of the terrible spectacle: "The gallows with its victims stood out black and terrible," "The moon and the stars shone brightly, illuminating the square and the gallows," over and over again)—all of these are carnival props necessary to the main character, who plays the traditional role of the sovereign—a mixture of extreme cruelty with equally extreme magnanimity—to perfection, but who is even more captivating in his other role, in his own skin, that of a royal thief, author of his own terrible and entertaining life. For him, the main spectacle is still to come, and the gallows that accompanies the advance of the impostor guides us there, to the final act of the tragedy. Barely having begun his ascent, the impostor already knows what will happen in the finale and moves toward it without hesitating, knowing it is a denouement necessary to the plot, to his final spectacle.

> I dreamed that a steep staircase
> Led me to a tower; from that height
> Moscow looked like an anthill;
> Below, people bustled in the square
> And pointed at me with laughter,
> And I became ashamed and frightened . . .*

Laughter. Pity. Terror. Pushkin had to experience all this in his own life. No matter how hard he personally tried to avoid spectacle, preferring to put his self-acting characters on display, without advertising his authorship, their fate nonetheless caught up with him—because poetry is itself an uncommon spectacle, because he had raised the curtain and turned on the footlights a long time before, and it was no longer possible to remain invisible.

There may come a time when an author who his whole life long has remained out of sight, who has avoided speaking in his own name (for the sake of the innocent birdies about which he, in wonderful anonymity, has been chirping indistinct somethings in bird language), is in the end forced to take part in a spectacle not even of his own conception, as if he were some Byron or other of the sort he should have had nothing to do with and avoided like the plague. "The noise died down. I stepped out onto the stage."*

It was even more impossible for Pushkin to leave this life quietly and unnoticed, as he would have liked, because every street urchin recognized him from afar and chanted: "Having crossed the bridge, Kokushkin . . ."* (what follows is unprintable).[13] His photogenic personality had already become a topic of gossip. Everyone knew for a fact from his own words—with whom, when, where, and about whom—they were au courant, kept him in their sights, and waited to see what would happen next. "The folk demand strong sensations, for them even an execution is a spectacle." He had to die in public, in the street.

Tynyanov,* it seems, was upset that Pushkin's duel—studied in minute detail and blown out of all proportion by swarms of biographers, lyrical responses, solemn oaths to avenge him, plays, movies, and just plain idle conjecture—concealed from the audience the work of the poet, the artist. As if it were not the artist himself who had staged it all. As if it were not the result of his efforts!

And perhaps it wasn't. How can we know? Perhaps it was the man who fired the shot, driven to his wits' end, forced by the poet into a blind alley, into a situation from which there was no way out. Because it was the poet who first started the rumor that drove him to his grave. It was he who organized and arranged everything so that the man became everyone's buddy, go-between, and well-wisher, poking his nose in everywhere and getting his ears boxed in public. It was he, the poet, who forced the man to bow and smile, to strike up conversations with every passerby: "Hm, hm! My noble reader, are all your relatives in good health?" To which the reader eagerly responds: And how 'bout you, Pushkin, are all your relatives well?

Oh, how risky it is to let your biography into poetry, to show your face on the stage. This is imposture! They'll start trying to find out who you are, who you're married to, why you fought the duel.

> "Who do you think I am, in your opinion?"
> "God only knows, but whoever you are, you're playing with fire."*

The rumor, started by the poet, grew to a fury.* But the main disgrace still lay ahead, beyond death, beyond the duel, which—and he

13. This can be replaced by any other quotation, to suit the reader's taste. For example, "Whether I wander through noisy streets . . ."

suspected this, shuddering in advance—would light up like a search-light all the nooks and crannies of his brilliantly interrupted life and turn every little spot of blood on his vest into a coarsely painted ace.* With the duel, all the interest that had smoldered for so long in his entertaining personality, in the rumors about him, in the family members who served as the pretext, reached a weight so incredible that it was more than the man could bear.

Can it be—I'm asking directly because life is short and the gauntlet has been thrown down and evasions won't help anymore—can it be that Pushkin, who knew his own worth, didn't know that for centuries and centuries all humanity, hearing of him, whether indifferent toward him or filled with admiration, whether readers or illiterates, would ask: But after all, cross your heart, tell the truth, did she put out or didn't she? Did anything really happen or did Pushkin get all worked up over nothing? Even if people are too well bred to ask out loud, they imply it in their journals and textbooks. Because Pushkin didn't die in bed but on stage, because it wasn't at a country house but on the executioner's block that Natalya Nikolaevna kissed or didn't kiss the handsome cavalry officer. The shot lit up the trio with a burst of Bengal fire.

Well, but after all? . . .

The very thought makes you . . . "Just you wait, miracle worker, I'll show you . . ."*

We don't know who fired the shot. Maybe it was the man, Evgeny, crazy Evgeny, shooting at the Poet, at the Bronze Horseman. And the bullet bounced off.

After all, you can't kill the Poet, you can't puncture him. He'll grow, flourish, gain fame, spread disgraceful rumors about Pushkin all over the planet in every existing tongue.* "Just you wait, miracle worker . . ." But it's the man who has to die.

"He recognized him in the crowd and nodded his head to him, the head that a minute later, dead and bloody, would be displayed to the people."*

No, I can't, I have no right to agree with Tynyanov. No matter what Pushkin dreamed up—even if it be to fight a duel or to disgrace himself for all ages—art puts everything to use—death, the duel—art transforms everything into spectacle, striking the three chords of our imagination: laughter, pity, and terror. The drama he played out in public before the curtain fell does not eclipse Pushkin's poetry but, on the contrary, crowns it, carrying its fiery breath to everyone right down to the last street urchin. And in its carnival form (from which it's impossible to figure out—and anyway it's not important—who was shooting at whom, all that's important is that there was shooting) it accurately corresponds to our general conception of Pushkin the artist. If you want to find out more, read his poems and letters, but the duel is enough to give you the first—the most general and truest—impression. The duel, in its overblown and gaudy style, provides a sufficiently faithful and juicy portrait of him: "Rather than eat carrion for three hundred years I'd drink warm blood once, and then let it be as God wills!" (Pugachov's parable).

That's how the figure of Pushkin has remained in our consciousness—with a pistol in his hand. A little Pushkin with a big, big gun. A civilian, but more famous than any military man. A general. An ace. Pushkin!

It's crude, but accurate. He was the first poet with his own biography—how else would you have had him bite the dust, the first poet who wrote himself into the history of art with blood and gunpowder?

See what we can do! Civilians rejoiced. It was the beginning of literature as a serious—not just scribbling verses—spectacle, where money was no object. With that single step—to the barrier!—he overtook himself and left for posterity a recipe for the poet. With that one shot, he said everything he had to say and responded to all his hypostases: Negro, tsar, impostor! . . .

The man had to pay up for all of them.

But there was one other, whom all the shooting, the fuss, all the laughter and moaning didn't reach. As he had stood in prostration, so he remained. He is always what is left, beyond death, beyond life, beyond spectacle. The gossip did not anger nor the fame gladden him. It's all the same to him.

> Not for ordinary worries,
> Not for profit, not for battles,
> We are born for inspiration,
> For sweet sounds and prayers . . .*

Perhaps it was even he who gave the signal—Fire! Not in order to intervene in the game, but simply to put the one on earth out of his misery. Perhaps the time had come—it was time for him to go to his rest.

Everything in Pushkin originates in and is a continuation of him, but he himself participates in nothing, allowing everything to run its own course. Perhaps, only by his silent presence, he sometimes injects discordances into the compositions of the author, whose personality, as soon as it remembers him, begins to deny itself and contradict itself at almost every turn. Discrepancies begin to crop up.

The most accessible writer in the world, understandable even to a child, suddenly introduces himself as "not understood by anyone." The most companionable, the most sociable Pushkin suddenly turns to stone: "live alone." The most fun-loving and talkative of authors announces that he has taken an oath of silence: "despondent and mute." * The most ardent and eccentric of people declares, "But you remain steadfast, calm, and grim."

What's going on here? What was the name? We don't know. "A damned incognito."

Once he had produced everything in Pushkin, once he had tuned everything in Pushkin's key, he immediately dissociated himself from him, repeating over and over: that's not right, not like that, I'm not like that. This sort of negative definition of his own nature and image by an artist is called *pure art*.

That's all we needed! Art "pure"? Nonsense. Art's relationship to life is extremely suspect as it is, and now you want to add "pure"! Is it possible, is it becoming to art to be pure? Never. It has to be either one thing or the other. Those who say there never has been and never can be pure art are right. Just take Pushkin himself. Didn't he encourage the Decembrists? Didn't he try to talk some sense into the little father Tsar? Didn't he cross swords with the slanderers of Russia? Didn't he call for mercy for those who had fallen? Didn't he scorch people's hearts with his Word? * Where's the pure art here?

The idol holds his peace. He just stares blankly. Only once in a hundred years does he let one fly that would make a sailor blush:

> He sings for his own amusement,
> Without further intentions; he knows neither fame,
> Nor fear, nor hope . . . *

Or he shuts up one of his own friends when that friend tries to impose on poets the responsibility "to inspire people with love of virtue and fire them with hatred toward vice": "Not at all. Poetry is above morality—or at least it is an entirely different matter" ("Notes in the

Margins of P. A. Vyazemsky's Article 'On the Life and Works of V. A. Ozerov' ").

Pushkin did not come to the idea of pure art right away, and at first, as we've said, he attributed to his trifles only the auxiliary, applied significance of serving the everyday needs of his circle of friends and lovers. He only wrote to sign albums, to entertain at table, to finagle kisses. But even behind these obviously lightened tasks of creation could be discerned the negative position of the author, who preferred to work for ladies in order to evade more demanding clients. Pushkin hid in the embraces of women from the eyes of authority, from the didactic tradition of the eighteenth century, which, even in the new century, kept trying to pigeonhole the poet. Behind the dedication to *Ruslan*— "For you, queens of my heart, my beauties, for you alone"—stands a very transparent negative addressee: it is *not* for epic heroes. Lyudmila gently guided Ruslan, opening up a loophole to independent art.

Soon, however, even that seemed too little for him: "I am not one of our writers of the eighteenth century: I write for myself and publish for money,* not at all for the sake of the smiles of the fairer sex" (Letter to P. A. Vyazemsky, March 8, 1824).

A false accusation is leveled against our writers of the past century here. Even when they did write for the smiles of the fairer sex, it was generally for crowned members of that sex. After all, at that time literature was more often than not under the patronage of empresses. Pushkin was another matter: he made his fortune off women, who provided him with room and board. Was it so long ago, "for you alone"? Was it so long ago that he was falling all over himself to prove, "No poem could ever be worth as much as a smile on lustful lips"?* And now all smiles are given short shrift (how can you believe him after that?). "For myself and for money." What a skinflint!

He really did need money desperately. But besides providing him with material support, money, like women, served as a cover, a screen of respectability. In a semi-official letter Pushkin called his activities as a writer "a branch of honest industry" that provided him with a decent income. Industry sounded solid, it enjoyed privileges, it presupposed free private enterprise. Under this trademark he really got going, preferring to be considered a businessman to serving anyone whatsoever. He traded in manuscripts at full tilt so as not to sell out inspiration.

On the other hand, money freed him completely from the narrowly utilitarian goals of his earlier period. Once he had set up large-scale literary production, Pushkin began to look down his nose at his practical duties, at the "repose of a sensitive man" as he now contemptuously called the habit of using poetic means to embellish leisure time, to entertain himself and his domestic circle.

Finally, the emphasis on "for money" meant—not for fame, not for poetic laurels.

We see how, by substituting some motives for others (women for service to society, money for women, amusement for lofty tasks, entrepreneurship for amusement), Pushkin gradually renounced, without exception, all the conceivable purposes that are generally imposed on art and opened up the way to an understanding of poetry—negative to its very core—according to which it, "by its nature lofty and free, must have no other aim but poetry itself." He made an unnecessary fuss and organized his business in such a way that all the capital earned and accumulated in it went up in smoke. For no reason. Just like that. Because the lofty nature of poetry demanded it.

Pure art bears a remote resemblance to religion, which, viewed in the broader perspective, it succeeds, filling the vacuum created with a new aesthetic cult that, having replaced revelation with inspiration, promotes the artist into the place of the ascetic. With the decline of traditional foundations, it becomes almost the only haven for intense self-contemplation, which has renounced the vanity of the world but still remembers its ancient kinship with prayer and nature, with prophecy and dreams, and tries to prattle something about heaven and miracles. Because there are no other altars, art becomes a temple for solitary, spiritually gifted individuals who gather around them a generous and grateful flock. It is art that provides a haven for the remnants of the liturgy and at the same time profanes it as is customary for all new fashions. The consciousness of spiritual primogeniture merges with the egoism of individual authorship, which promises the poet immortality in his creations, in which his soul ("no, not all of me will die")* will be reincarnated, not believing in paradise and therefore all the more ardently grasping at the artistic palliative. Strictly speaking, the deified creation feeds on itself, suffices unto itself and is an end in itself, being defined as a deity to a large extent negatively: it needs nothing, shines from within, and is pure and purposeless.

All this would inevitably degenerate into the cruelest parody (and for all practical purposes it does degenerate as soon as the spiritual source weakens or dries up, turning the newly appeared clergy into ordinary bohemians) if art did not in fact apparently have at its disposal a potential that allows it, even when immersed up to its ears in banality, suddenly, spontaneously to catch fire and soar. Just give it an excuse and although estranged from everything, although having forgotten all about heavenly gifts, it will reveal "divinity, and inspiration, and life, and tears, and love" in the soul.

Inspiration is given a very precise place in this series—somewhere between divinity and love. Besides religious emotions, there is always a hint of depravity in pure art. The ungracious formula that was applied in passing to Akhmatova, "a spoiled gentlewoman, rushing back and forth between the chapel and the boudoir,"* aptly defines the nature of poetry, poetry in general, as such, conveying the unstable essence of art as a whole. Pushkin's Muse was just such a gentlewoman.

Trying to find a definition for the emotional state that leads to scientific discoveries (which in this respect have a great deal in common with art just as this state does with poetic inspiration), Albert Einstein explained that it resembles religious ecstasy or the state of being in love: "constant activity arises not by premeditation nor according to some program but by the force of natural necessity" (Letter to Max Plank, 1918). It's especially gratifying to hear such a confirmation of Pushkin's (and of many other pure poets') thoughts devoted to the same riddle come out of the mouth of a scientist.

Is it not to this vacillation between religion and eroticism (or perhaps to their combinations in various doses and forms) that we are indebted for the aura that seems to emanate from the person of an artist and his creations as a specific aroma, a fragrance (to which women, like bees, are particularly susceptible)? The state of involuntary activity, of eternal, objectless infatuation, of felicitous completeness coexists in poets with a monastic thirst for peace and inward concentration, with abstinence that saps the strength and heeds nothing but its own bliss. Just compare: on the one hand, conflict with the world, a break with morality and society; on the other, the near saintliness and blessedness that mark people of art, their strange influence and social authority. Pushkin! Isn't it almost a government decree, a cornerstone of the universal human family and the world order? This is the same Pushkin who said, "Go away! What do I, a peaceful poet, care about you?"* We are not offended, we all care about him and recognize his power over us and his right to judge everything from his own narrow-minded point of view.

Pure art is not a doctrine Pushkin thought up to make life easier, it's not the sum of opinions nor the fruit of many years of seeking; it is a force that was born in the heart, without purpose or premeditation, like love, like religious feeling, impervious to control or coercion. He did not deduce it intellectually but noticed it in the course of his experience, that very experience he presents to us as a free outpouring independent of everything and everyone, even the will of the author. Pure art pours out of the word as a sign of its fluidity. The spirit wafts where it will.

> And I forget the world—and in the sweet silence
> I am sweetly lulled by my imagination,
> And poetry is awakened inside me:
> My soul is constrained by lyrical agitation,
> It trembles and resounds and searches, as if in a dream,
> For a way to pour itself out freely at last.*

Just try to find a place here for some purpose, to limit the process or make it conditional . . . But precisely because this art is free and obeys only "the movement of momentary, free feeling" (as Pushkin called inspiration) it has a habit of slipping through fingers that embrace it too tenaciously, even if they are the fingers of those who worship the beautiful, and it does not fit into its own pure definitions. Pushkin's nods and bows to the good of the fatherland, virtue, mercy, et cetera, are neither concessions nor a betrayal of his principles of freedom, but a consistent and vital application of them. His art is so purposeless that it pokes its nose into every nook and cranny it happens to come across on its way and doesn't shrink from asking questions about things that are none of its business but that for some reason attract the author's attention. He is free enough to allow himself to write about anything that comes into his head without turning into a doctrinaire of any single idea—even a purposeless one.

> Along a free road,
> Go where your free mind leads you.*

The landscape changes, the road zigzags. In the broad sense Pushkin's road embodies the mobility and elusiveness of art, which is inclined to shift and therefore is not subject to strict rules with regard to where to go and why. Your way today, ours tomorrow. Art strolls. How touching that Pushkin stipulated the right to stroll in a special paragraph of his constitution, his understanding of freedom.

> To wander here and there following my fancy,
> Wondering at the divine beauty of nature . . .
>
> . . . .
>
> That is happiness! Those are rights . . .*

Art depends on everything—food, weather, time, and mood. Nevertheless it is inclined to free itself from everything in the world. It leaves aestheticism for utilitarianism in order to remain pure and, not wanting to cater to anyone, it takes to flattering one bigshot to spite another, it calls to arms, forms oppositions, becomes sometimes impertinent, sometimes naive, and sometimes plays the fool. Every time it changes course, it is perceived—sometimes even by authors themselves—as the definitive direction, and some term, the name of some artistic movement, is pasted onto it, and people say that art serves, guides, reflects, and enlightens. And it does all that—as far as the first milepost, then it turns and—

> Is gone like the wind in the field.

Some people think it's possible to live with Pushkin. I don't know, I've never tried. But it is possible to stroll with him.

1966–1968, Dubrovlag

NOTES

blur with sidewhiskers / Pushkin, who followed the latest trends in fashion, had prominent sidewhiskers, which became an obligatory element of his portraits. O. Kiprensky's portrait, painted in 1829, occupies a special place. In the Soviet period it became the canonical representation of Pushkin and was included in textbooks, anthologies, and editions of Pushkin's collected works. Reproductions of the portrait often adorn the walls of schools, cafeterias, and other public places.

Nothing more / From the poem *The Little House in Kolomna* (1830).

Pushkin Academy of Sciences and Arts / There is no such place. Sinyavsky invents it to spoof the mindless idolization of the poet in Soviet Russia. There is, however, Pushkin House, a literary research institution attached to the Academy of Sciences in St. Petersburg. It was established in 1905 as a museum and center for Pushkin studies and became part of the Academy of Sciences in 1918. It holds all of Pushkin's manuscripts and his library.

Pushkinspieler! Pushkinstein! / A reference to colloquial punning on Pushkin's name. The names given in the Russian text—Pushkinshuler and Pushkinzon—connote a card-sharp and a scoundrel, respectively. They sound unmistakably Jewish.

Neva Spectator / A Russian monthly, published in St. Petersburg in 1820–1821 with the active participation of the future Decembrists Kondraty Ryleev and Wilhelm Kyukhelbeker. It was an organ of the liberal segment of Russian society. The journal published Pushkin's "To Dorida," "To Kyukhelbeker," "To the Enchantress," and an excerpt from *Ruslan and Lyudmila*. In 1821 Bestuzhev-Marlinsky published his review of *Ruslan and Lyudmila* there.

Son of the Fatherland / A conservative weekly, published from 1812 to 1840 by N. I. Grech. In 1825 it merged with Faddei Bulgarin's *Northern Archive* and published articles directed against Pushkin.

there was Batyushkov, there was Zhukovsky / Konstantin Batyushkov (1787–1855) was one of the leading poets of early romanticism in Russia. He was the main representative of so-called light poetry, which continued the eighteenth-century tradition of Anacreontic poetry. His poems were concerned with the joys of earthly life, friendship, and love. Later, under the influence of the tragic experience of the 1812 war, Batyushkov's poetry assumed pessimistic overtones that reflected the poet's spiritual crisis. Vasily Zhukovsky (1783–1852) is often referred to as the father of Russian romanticism. He introduced new forms and rhymes into Russian poetry in his adaptation of Thomas Grey's "Elegy Written in a Country Churchyard" (1801). In his poetry, cold, classical structures give way to an emotional perception of the world, vivid and tangible imagery, and a wealth of poetic meter.

She/Touching the floor with one foot / From *Evgeny Onegin*, chapter 1, stanza xx, in which Pushkin describes the ballet of his time. Pushkin himself was an avid theatergoer and balletomane. His interest in theater included participation in behind-the-stage life, patronage of actors, and numerous love affairs with actresses and dancers. Avdotya Istomina (1799–1848) was a prima ballerina of the Petersburg ballet. Pushkin was at one time romantically involved with her.

Summon me no longer / From "To Turgenev" (1817). Aleksandr Turgenev (1784–1845) was a statesman and a friend of Pushkin. In the poem Pushkin responds to Turgenev's urging him to continue his work on *Ruslan and Lyudmila.*

the fruits of merry leisure / From the poem "To My Aristarchus" (1815). Pushkin's Aristarchus was Nikolai Fyodorovich Koshansky (1785–1830), an instructor of literature at the lycée at Tsarskoe Selo who was famous for his critical attitude toward the compositions of his students. Aristarchus (ca. 217–145 B.C.) was a prominent Greek scholar and a commentator on classical Greek poets. His name became synonymous for Pushkin and his friends with strict, pedantic criticism. Pushkin could expect that Koshansky would disapprove of the frivolous tone and subject of his "flitting epistles" and to deviations from classical metrical norms.

When I'm in this lazy pose / Also from "To My Aristarchus."

Rossiad / A lengthy poem (nine thousand lines) by Mikhail Kheraskov on which the poet worked for more than eight years, from 1771 to 1779. Written during the reign of Catherine the Great, the *Rossiad* clearly shows the influence of ideas common to the period of the Enlightenment: the demand for an enlightened monarch, patriotic pathos, and a warning against the dangers of despotism. The *Rossiad* was an attempt to create a national epic. It is based on the events of the capture of Kazan by the army of Ivan the Terrible in 1552.

where Mayakovsky ended / The theory of "art in production" was proclaimed by the Russian formalists, who were grouped around the journal LEF (Left Front of Art) in the mid-1920s. As Sinyavsky writes in *Soviet Civilization,* "the revolution had furnished Futurism with a purpose that conformed to . . . the creation of useful things as opposed to form pure and simple. . . . This movement of left-wing abstract artists dedicated to production was dubbed 'design' in the West. But Russian 'design' of that period distinguished itself in that it was not confined to the aesthetics of contemporary industrial and technological culture. It was art sacrificed to production, to a socialist production that encompassed all of life in its march toward the future." A. Siniavsky, *Soviet Civilization* (New York: Arcade Publishing, 1990), 46.

Nowadays I dash off after my own fashion / From the poem "To Prince A. M. Gorchakov" (1814). A. M. Gorchakov (1798–1883) was one of Pushkin's classmates at the lycée. Later he became a prominent statesman. The poem was written on the occasion of Gorchakov's birthday on August 30, 1814.

some stanzas as a gift / Yakov Tolstoy (1791–1867) was one of the organizers of the Green Lamp literary circle. He participated in the war of 1812. In 1823 he went to Europe for medical reasons and stayed there after he found out that he was to be put on trial in connection with his association with the Decembrists. To clear his name, Tolstoy agreed to become an informer for the Russian government, and after he returned to Russia in 1837 he became an official in the Ministry of Education and an agent of the Third Section (secret police). The stanzas mentioned here are "Stanzas for Tolstoy," written in 1819.

Don't think, my gloomy censor / An inexact quotation from "To My Aristarchus": "laziness" (*len'yu*) should be "rest" (*pokoem*).

Baratynsky / Evgeny Baratynsky (1800–1844) was one of the most prominent poets of Pushkin's time. He was often considered Pushkin's rival, and his attitude toward Pushkin ranged from admiration to envy and hate.

Pushkin in Moscow / Ivan Turgenev delivered his speech on Pushkin on the occasion of the opening of the monument to Pushkin in Moscow in 1880. In his speech Turgenev pointed out that it had become necessary to establish links between the younger generation of the 1860s and the older generation of the 1840s. He argued that the rejection of Pushkin and of art in general that was typical of the young radicals was a temporary and justifiable stage in Russian historical development but that the time had come to turn once again to the Russian poet, who would serve as a point of reconciliation between the generations.

Russian Antiquity / A historical monthly, which came out in Petersburg from 1870 to 1918. The journal published materials on Russian history and the history of Russian literature and art, primarily of the eighteenth and nineteenth centuries.

why am I not Pushkin! / The poem "To the Beauty Who Was Sniffing Tobacco," written in 1814 when Pushkin was fifteen years old, ends with the following lines:

> Ah, if, transformed into tobacco,
> In the captivity of your snuff-box,
> I could be caught in your tender fingers,
> Then in sweet delight
> I would spill myself under the silk kerchief on your bosom
> And, maybe, even onto . . . But, alas! it's just an empty dream.
> It will never be.
> Fate is jealous and cruel.
> Oh, why am I not that tobacco! . . .

At times I turn a verse sharply / From a draft of *Little House in Kolomna.*

I almost came to hate my native land / From "An Inexperienced Lover of Distant Lands" (1817). Princess E. I. Golitsyna (1780–1850) was a beautiful socialite. Pushkin visited her salon during 1817–1820 when he lived in St. Petersburg.

divinity . . . and love / From Pushkin's most famous love poem, "To ———" (To A. P. Kern), written in 1825 and published in 1827 in the almanac *Northern Flowers.*

> I remember a wondrous moment
> You appeared before me
> Like a fleeting apparition,
> Like the genius of pure beauty.
>
> In the longing of hopeless grief,
> In the anxiety of noisy vanity,
> I listened to your tender voice for a long time,
> And your dear face appeared in my dreams.
>
> Years passed. The stormy gust
> Scattered my former dreams,
> And I forgot your tender voice,
> Your heavenly features.

> In the wilderness, in the darkness of captivity,
> My days quietly dragged along
> Without divinity, without inspiration,
> Without tears, life, or love.
>
> My soul suddenly awakened,
> And you again appeared before me
> Like a fleeting apparition,
> Like the genius of pure beauty.
>
> My heart beats in exultation,
> For in it have been revived again
> Divinity and inspiration,
> And life, and tears, and love.

Pushkin twice met Anna Petrovna Kern (1800–1880), the wife of General E. F. Kern and the niece of P. A. Osipova: the first time in 1819 at a ball in St. Petersburg, and the second time in the summer of 1825 when she was visiting her aunt at Trigorskoe, an estate near Pushkin's.

rosy and lily-white little feet / A reference to Pushkin's fascination with women's feet, which he immortalized in *Evgeny Onegin* (1, xxx–xxxii). Pushkin writes about his passion for balls:

> I like their maddening youth,
> The crush, the glitter, and the happiness,
> I like the ladies' carefully chosen dresses,
> I like their little feet . . .

Then he recalls a pair of feet, to which are devoted his most famous passage on the subject:

> Ah, little feet, little feet! Where are you now?
> Where do you trample fresh spring flowers?

And he concludes:

> Diana's bosom, Flora's cheeks,
> Are charming, dear friends!
> But Terpsichore's little feet
> Are somehow more beautiful to me.

She, like a spirit, passes by / From *The Fountain of Bakhchisarai*. "She" is Maria, the captive Polish princess, passing like a spirit before Khan Girei's eyes.

Byron / The comparison with Byron is quite natural here since *The Fountain of Bakhchisarai* is one of the "Byronic" poems written by Pushkin in the early 1820s. Sinyavsky refers to the episode in Byron's *Don Juan* in which Juan dresses as a woman and steals into a Turkish harem. We find a similar situation in Pushkin's poem *The Little House in Kolomna* (1830), where a man pretends to be a female cook in order to get a job at the house of the woman he wishes to seduce. The mistress discovers the deception when she sees him shaving, after which he flees the house. Sinyavsky is quite right that there is no uhlan in the poem. Quoting from memory, he probably confused *The Little House in Kolomna* with Lermontov's "The Tambov Treasurer's Wife," written, according to Lermontov himself, in imitation of Pushkin's *Little House in Kolomna* and *Count Nulin*. There is indeed an uhlan in the Lermontov poem. This one is after the flirtatious wife of the town's treasurer. He wins her in a card game and flees with her at the end of the poem.

Polar Star / A literary almanac published by Aleksandr Bestuzhev-Marlinsky and Kondraty Ryleev in 1823–1825 in St. Petersburg. The publication was distinguished by its clearly defined expression of the political and ideological views of the Decembrists and by its tendency to unite all the progressive forces of the epoch, publishing works by Pushkin and other important writers of the period. Yearly critical surveys of Russian literature by Bestuzhev-Marlinsky, published under the rubric "A View of the Old and the New Literature in Russia," defined the journal's ideological bent.

What the devil! I thought: now / From Pushkin's poem "The Hussar" (1833), in which a soldier tells the story of how he stayed at the house of an attractive woman who turned out to be a witch.

Ruslan and Lyudmila / A long poem (1817–1820) about a fairy-tale land filled with fantastic creatures from Russian folklore. This is one of the first poems that Russian children read.

the prologue / The introductory stanzas of *Ruslan and Lyudmila* are among the best-known verses to Russians, and schoolchildren are often made to memorize them. The first lines are, "A green oak stands at the curved seashore,/A golden chain hangs on that oak."

hunters at rest / Sinyavsky lists here popular emblems of Russian and Soviet life. A kokoshnik is a type of headdress worn over the forehead by Russian peasant women. It is usually triangular in form and embroidered with golden thread and semiprecious stones. Sugar-coated hawthorn berries were a treat popular among Russian children, as were honey cakes and gingerbread cakes, which were sold in the streets. Moscow and Tula honey cakes had an imprint of Saint George on them, thus becoming gingerbread knights in Sinyavsky's text. The bears on bicycles come from Kornei Chukovsky's children's tale in verse "The Cockroach." It was rumored that the frightening cockroach was an allusion to Stalin, its whiskers calling to mind Stalin's moustache. "Hunters at Rest" is the title of a realist painting by Vasily Perov, reproductions of which hung in many public places in the Soviet Union.

breathed out by Zhukovsky / Sinyavsky refers here to Zhukovsky's ballad "Lyudmila" (1808), which was considered one of the most important works of Russian romanticism. Zhukovsky's poem was an adaptation of Gottfried August Bürger's "Lenore." The elevated diction of the ballad, which is constructed around rhetorical questions and exclamations, led younger contemporaries of Zhukovsky, like Pushkin in *Ruslan and Lyudmila*, to parody the elder poet's sentimental style.

The ephemeral range of clouds grows thin / The opening line of an elegy (1820) dedicated to one of General Raevsky's daughters.

at least got warm / Sinyavsky refers here to a joke about a rooster that wants to have his way with a hen and so chases her around the yard. After the rooster fails to catch the hen, he is asked how he feels. The rooster answers that although he did not get what he wanted, he did get warm.

Love of poetry, love of my freedom / From "To Zhukovsky" (1818).

Ninette or Temira or even Parasha / Ninette, Temira, and Parasha are women's names that appear frequently in Pushkin's poetry—especially Parasha. Not only does the name Parasha appear in Pushkin's lyrics, but the main female character in *The Little House in Kolomna* and Evgeny's beloved in *The Bronze Horseman* both bear that name.

We await the moment of sacred freedom / From "To Chaadaev" (1818). Pyotr Chaadaev (1794–1856) was a writer and philosopher as well as Pushkin's friend and mentor at the time of the poet's studies at the lycée.

By you, by you alone / From the poem that begins "High gloom lies on the hills of Georgia," written in 1829 during Pushkin's trip to Erzerum and published in *Northern Flowers* in 1831.

Marina Mnishek / A Polish princess who figures as a character in Pushkin's drama *Boris Godunov.*

better than any other woman / A reference to the beginning of the eighth and final chapter of *Evgeny Onegin.* The chapter opens with an account of Pushkin's relationship with his Muse, embodied in the heroines of his works—from "the gardens of the lycée" through "the cliffs of the Caucasus" and "the wilderness of sad Moldavia" to his own garden, where the Muse appears to him as a provincial noble maiden "with a sad thought in her eyes,/With a French book in her hands"—like Tatyana Larina, the heroine of *Onegin.*

All my life was a pledge / From Tatyana's letter to Onegin (3, xxxi).

to the black sky, to the whole wide world / In Russian there is a play here on the opposition between black and white. The folkloric expression *belyi svet* can mean "white light" as well as "the whole wide world." This may be viewed as an allusion to the main visual image in Aleksandr Blok's 1918 poem *The Twelve*, the opening stanza of which reads:

> Black wind,
> White snow.
> Wind, wind!
> A person cannot stand up.
> Wind, wind—
> On the whole wide world.

Who imbued her with this tenderness / *Evgeny Onegin*, 3, xxxi. Pushkin's narrator's comment on reading Tatyana's letter.

wrote the letter in French / *Evgeny Onegin*, 3, xxvi. French was an obligatory component of the education of children of the Russian nobility. Russian was used in daily conversations (especially with servants), whereas French was used for correspondence, since Russian did not have as developed an epistolary style. Pushkin himself wrote letters in French. As one of Pushkin's contemporaries quipped, "We philosophize in German, joke in French, and use Russian only for praying to God and scolding our servants."

Here is/An incomplete and weak translation / *Evgeny Onegin*, 3, xxxi.

From morning till evening / From the poem "The Muse" (1821).

Ruslan . . . "The Queen of Spades" / Ruslan dreams of his death at the hand of his rival, Farlaf, and of the loss of Lyudmila. The dreams of Aleko, the main character of the narrative poem *The Gypsies*, "are strange and disturbing" because he is dissatisfied with his life with the gypsies and jealous about his wife Zemfira. Tatyana in *Evgeny Onegin* has a dream about Onegin in which he appears as the leader of a gang of grotesque creatures. The dream serves as a premonition of the duel between Onegin and Lensky in which Lensky is killed. In *Boris Godunov*, Grigory Otrepev, the fugitive monk who aspires to become the tsar of Russia, dreams of a staircase going upward by which he ascends to the throne. Grinyov, the main character of the novel, *The Captain's Daughter*, has a dream which, in his own words, he "cannot forget and in which he . . . sees something prophetic." In his dream he returns home and finds his father ill, but when he goes up to him, he sees a black-bearded man lying in the bed instead of his father. The man is Pugachov, whom Grinyov will meet later. In the poem "The Song of Oleg the Seer," a magician predicts that Prince Oleg will meet his death through his horse. In the "little tragedy" *Mozart and Salieri*, Mozart is visited by a man in black who commissions him to compose a requiem. It becomes a requiem for Mozart himself when Salieri poisons him. In "The Queen of Spades," the old countess appears to Hermann in a dream and reveals the secret of three cards that can win money in a card game.

All earthly joys are in our dreams! / The concluding lines of "The Epistle to Yudin" (1815). Pavel Yudin (1798–1852) was a classmate of Pushkin at the lycée.

And fatal passions are everywhere / The concluding lines of the narrative poem *The Gypsies* (1824).

We are not the masters of our fate / From "To the Album of Illichevsky" (1817). Aleksei Illichevsky (1798–1837) was a classmate of Pushkin at the lycée.

broken trough / A reference to Pushkin's *Tale of the Fisherman and the Golden Fish*. In this verse tale a poor fisherman accidentally catches a magical golden fish. The fish asks him in a human voice to let it go and promises to grant him a wish in return. The kind fisherman lets the fish go, returns to his wife, and tells her what has happened. His wife becomes angry with him for not asking the fish for something, not even a new trough, and sends her husband back to the seashore. The fisherman goes back, summons the golden fish, and asks it for a new trough. His wife is still not satisfied with this small gift and demands again and again that the fisherman go back and ask the fish to grant ever grander requests. The fish becomes angrier with each new demand and finally ends by taking everything it gave her away, leaving her only with the broken trough she had at the beginning of the story. The expression has become such a popular saying that the Oxford Russian-English Dictionary includes it in its entry for *koryto* (trough), giving the English equivalents "to be no better off than before" and "to be back where one started."

Now, Naina, you are mine! / From *Ruslan and Lyudmila*.

He to whom irresistible fate / From *Ruslan and Lyudmila*.

Only I, subservient / From the poem "Farewell" (1817).

blood and deception / A reference to the "little tragedy" *Mozart and Salieri* (1830). Pushkin represents Mozart as a genius by the grace of God, a true artist, and Salieri as an untalented artisan who decides to assume the role of a defender of art. In the play Salieri explains that he must kill Mozart to save art from the human Mozart. By killing him, Salieri can transform Mozart into a god of music who cannot be soiled by the unclean hands of his human incarnation.

Aleko . . . Godunov . . . Hermann / Aleko, the main character of the narrative poem *The Gypsies*, murders his wife and her lover. Boris Godunov is called a usurper because he supposedly ordered the murder of the young tsarevich Dmitry, the youngest son of Ivan the Terrible, in order to become tsar himself. Hermann is called a petty thief for stealing the secret of the three cards.

its own whimsically created being / The story "The Snowstorm" is one of the *Tales of Belkin*, which Pushkin wrote during his stay at Boldino in 1830. The story begins with a young noblewoman, Masha, who was raised on French novels and falls in love with her neighbor Vladimir. They decide to run away and get married. On the appointed day Masha arrives at the church where they have agreed to meet, but Vladimir loses his way in the blizzard. Masha returns to her parents' home feeling feverish and becomes seriously ill. Vladimir leaves for the front and is killed soon after at Borodino. Several years later Masha meets Colonel Burmin, who falls in love with her but says he cannot marry her because he is already married. He tells her that once he was lost in a blizzard and stopped at a church where he found a young lady and her maid waiting for someone. The lady was delirious and did not quite know where she was. The maid ushered him to her, and the priest performed the marriage ceremony. When he pronounced them husband and wife, the girl looked at Burmin, cried, "He is the wrong man," and fainted. It turns out that Masha was that girl and that now the husband and wife have found each other.

like a black ribbon / From the poem "The Song of Oleg the Seer," published in *Northern Flowers* in 1825. It narrates the fulfillment of the prophecy made to Prince Oleg that he would die because of his horse. The prince, trying to avoid his destiny, orders his horse taken far away from him. Several years later he learns that the steed is dead. Prince Oleg thinks that this proves that the prophecy was wrong and goes to see the remains of his horse. The "black ribbon" in the lines cited refers to the snake that was hiding in the skull of the prince's horse. It bites the prince, and he dies.

the realm of the supernatural / In "The Queen of Spades" a young officer named Tomsky tells a story about his grandmother, an old countess, who came into possession of the secret of three cards that could guarantee three successive wins in a card game. The secret was revealed to her by the French alchemist St. Germaine, who wanted to help her win back money she had lost in a card game. Since that time the countess had not played cards and had divulged the secret to no one. The story makes a strong impression on a military engineer named Hermann, who decides to ask the countess to reveal the secret to him. For this purpose Hermann begins to court the countess's ward Lizaveta. Lizaveta, thinking that he is in love with her, arranges a rendezvous with him: Hermann is supposed to sneak into her room while she and the countess are at a ball. Instead of going to Lizaveta's room, Hermann hides in the countess's bedroom. When she returns, Hermann implores her to reveal the secret to him, but the countess remains silent. Then Hermann pulls out a revolver and threatens to kill her. The countess dies of fright, and Hermann leaves in despair. Several days later, the countess appears to him in a dream and says that she will reveal the secret to him, but he must marry Lizaveta. The three cards that will win for him are the three, the seven, and the ace. Hermann plays the three and wins. The next day he plays the seven and wins again, but when he plays the ace, the queen of spades is dealt to him instead. It seems to him that the queen of spades is the old countess. He loses all his money, goes mad, and ends up in an asylum.

Futile gift, gift of chance / The opening lines of a poem written by Pushkin on May 26, 1828, on the occasion of his birthday. At the end of the poem, Pushkin says that he has no goal in life, that his heart is empty, his mind is idle, and the monotonous world bores him.

the hairsplitting metropolitan Filaret / Filaret, the metropolitan of Moscow, was an educated man respected for his eloquence even by Pushkin. He published his poem in the almanac *Northern Flowers* in 1830 as a response to Pushkin's. Retaining almost entirely the form of the Pushkin poem, Filaret changed the text slightly, adding a religious note to the poet's words: life is given to us not accidentally and not in vain, without God's will life would perish, and the poet is responsible for the way he lives his life.

heads or tails / The game of heads or tails is played differently in Russia than it is in the United States. The object of the game in Russia is to flip your opponent's coins to the opposite side—from heads to tails and vice versa. In order to do so, you have to hit smaller coins with heavier ones.

perhaps, a pledge of immortality / From the last "little tragedy," *Feast in Time of Plague.* The words are taken from the Chairman's "Hymn in Honor of the Plague."

and what if Bonaparte / A reference to the rumor that Napoleon had a cold during the battle of Waterloo and that it affected his ability to react alertly to events, leading him to make tactical errors and, ultimately, lose the battle.

If you drew the wrong queen / A reference to the final scene of "The Queen of Spades."

all is permitted! / Raskolnikov, the main character of Dostoevsky's *Crime and Punishment,* conceives the idea of a superman who stands above everyone else, above ordinary laws, and morality. "All is permitted" becomes his motto. In order to prove his idea is true, he murders an old pawnbroker.

Count Nulin / A narrative poem in which the title character, a young nobleman returning from Paris, has an accident near the estate of a landowner and is invited to spend the night there. The landowner's young wife flirts with him and appears willing to offer him further "hospitality." But when he goes to her bedroom later that night, she resists his advances and slaps him. Ashamed, he departs the next morning.

the echo mimics us / A reference to the poem "Echo" (1831).

Gabrieliad . . . "The Undertaker" / *The Gabrieliad* is a satiric poem written by Pushkin in 1821. It created a scandal because in it Pushkin made fun of the immaculate conception. Ludovico Ariosto (1474–1553) was an Italian poet of the Renaissance. His long narrative poem *Orlando Furioso* was one of the most popular works of the romantic period. *Ruslan and Lyudmila* is a parody of the traditional romantic poems of Zhukovsky. "Poor Liza" is a sentimentalist tale by Nikolai Karamzin, one of the most popular works in Russia at the end of the eighteenth and the beginning of the nineteenth century. It tells the story of a poor peasant maiden who falls in love with a nobleman. When he marries another woman, she commits suicide. Despite the fact that she is supposed to be a peasant girl, Karamzin gives her the speech and social graces of a noblewoman. In Pushkin's "Mistress into Maid" the roles are reversed, and the plot revolves around a noblewoman who pretends to be a peasant maiden. *The Stone Guest* is one of Pushkin's "little tragedies" and is based on the story of Don Juan. In "The Undertaker," one of the *Tales of Belkin*, a coffin maker named Adrian Prokhorov is invited to a party at his neighbor Gottlieb Schultz's house. When the guests begin to drink to the health of everyone present and then to the health of people they work for, one of the guests jokingly suggests that Adrian drink to the health of his corpses. Adrian becomes angry, leaves the party, and goes home to sleep. Soon he is awakened and summoned to the house of a merchant's wife who has just died. He goes there, takes measurements for the coffin, and returns home. There, to his astonishment and horror, he sees that he too has guests; the dead he has buried have come to thank him for his work. Horrified, Adrian pushes one of the skeletons away from him, and the skeleton crumbles. The dead are outraged and begin to shout at Adrian. He faints and wakes up the next morning wondering what has happened. It turns out that it has all been nothing but a dream.

The unexpected event amazed all of us / From "The Shot," one of the *Tales of Belkin*.

table of ranks / Introduced by Peter the Great in January 1722. Government service had hitherto been the prerogative and duty of the hereditary nobility alone. Peter, who was fond of promoting people from diverse social groups, wanted to make it possible for his protégés to attain the highest ranks in the realm. The table of ranks arranged all offices in both the armed forces and the civil service into fourteen classes in hierarchical order. A soldier who had achieved the lowest officer's rank and a civil servant who had attained rank 8 gained membership in the nobility.

I am Dubrovsky / Dubrovsky is the main character of Pushkin's unfinished novel of the same name. He is the son of a Russian landowner who was ruined by his rich neighbor. Dubrovsky vows to avenge his father and becomes a bandit (a sort of Robin Hood). The matter is complicated by Dubrovsky's love for the daughter of his enemy.

Mérimée . . . a given epoch / The French novelist Prosper Mérimée (1803–1870) was also a prolific translator of Russian works. The quotation is from the preface to his historical novel *Chronicle of the Reign of Charles IX*. Our thanks to Charles Porter of Yale University for identifying the source.

Ivan Khmelnitsky / Eighteenth-century Ukrainian writer and philosopher. He was a direct descendant of Hetman Bogdan Khmelnitsky. Ivan studied at the Kiev Seminary and later at Koenigsburg University, where in 1762 he defended his dissertation, "Discourse on Primary Philosophical Principles." He translated *The Light Seen through Personifications* from the German.

a rabbitskin coat / While collecting materials for his life of Peter the Great, Pushkin came across secret documents about the Pugachov rebellion and decided to write *A History of Pugachov*. He traveled to Orenburg and Kazan—the sites of the peasant uprising—examined documents, and interviewed participants. His investigation resulted not only in a historical account of the events but also in a short novel entitled *The Captain's Daughter*, in which a young officer, Grinyov, while traveling to his post, meets Pugachov, the future leader of the peasant army fighting the army of Catherine the Great. Grinyov gives him his rabbitskin coat in payment for his services. Later, when Pugachov's army captures the fort where Grinyov is stationed, his life is spared by Pugachov, who remembers Grinyov and his gift to him.

Wishing to pay back the debt, Pugachov gives Grinyov a sheepskin coat off his own shoulders.

its handshake / A reference to the ending of the "little tragedy" *The Stone Guest*, in which the statue of the commander takes Don Juan by the hand and drags him into hell.

But luck toys with me maliciously / From the poem "To Yazykov" (1824). Nikolai Yazykov (1803–1846) was a poet close in his philosophy to the ideas of the Decembrists. He met Pushkin in 1826 when he visited the exiled poet at Mikhailovskoe.

his uncle / Pushkin's uncle Vasily Lvovich Pushkin (1767–1830) was a minor poet, known mostly for his epigrams and fables. His most important work, a comic poem entitled "A Dangerous Neighbor," circulated in manuscript form in intellectual circles of the time. He played a very important role in Pushkin's biography. Vasily Pushkin introduced his nephew to the literary society Arzamas, which marked the beginning of Pushkin's literary career. Sinyavsky is not referring here to a specific incident but is merely alluding to the general atmosphere of literary gatherings of the time.

At first I was just playing / From the poem "To Delvig (A Response)" (1815).

Generals and privy counsellors / From "The Queen of Spades." Hermann plays his last card against his opponent, Chekalinsky. The game is cast as a battle with fate.

P. A. Vyazemsky / Prince Vyazemsky (1792–1878) was a poet and literary critic and Pushkin's close friend.

d'Anthès' button / According to an account of the duel between Pushkin and d'Anthès recorded in Veresaev's *Pushkin in Life*, the seriously wounded Pushkin demanded the right to take his shot. After he was given a new revolver, he aimed and fired. The bullet went through d'Anthès' hand, which he had pressed to his heart, and hit a metal button on his uniform, which saved his life.

But the days are flying / The concluding lines of *The Gabrieliad*.

The horse's move . . . sound the fanfare! / Pushkin creates a pun here. In Russian the "knight" chess piece is called a "horse" or "steed." A "move with the horse" in chess terms generally means moving around or over another piece and thus suggests a sneaky action. In the poem "The Song of Oleg the Seer" the prince's death comes from a snake hiding in his dead horse's skull.

The warriors remember / The concluding lines of "The Song of Oleg the Seer."

A state of freedom and peace comes / A reference to a poem of 1833, which contains the lines: "There is no happiness in life,/But there is peace and freedom."

now lettest thou thy servant depart / From the blessing of Simeon on the presentation of the child Jesus at the Temple in Jerusalem (Luke 2:29–32). It symbolizes the point at which the Old Testament ends and the New Testament begins.

It's time to ride / From *Ruslan and Lyudmila*. The four rivals—Ruslan, Farlaf, Rogdai, and Rotmir—set out in search of Lyudmila, who has been abducted by the wizard Chernomor.

The Gypsies / Pushkin's last "romantic" narrative poem focuses on the question of freedom. A romantic hero, the "proud man" Aleko, rebels against civilization and leaves it to join the free life of the gypsies. He falls in love and marries a beautiful gypsy woman, Zemfira. In the poem the author contrasts two notions of freedom: the logical construction of freedom that underlies Aleko's rebellion against civilization and society and the absolute freedom of the gypsies, who live in harmony with nature, with the boundless expanse of the steppes. Aleko is unable to understand and accept the total freedom of the natural life. He wants Zemfira to belong to him alone. When she falls in love with another man, Aleko kills her and her lover. The gypsies demand that he leave them.

like the moon in oil / A reference to the Russian saying "to slide like cheese in butter" ("oil" and "butter" are the same word, *maslo*, in Russian), which means to be well off, to live the good life.

Friends! Does it make any difference / The closing lines of the poem "To a Kalmyk Woman" (1830), which Pushkin wrote shortly after returning from his trip to Erzerum.

and the Finn / From Pushkin's 1836 poem that begins, "I raised a monument to myself not made by hand." In Russia it became famous as Pushkin's literary testament under the name "The Monument" (1836). In English translations it is often called "Exigi monumentum," following the epigraph from Horace.

The Robber Brothers / A narrative poem, published in 1825, that Pushkin wrote during his romantic or "Byronic" period. It begins with a gathering of bandits, among whom we see "a mixture of clothes and faces" of "fugitives from the banks of the militant Don," of Jews with black hair, of "wild sons of the steppes—Kalmyks and Bashkirs," of red-haired Finns, and of gypsies. An old robber tells the story of his and his brother's escape from prison and of his brother's death.

Paskevich, Ermolov / A reference to Pushkin's journey to Erzerum in the Caucasus Mountains in 1829. On his way to General Paskevich's forces, Pushkin visited General Aleksei Ermolov, who was living in retirement. I. F. Paskevich (1782–1856) fought in the war of 1812. In 1828–1829 he was in charge of military activities against the Turks, for which he received the title of Count of Erevan and later the rank of commander in chief. He was also in charge of the suppression of the Polish uprising of 1831. A. P. Ermolov (1772–1861) was a participant in the Napoleonic Wars and a commander of a special Caucasus corps. In 1817 he became the governor of Georgia. Ermolov opposed the policies of Alexander I and, because of that, was popular among the Decembrists. He retired and moved to Moscow in 1827.

So my Muse / The opening lines of the epilogue of the narrative poem *The Prisoner of the Caucasus* (1821).

A. O. Smirnova-Rosset / Before her marriage, Aleksandra Smirnova, née Rosset (1809–1882), was a lady-in-waiting to the emperor's wife Aleksandra. Smirnova-Rosset was a highly educated woman, a graduate of the Catherine Institute. Her wit, beauty, and independence of thought attracted many prominent people of her time, including Zhukovsky, Turgenev, and Lermontov. She met Pushkin in 1828, and they became good friends. Pushkin valued Smirnova-Rosset's literary taste, read his new works to her, and in 1832 suggested that she keep a diary, giving her an album inscribed with the facetious title "The Historic Notes of A. O. Smirnova."

and the underwater movement / From the poem "The Prophet" (1826).

Holding my nose, I turned away my face / From the poem "And we went further— and fear seized me . . ." (1832).

Pellico's book / Silvio Pellico (1789–1854) was an Italian writer close to the revolutionary group of the Carbonari. In 1820 he was arrested by the Austrian police and spent ten years in prison. His memoir *My Prisons* was extremely popular among young Russian radicals. *On the Obligations of Man* appeared in 1834, and Pushkin reviewed the book in his journal the *Contemporary*.

Winter! / From one of the lyrical digressions in *Evgeny Onegin* (5, ii).

Why are you neighing / The opening line of the poem "The Steed," one of the poems in the cycle "The Songs of the Western Slavs" (1834).

My uncle / The opening line of *Evgeny Onegin*.

"Borodino" / Mikhail Lermontov's poem "Borodino" is about the battle between the Russian and French armies at the village of Borodino, not far from Moscow. The poem begins with a young soldier asking an old one: "Tell me, uncle, is it not in vain/That Moscow was surrendered to the French?" Lermontov's poetry is characterized by a pessimistic tone of disillusionment with life, love, friendship, and society.

The Ukrainian night is quiet / From *Poltava* (1828), one of Pushkin's historical poems about Peter the Great. Historically, Poltava was the place of the decisive victory of the Russian army led by Peter over the Swedish army of Charles IX. Charles made a treaty with the Ukrainian hetman Mazepa, who promised to help him in exchange for the independence of Ukraine. The main characters of the poem are Kochubei and his daughter Mariya. Fascinated with the power the hetman possesses, Mariya falls in love with Mazepa in spite of the fact that he is much older than she, and she eventually marries him against her father's will. At the beginning Kochubei is a close friend of Mazepa. But when he learns about the pact between the hetman and Charles IX, he denounces his former friend to Peter. Mazepa captures and executes Kochubei. After she learns about her father's fate, Mariya leaves her husband.

Kochubei is rich and famous / The opening line of *Poltava*.

The children ran to the cottage / The opening lines of the poem "The Drowned Man" (1828). The children run to their father after they discover a drowned man tangled in his fishing net. The peasant decides to get rid of the body and pushes it back into the water. From then on, the drowned man comes every year to haunt the peasant.

Godspeed on your long journey! / The opening lines of the poem "The Funeral Dirge of Iakinf Maglanovich," from the cycle "The Songs of the Western Slavs" (1834).

So—praise to you, Plague! / From the "little tragedy" *Feast in Time of Plague*. The Chairman sings a hymn in which he challenges death, the Plague.

the coming of autumn / The ode was the main genre of neoclassical poetry, belonging to the "high style" in the hierarchy of genres of that period. Sinyavsky here refers to Pushkin's poems "To My Inkwell" (1821) and "Autumn (An Excerpt)" (1833).

Frost and sun / The opening stanza of the poem "A Winter Morning" (1829).

The Bronze Horseman . . . The Covetous Knight . . . "The Stationmaster" . . . "The Shot" / In *The Bronze Horseman* "poor" Evgeny rebels against Peter the Great, the founder of St. Petersburg. In the "little tragedy" *The Covetous Knight* the miserly baron and his son Albert argue over the baron's money. In one of the Belkin tales,

"The Stationmaster," the daughter of a stationmaster leaves her father to live in the city with a handsome hussar. The father is heartbroken and tries to bring her back. She loves her father but refuses to return to him. The father dies from grief. In "The Shot," another Belkin tale, a magnanimous count, while fighting a duel with an officer named Silvio, offers his opponent the right to shoot at him whenever he wants—Silvio is unwilling to shoot now because he sees that the count is not afraid to die. Silvio appears at the count's estate several years after the duel when the count, now happily married, is enjoying the best time of his life. But instead of taking the count's life, Silvio, observing the count's fear, nobly shoots at a painting in the count's study.

An exchange of fire / From the poem "The Banner" (1829).

God help you, my friends / This poem, written in 1827, is one of the series of "October 19" poems that Pushkin wrote throughout his life to commemorate the anniversary of the opening of the lycée at Tsarskoe Selo.

the Decembrists / The Decembrist revolt took place on December 14, 1825, when a group of officers led a regiment of soldiers to Senate Square in St. Petersburg and demanded political reforms. The revolt was severely suppressed: five leaders were executed, and the rest of the participants—many of them friends of Pushkin—were exiled to Siberia or sent into active army duty in the Caucasus.

Was it not we / From the unfinished poem "What a night! The ringing frost" (1827), about an oprichnik (called in the text of the poem *kromeshnik*), a member of Ivan the Terrible's personal guard. The poem is based on Karamzin's *History of the Russian State* and describes mass executions during Ivan's reign.

epistle to Siberia / A reference to "In the Depths of Siberian Mines" (1827), which Pushkin wrote to his friends Ivan Pushchin and Wilhelm Kyukhelbeker. The poem became known as "An Epistle to Siberia."

send him away empty-handed / A reference to "What a night! The ringing frost."

Pushchin complained about him / Ivan Pushchin (1798–1859) was one of Pushkin's closest friends and had been a classmate in the Tsarskoe Selo lycée. For his part in the Decembrist uprising Pushchin was exiled to Siberia from 1826 to 1856. Pushchin's *Reminiscences of Pushkin* are considered one of the best memoirs about the poet.

touchingly . . . from under a mantilla / From the poem "To the Grandee" (1830), which has the subtitle "An Epistle to PNBY," that is, to Prince Nikolai Borisovich Yusupov. Prince Yusupov (1751–1831) was a Russian statesman during the reign of Catherine the Great. He lived in Arkhangelskoe near Moscow, where Pushkin visited him. Yusupov's service to Catherine included traveling to European courts with diplomatic missions and managing the Imperial Theater and the Hermitage.

Kolobok slipped away from the old man and woman / A reference to the Russian fairy tale about Kolobok, a round loaf of bread. When the old woman in the tale puts Kolobok on a windowsill to cool, it escapes and rolls down a path, meeting various animals on its way, including a rabbit, a wolf, and a bear. Kolobok taunts each of them in turn, bragging that it got away from the old woman and the old man and can get away from them as well. Finally a fox tricks Kolobok and eats it.

God, don't let me go out of my mind / The opening line of an untitled poem (1833).

They dragged me / From *The Captain's Daughter.*

a disposition of the soul / This statement of Pushkin's is cited by Blok in his speech "On the Calling of the Poet," which may be where Sinyavsky remembered it from.

his own crooked nose / The great satiric writer Nikolai Gogol was a younger contemporary of Pushkin. His style is marked by a complex mixture of realistic details and fantastic occurrences. One of his most famous works is the short story "The Nose," in which the central character wakes up one morning to discover that his nose has disappeared. He later meets his nose, which is wearing the uniform of an important government official. Noses are mentioned frequently in Gogol's other writings, including *Dead Souls* and "Nevsky Prospect." Sinyavsky is also alluding to Gogol's own very long nose. According to rumors, Gogol could touch the tip of his nose with his tongue.

Is a beast howling / The opening lines of the poem "The Echo" (1831).

Don Juan / As portrayed in Pushkin's *The Stone Guest.*

You're beautiful! / A reference to Mephistopheles' words to Faustus in *A Scene from "Faustus"* (1825).

Having reveled in pleasure / From *The Stone Guest.*

The clouds rush, the clouds whirl / From "The Devils" (1830). In the poem a traveler is caught in a blizzard while on the road. In the flying clouds that cover the moon and make it invisible, he sees a devils' Sabbath. Dostoevsky borrowed the title of the poem for his novel *The Devils,* best known in English translation as *The Possessed.*

"The Queen of Spades" . . . Boris Godunov / In "The Queen of Spades" the ghost of the dead countess appears twice to Hermann: first in his dream, in which she reveals the secret of the three cards, and the second time on the face of the card Hermann plays at the end of the story. It also seems to Hermann that during the funeral the dead countess winks at him. In *Boris Godunov* the tsarevich, Dmitry, murdered on Godunov's orders, is mentioned over and over in speeches made by various characters. It seems as if he and not the Pretender becomes Godunov's true opponent. Dmitry lived with his mother in Uglich and was killed there.

The clever Shuisky / Vasily Shuisky was a Russian boyar. He was an adviser to Tsar Fyodor and, to some extent, a rival of Boris Godunov. He even joined the Pretender's army to overthrow Boris. After Godunov's death and the Pretender's ascent to the throne, Shuisky organized a boyars' revolt against him. The Pretender was killed, his body burned, and the ashes shot from a cannon to the four winds. Shuisky proclaimed himself tsar, although he was not elected by the Zemsky Sobor, as was customary at the time, but only nominated by his associates. Shuisky remained the ruler of Muscovy (if not much more than that) for three years, overcoming peasant rebellions, war with Poland, and internal strife.

The healer came to Yakubovich / From the poem "Marko Yakubovich," which belongs to the cycle of poems "Songs of the Western Slavs."

Zaretsky carefully laid / From *Evgeny Onegin,* 6, xxxv. The duel between the friends Onegin and Lensky stands at the center of the novel, dividing it into two parts. Toward the beginning, after Onegin comes to live in the country, Tatyana, under the influence of romantic and sentimentalist novels, falls in love with him and openly declares her feelings in a letter to Onegin. Onegin rejects her. After the duel Onegin has to leave Russia. He returns to St. Petersburg, after traveling in Europe for several years, and meets Tatyana there. She is now married to a general. Onegin falls in love with her and declares himself to her in a letter. Tatyana rejects him.

And having recognized the naked guest / From "The Drowned Man" (1828).

more useful than poetry / The literary critic D. I. Pisarev (1840–1868) was one of the most prominent of the radical critics. In his articles "Pushkin and Belinsky," "The Destruction of Criticism," and "We'll See," Pisarev launched an attack on Pushkin from the utilitarian position. He ridiculed Pushkin's *Evgeny Onegin*, taking quotes out of context and commenting on them with the simple-heartedness of a plebeian. Pisarev drowned while swimming in the Baltic Sea in June 1868.

There is a high mountain / From "The Tale of the Dead Tsarevna and the Seven Bogatyrs," written at Boldino in 1830.

The entrance to the grave / From the closing stanza of "Whether I wander through noisy streets" (1829).

The Feast in Time of Plague / The last of Pushkin's "little tragedies" is based on a scene from John Wilson's poem *The City of Plague*. The main idea of Pushkin's play is conquering fear of death. Surrounded by a raging plague, a group of survivors led by the Chairman celebrate the last days of their lives. One of them, a young woman named Mary, sings a song about two lovers—Jenny and Edmund—who overcome death through the memory of their faithful love. The other way to defeat death is to fight it. In his "Hymn to the Plague" the Chairman challenges death, opposing the fullness of life to submission to death.

Michael Psellus / An eleventh-century Byzantine scholar who became very popular among Soviet intellectuals in the 1960s because of the duality of his philosophy. Psellus was a devoted Christian, but at the same time he admired pagan Greek philosophy. His duality corresponded to the duality of life in the Soviet Union, where people were living two lives—one official and one private—and was reflected in the duality of Sinyavsky-Tertz as well.

For a long time / From "To Yazykov" (1828). The Kiselyov mentioned in the poem is Nikolai Dmitrievich Kiselyov (1802–1869), Yazykov's friend at Derpt (now Tartu) University. In 1828 he was going on a diplomatic mission to Vienna and was supposed to stop in Carlsbad.

Tungus / A Siberian ethnic group that includes the Evenki and the Lamut. In Pushkin's time to call someone a Tungus was to call him a savage or primitive.

Having donned a wide-brimmed bolivar / From *Evgeny Onegin*, 1, xv–xvi.

Belinsky . . . a whole encyclopedia / Vissarion Belinsky (1811–1848) was the leading Russian literary critic of the 1830s and 1840s. His most significant work was a series of eleven articles on the works of Pushkin (1843–1846). The eighth and ninth articles are dedicated to *Evgeny Onegin*. Belinsky writes that Pushkin depicts the whole epoch in his novel, showing not only details of the everyday life of Russian society but also the entire scope of ideas and problems characteristic of it. In his conclusion, Belinsky calls the novel an "encyclopedia of Russian life." This became a cliché that was hammered into the heads of Soviet schoolchildren.

we've all studied something a little bit somewhere / *Evgeny Onegin*, 1, v.

The closed sleigh rushed / The description of the Larins' arrival in Moscow, *Evgeny Onegin*, 7, xxxviii.

Plyushkin / A character from Gogol's novel *Dead Souls*. His name has become synonymous in Russian with "miser." Plyushkin collects everything. Describing his house, Gogol depicts rooms piled with things that are decaying because Plyushkin never uses them.

toilet water he used / A reference to the description of Onegin's dressing room (1, xxiii–xxvi), which especially outraged Pisarev.

Belkin / Sinyavsky deliberately confuses time periods here, placing Chekhov—who lived and wrote in the 1880s and the 1890s, "the decades of little deeds and mediocre people," and was noted for describing the flow of everyday life in his stories—chronologically before Pushkin, who according to Sinyavsky did the same sixty years earlier. Belkin is the fictional narrator of Pushkin's *Tales of Belkin*, which were among Pushkin's earliest attempts at writing prose. The probable parallel with Chekhov in this respect is Belikov from Chekhov's story "The Man in a Case."

Of course, Evgeny was not the only one / From *Evgeny Onegin*, 5, xxxii.

sieves of ellipsis points / There are several instances in *Evgeny Onegin* where in place of verses we find lines of dots. Politically radical contemporaries and Soviet literary critics have insisted that these indicate lines that were omitted because of the censorship.

My tongue is my enemy / From the draft of chapter 1 of *Evgeny Onegin*.

the famous tenth chapter / A hypothetical chapter 10 of *Evgeny Onegin*, describing Onegin's political activities, was purportedly omitted from the novel under pressure from the censor.

And in order to open up / From *The Little House in Kolomna*.

Devout Shikhmatov / From *The Little House in Kolomna*. Prince S. A. Shirinsky-Shikhmatov (1783–1837) was a poet and a member of A. S. Shishkov's conservative-minded Colloquy of Lovers of the Russian Word. In 1830 he took holy vows as a monk.

O, dreams . . . Ta-tá . . . / *Evgeny Onegin*, 6, xliv, and 4, xlii. These lines may be considered an instance of self-parody on Pushkin's part, since he is poking fun at rhymes he himself used in earlier works.

Poor Folk / Dostoevsky's first novel (1844–1845). *Dead Souls* / Gogol's epic novel (1841). *An Ordinary Story* / A short novel (1847) by Goncharov. *A Boring Story* / A short novel (1889) by Chekhov.

Life . . . War and Peace . . . / There is no well-known novel in Russian literature entitled *Life*. Sinyavsky may be alluding here to works like Leonid Andreev's *Life of Man* or Maksim Gorky's *Life of Klim Samgin*. One cannot help noticing the blithe juxtaposition of this obscure *Life* and perhaps the most famous of Russian novels, *War and Peace*. The "other" artist, incidentally, is Lev Tolstoy.

even the miser a knight / A reference to the title character in the "little tragedy" *The Covetous Knight*.

the Contemporary / A literary and historical journal that Pushkin founded in 1836. He remained its editor until his death in 1837.

"moralistic and decorous" novel / From *Count Nulin:* a reference to the type of novel Natalya Pavlovna reads.

Natalya Pavlovna at first / From *Count Nulin.*

Anton Goremyko . . . Pushkin's stationmaster / "The Stationmaster" is a parody of sentimentalist literature. The main character of the story cries over the loss of his daughter, who has abandoned him for a traveling hussar. "Bad-Luck Anton" is a story by Dmitry Grigorovich (1822–1899), a representative of the "natural school." The main character of the story, a poor peasant named Anton, is at first patient and obedient. When he tries to correct an injustice and complains to a landowner about the steward of his village, he is put in jail. The story was seen as a protest against the inhuman treatment of people, and Anton became a symbol of the best qualities of the Russian national character. P. A. Kropotkin wrote: "In the days of my youth and even later on, every educated person of that time could neither read without tears about Anton's misfortune nor remain indifferent to the horrors of serfdom."

today he's here, tomorrow there / From a Russian children's song.

like a Swede at Poltava / A reference to the crushing defeat that the Russian army of Peter the Great dealt to the Swedish army of Charles IX at Poltava. The expression, "You won't perish like a Swede at Poltava," became a popular saying.

When youth sweeps away / From the poem "Good Advice" (1817–1820), which exists in a manuscript by Pushkin's brother Lev.

a faithful wife and a virtuous mother / From *Evgeny Onegin,* 3, xxi (Tatyana's letter). Sinyavsky refers here to Lev Tolstoy's *Anna Karenina,* in which Tolstoy chronicles the trials of married life and the disintegration of a family.

For everything there is a time / From the poem "To Kaverin," written in 1817 but published only in 1828. Pyotr Pavlovich Kaverin (1794–1855) was a Hussar officer. In 1816 his regiment was stationed at Tsarskoe Selo, where Pushkin met him. Later Kaverin was a member of the Decembrist association the Union of Welfare.

Sleep comes in its turn / "Autumn (An Excerpt)" (1833).

Joy is granted / From *The Gypsies.*

Gavrila and Afanasy / Gavrila Pushkin and his nephew Afanasy were Pushkin's ancestors on his father's side of the family. The Soviet Pushkin scholar D. Blagoi points out that in his *Blackamoor of Peter the Great* Pushkin portrays another relative on his mother's side, Gavrila Afanasevich Rzhevsky, combining in his name the names of the two other relatives. Including them in the plot of *Boris Godunov,* Pushkin cast them as opponents of the tsar. For Pushkin, Gavrila was the most characteristic representative of "the rebellious kin of the Pushkins," and he compared him directly to members of the French revolutionary National Convention.

entrance into history / Sinyavsky here refers to Vladimir Mayakovsky's "First Introduction to a Poem. 'At the Top of My Voice'" (1929–1930). Mayakovsky never completed the poem, which was supposed to be about the first five-year plan initiated by Stalin. The Introduction was presented as the poet's report to his reader about what he was doing. At the end of the Introduction, Mayakovsky directly addresses future generations: "Over the gang of skinflints and grabbers of poetry, I will raise like a Bolshevik party card, all hundred volumes of my party books."

My forefather did not get on with Peter / From the poem "My Pedigree" (1830).

poem about the resurrection of the dead / These words belong to Chichikov, the main character of Gogol's *Dead Souls*, who is describing the collection of things he sees in Plyushkin's house. Gogol intended to write a trilogy modeled on the *Iliad* and the *Divine Comedy*, which is one reason why *Dead Souls* bears the subtitle *A Poem*. Gogol published only the first part of his intended trilogy. He burned the second part shortly after its completion because he was dissatisfied with it.

times of chivalry / Sinyavsky here refers to subtitles of Pushkin's works, including, for example, the poem "Autumn. A Fragment" and the dramatic works *A Scene from "Faustus"* and *Scenes from the Times of Chivalry*.

The fragmentariness of Onegin . . . the "little tragedies" and Godunov / *Evgeny Onegin* ends with the "thunderstruck" Onegin left standing alone after Tatyana rejects his love. Tatyana's husband appears, and the narrator's closing words are: "And here . . . we will leave my hero . . . for a long time . . . forever." In *The Covetous Knight* it remains unclear what will happen to the baron's son, Albert. *Mozart and Salieri* ends with Salieri's question, "And was not the creator of the Vatican a murderer?" In *The Stone Guest*, after Don Juan is taken to hell by the statue of the commander, we are left wondering about the fate of Doña Anna, to whom Don Juan's last words are addressed. At the end of *The Feast in Time of Plague* the Chairman is left "lost in thoughts." *Boris Godunov* ends with the famous stage direction, "The folk are silent."

I loved you so honestly / The concluding lines of Pushkin's famous poem "I loved you" (1829).

That is why in this joyous hour / From the poem "The Feast of Peter I" (1835).

She paused for a moment / From the unfinished poem "Critias, a Magnificent Citizen" (1829).

I loved the sound of clear water and leaves / The middle and concluding stanzas of the poem "At the beginning of life, I remember school" (1830).

The maiden sits eternally / From the poem "A Statue at Tsarskoe Selo" (1830). On statues in Pushkin's works, see Roman Jakobson, *Puškin and His Sculptural Myth*.

meekly presses to his heart / A reference to the pose of the Bronze Horseman, the Falconet statue of Peter the Great, which stands on the banks of the Neva River in St. Petersburg. Evgeny survives the flood by sitting on one of two statues of lions that stand in front of a house on Admiralty Prospect. At the time the poem was written there was a clear sight line between the statues of the lions and the statue of Peter the Great, although that is no longer the case today.

Pimen / The monk Pimen is a chronicler in *Boris Godunov*. Sinyavsky here refers to Grigory's words when he wakes up and sees Pimen: "And by the candle/The old man sits and keeps writing."

The Chairman remains / The closing stage direction of *The Feast in Time of Plague*.

I am involuntarily drawn / From the Prince's monologue in Pushkin's drama *The Mermaid* (1833).

Memory silently unfolds / From the poem "Recollection" (1828).

But I can't wash away / The closing line of the poem "Recollection."

I gaze like a madman / From the poem "The Black Shawl" (1820).

A withered and scentless flower / From the poem "A Flower" (1828).

Chaadaev, do you remember the old days? / From "To Chaadaev" (1824).

Once again I visited / The opening line of a poem written to commemorate Pushkin's last visit to Mikhailovskoe in 1835, in which the poet recalls the Black Sea, Kishinyov, and Odessa.

"behold" and "arise" / A reference to the poem "The Prophet" (1826), in which an angel tells the poet: "Arise, prophet, and behold and understand."

Your eyes gleam / An inexact quotation from the poem "Night" (1823). Instead of *sverkayut* (gleam) it should read *blistayut* (shine).

in the dark of the night / A reference to the last part of the poem "Once again I visited," in which Pushkin addresses the trees saying that "my grandson . . . will pass by you in the dark of the night and will remember me."

Appear, beloved shade / From the poem "Incantation" (1830).

visions of days primordial and innocent / From the poem "Resurrection" (1819).

And reveal the bright distance / From the poem "The Dreamer" (1815).

The profound darkness dissipated in the sky / The closing scene of Pushkin's romantic poem *The Prisoner of the Caucasus*. In it a young Russian is captured by the Cherkess, a mountain people at war with Russia. The prisoner is wounded. A beautiful Cherkess girl tends to his wound, and they fall in love. She helps him to escape, knowing that they will never see each other again.

They remind me / From the poem "Once again I visited . . ."

Your voice, my darling / From *The Feast in Time of Plague*.

The folk are silent / The closing stage direction of *Boris Godunov*.

And was not the creator of the Vatican a murderer? / The closing line of *Mozart and Salieri*. Salieri is referring to the rumor that Michelangelo ordered a young man crucified to serve as a model for the suffering Christ in a painting of the Crucifixion.

And the sails swelled / The closing lines of the poem "Autumn (An Excerpt)" (1833).

senior tutor at the court / Batyushkov was an officer in the Russian army and participated in three wars, including the campaign of 1814 against Napoleon. Zhukovsky served as tutor to the heir to the Russian throne, the future Alexander II, at the court of Nicholas I.

Everyone worshiped him / Gavriil Derzhavin (1743–1816) was the major literary figure of the late 1780s and 1790s as well as "by an irony of fate, a professional soldier and administrator and one of the great 'magnates' [*vel'mozhi*] clustered around the throne of Catherine II" (William Edward Brown, *A History of Russian Literature* [Ann Arbor, Mich.: Ardis, 1980], p. 381). Derzhavin's career soared when he wrote his ode "Felitsa" (1783), dedicated to Catherine the Great. The empress was so pleased that she made Derzhavin an "actual state councillor" and appointed him to the governorship of Olonets Province in northern Russia.

To be a clerk or an uhlan / From the poem "Farewell" (1817).

You don't have to be a poet / Actually, these words belong to the "civic poet" of the 1860s, Nikolai Nekrasov. Sinyavsky playfully ascribes them to Mikhailo Lomonosov

(1711–65), who, inspired by Enlightenment ideals, was one of the first to invoke in poetry the pathos of civic service and the enthusiasm of building the new state.

Stillness is dear to my heart / From "The Dreamer."

I like war's bloody entertainments / From the poem "I am acquainted with fighting— I love the sound of swords" (1820).

these same nerves / Lermontov often wrote about war and death, depicting them in expressive terms.

Bulgarin / Faddei Bulgarin (1789–1859) was a liberal literary critic before the Decembrist revolt of 1825. In 1826 he became a mouthpiece for monarchism and reaction and even received praise from Count Benkendorf for being a capable police informer. In 1825 Bulgarin became the editor of the political and literary newspaper the *Northern Bee*, which in the 1820s and 1830s published some works by Pushkin, Ivan Krylov, and Aleksandr Griboedov, but after the first issue of the *Contemporary* appeared he launched an attack on Pushkin.

My soul is bored / From *Ruslan and Lyudmila.*

kyukhelbekerish / Wilhelm Kyukhelbeker (1799–1846) was a poet and a close friend of Pushkin's from his lycée days. He participated in the Decembrist revolt and was arrested and sentenced to death. The sentence was later commuted to exile to Siberia for life. Sinyavsky here refers to Pushkin's epigram, "At dinner I over-ate/And Yakov locked the door by mistake/Because of that, my friends,/I felt both kyukhelbekerish and wretched."

Delvig / Baron A. A. Delvig (1798–1831) was a close friend of Pushkin's from his lyceé days. He was a poet, a member of the Society of Lovers of Literature, Sciences, and Arts, of the Free Society of Russian Literature, and of the Green Lamp literary circle. Delvig published a literary almanac called *Northern Flowers* and edited the *Literary Gazette*, in which Pushkin published several of his works. Delvig visited Pushkin in exile at Mikhailovskoe, and Pushkin dedicated several of his poems to him.

The Raevskys / Pushkin had a very close relationship with the Raevsky family. In 1820, on his way into exile in Odessa, he spent about three months with General N. N. Raevsky's family in the Caucasus and the Crimea. At that time Pushkin be-came especially close with the sons and daughters of the general: Aleksandr and Nikolai, both officers and participants in the war of 1812, and Ekaterina and Eliza-veta, with whom Pushkin spent three weeks in the Crimean city of Gurzuf. Later Pushkin met Ekaterina in Kishinyov, where she lived with her husband, General Orlov. Pushkin also knew the third daughter of Nikolai Raevsky, Mariya, married to the Decembrist Sergei Volkonsky, who followed her exiled husband to Siberia.

publish it as government legislation / A reference to *Selected Passages from Corre-spondence with Friends* (1842), in which Gogol, having experienced a spiritual crisis, proposed an extremely conservative plan for the reorganization of the Russian state based on theocratic ideas.

We remain the same / From the most famous of Pushkin's poems written on the occa-sion of the anniversary of the opening of the lycée at Tsarskoe Selo, "October 19" (1825), which begins with the line "The woods lose their crimson dress . . ."

Why shouldn't I write about him? / From *Evgeny Onegin*, 1, lix.

That the ardent agitation / An inexact quotation from the poem "It's Not That That I'm Proud of, My Bard" (1822). Instead of "thirst" (*zhazhdoi*) it should read "passion" (*strast'yu*).

The world's grown empty / From "To the Sea" (1824).

the Demon / The main character of Lermontov's long poem of the same name. He is a fallen angel doomed to live between heaven and earth. In him, Lermontov wanted to show the fate of the suffering individual.

When the poet is not called / The first stanza of "The Poet" (1827).

But as soon as the divine word / From "The Poet" (1827).

Pushkin's "Prophet" / In the poem "The Prophet" (1826) the poet, wandering through the desert, meets an angel, who replaces his eyes with those of an eagle and his tongue with that of a "wise snake." The angel touches his ears, and the poet gains the power to hear the hidden life of the world. Finally, the angel cuts open the poet's chest and replaces his human heart with a burning piece of coal. Thus the poet undergoes a rite of initiation: he dies as a man and rises as a prophet. At the end of the poem the angel calls to him: "Rise, prophet, see and hear,/Be filled with my will,/And going over seas and lands/Burn people's hearts with your words."

Lermontov's "Prophet" / Lermontov's poem "The Prophet" (1841) is essentially a realization of the saying, "No one is a prophet in his own land." From the moment that a person, by the will of the "eternal judge," becomes a prophet and begins to preach love and truth to people, all he can see in their eyes is anger and vice. People reject him and drive him away. As he is leaving, the elders point at him and say to children that he is an example of a proud man who wanted people to believe that God speaks through him, and now he is naked and poor, and everyone despises him.

The poet strummed his inspired lyre / The opening lines of the poem "The Poet and the Crowd" (1828).

Like a deity, it does not need / From the poem "A Conversation between the Bookseller and the Poet" (1824).

the Negro branch / Pushkin's great-grandfather on his mother's side was Ibrahim Hannibal (1697–1781). According to legend, he was the son of an Abyssinian prince. In 1705 he was stolen from the palace of a Turkish sultan where he was living as a hostage and presented to Peter the Great. In 1717 Peter sent him to France to study the military arts. In 1723 Hannibal returned to Russia, where he received the rank of engineer-lieutenant of an artillery company in the Preobrazhensky Regiment. In 1762 he retired with the rank of commander in chief.

Under the sky of my Africa / From *Evgeny Onegin*, 1, l.

Mayne Reid / A British writer who lived and worked as a journalist in the United States. He fought in the Spanish-American war of 1846–1848 and wrote adventure novels about Indians, Mexican rebels, hunters, and young people traveling to exotic countries in search of rare animals, flowers, and plants. Together with Jules Verne, Captain Mayne Reid has been the most popular writer among Russian children since 1860, when his novels (*The Headless Horseman, Oceola the Seminole, The Quadroon, The Plant Hunters,* and *The Cliff Climbers*) were translated into Russian.

a real Indian / When Russian children play cowboys and Indians, the roles are reversed in comparison with American culture: the Indians are the good guys. The cult of the noble savage was popularized in Russia by the works of such writers as James Fenimore Cooper and Sinclair Thompson (*The Little Savages*) as well as Mayne Reid.

Razuvaevka / A Russian town on the Moscow-Tashkent railway line where Sinyavsky spent summers with his grandparents when he was a boy.

At the sight of Ibrahim / The unfinished historical novel *The Blackamoor of Peter the Great* was Pushkin's first attempt at writing prose. It tells the story of how Peter married his godson Ibrahim Hannibal to a girl from an old Russian aristocratic family, the Rzhevskys.

And I, the eternally idle scapegrace / From the poem "To Yurev" (1820).

This skipper was that famous skipper / From the Post Scriptum to the poem "My Pedigree" (1830).

You are a tsar, live alone / From the poem "To the Poet" (1830).

I recruit an army / From *The Little House in Kolomna*.

Only a revolutionary thinker / This statement was written in 1823. In Pushkin's original text only initials are given where Sinyavsky supplies names.

On the bank by deserted waves / This is another example of Sinyavsky's intentional conflation of temporal coordinates. Any Russian would recognize these lines as the opening of Pushkin's *Bronze Horseman*, in which "he" refers to Peter the Great. The words, however, also begin Boris Pasternak's poem "Imitation," from his collection *Themes and Variations*, where the "he" becomes Pushkin.

Only you, Poltava's hero / From the concluding stanza of *Poltava*.

I have erected / The opening line of "The Monument" (1836).

My ideal now is a spouse / From "Onegin's Travels," the last chapter of *Evgeny Onegin*, published separately from the rest of the novel.

You have to find a use in everything / From "The Poet and the Crowd."

His eyes/Shine / From *Poltava*. Pushkin here describes Peter the Great at the battle of Poltava.

They were representations of two demons / From the poem "At the beginning of life, I remember school."

We press upon the Swedes / From *Poltava*.

the window that Peter cut / A reference to the introduction to *The Bronze Horseman*, in which Pushkin mentions Russia's ambition to open a way to Europe ("to cut a window into Europe") as Peter's main goal in building St. Petersburg on the Gulf of Finland.

The weather was growing ever fiercer / In *The Bronze Horseman* Pushkin describes the flood that engulfs St. Petersburg as a rebellion of nature against the will of man.

There is an ecstasy in battle / From *The Feast in Time of Plague*, the Chairman's "Hymn to the Plague."

I love you, creation of Peter / From *The Bronze Horseman*. Peter's creation is the city of St. Petersburg.

become Corsairs / The Corsair comes from Byron's poem of the same name, which was translated into Russian in 1825–1826. The poem was one of Byron's so-called oriental poems, filled with dramatic actions, fatal passions, and catastrophic finales. Along with Goethe's Werther and Byron's Childe Harold, The Corsair was viewed as one of the most typical of romantic heroes. The Corsair is a person who breaks all ties with his environment and takes the path of uncompromising struggle, revenge, and crime against the world of oppression and slavery. His individual revolt becomes an act of universal significance: rebelling against civilization, the hero challenges fate, the whole world, and God Himself.

I was embittered . . . his caustic arguments / From *Evgeny Onegin*, 1, xlv, xlvi. "He" is Onegin.

science of the tender passion / *Evgeny Onegin*, 1, viii.

an involuntary devotion to dreams / *Evgeny Onegin*, 1, xiv.

a superfluous man, a petty demon, a Carbonaro, or simply a minor / Sinyavsky here refers to typical characters of Russian literature. "Superfluous man" is a term that the critic Vissarion Belinsky applied to Evgeny Onegin, and it has since become a cliché. In his essay *On Socialist Realism* Sinyavsky writes that the central character of nineteenth-century Russian literature is called a superfluous man because "for all his generous impulses he is unable to find a destiny and he presents a lamentable example of purposelessness, which is of no use to anybody. He is, as a rule, a reflective character, with tendencies to self-analysis and self-flagellation. His life is full of unrealized projects, and his fate is sad and slightly ridiculous" (Abram Tertz [Sinyavsky], *On Socialist Realism*, trans. George Dennis [New York: Pantheon Books, 1960], pp. 61–66). The "petty demon" comes from Fyodor Sologub's novel of the same name. It is the *nedotykomka*, a little gray sprite that pesters the insane Peredonov, the main character of the novel. For Sologub's contemporaries, the *nedotykomka* became a symbol of all the ugliness that existed in Russia at the end of the nineteenth and the beginning of the twentieth centuries. The Carbonari were Italian rebels who around 1821 organized to drive out the Austrians and establish a united Italy. For Russian romantics "Carbonaro" became synonymous with "revolutionary." Interest in the Carbonari became even greater after the novel *The Gadfly* (Ovod), by the British writer Ethel Lillian Voynich, was published in Russia in 1897. It tells the story of a Carbonaro and his fight against political oppression as well as against the Catholic church. In the Soviet period it became obligatory reading for all schoolchildren. The minor Mitrofan is the main character of Denis Fonvizin's comedy *The Minor* (1782). He is the uneducated, rude, and obtuse son of an equally vile woman landowner. Written in the spirit of the Enlightenment, the play is a satire on the stagnation and corruption of the eighteenth-century Russian gentry.

empty, universal, and sincere / This characterization of Khlestakov in *The Inspector General* is given by the characters Bobchinsky and Dobchinsky, who think that he is an important government official.

Love knows no distinctions / From *The Inspector General*. Khlestakov flirts with both the mayor's daughter and wife. First he flirts with the daughter, Marya Antonovna, but when he is interrupted by her mother, Anna Andreevna, he switches allegiances. He declares his love for Anna Andreevna and, disregarding the fact that she is "in a certain sense . . . married," offers to run away with her and "withdraw beneath the canopy of streams." Then when Marya Antonovna returns and sees him on his knees in front of her mother, he switches again and immediately proclaims that he wants to marry her.

I confess that / Khlestakov in *The Inspector General.*

the lady became a peasant girl / The Belkin tale "Mistress into Maid" is a kind of unrealized *Romeo and Juliet.* It tells the story of a rivalry between two Russian land-owners: the "progressive" anglomaniac Muromsky and the conservatively Russian Berestov. After Muromsky's daughter, Lisa, hears from her maid Nastya about the arrival of Berestov's son, Aleksei, at his father's estate, she decides as a joke to meet him pretending to be a simple peasant girl named Akulina. They meet by accident in the forest, and Aleksei falls in love with the beautiful peasant girl. They begin to see each other often, and when the weather is bad they exchange letters. Mean-while their fathers have a chance meeting of their own. Muromsky's horse throws him, and Berestov takes him to his house to recover. Their enmity disappears and a friendship begins. They decide that their children should be married to one another. Aleksei is in despair. He has seen Lisa as herself only once when she, not wishing him to recognize her, put on heavy makeup and behaved like a spoiled brat. He goes to Muromsky's estate to announce his decision not to marry Muromsky's daughter, but when he arrives he sees Lisa and recognizes her as his beautiful Akulina. As Pushkin says, you can guess what happens next.

I couldn't help wondering / From *The Captain's Daughter.*

The shade of Ivan / From *Boris Godunov:* Grigory, in his conversation with Marina Mnishek.

Pugachov pulled exactly the same stunt / Emelyan Pugachov was a Don Cossack who claimed that he was Peter III, Catherine the Great's husband, who had suppos-edly been assassinated. He was arrested several times, and several times he escaped from both prison and the Russian army. In the autumn of 1773 he led a rebellion in the territory east of the Volga with the cities of Orenburg and Kazan as its centers. Pugachov found strong support among fugitives from serfdom, who were abundant in that area: dispossessed native tribesmen (like the Bashkirs), Old Believers, forced laborers in Ural mines, and of course the Cossacks, who were perpetually at odds with the central government. Pugachov's forces amounted to 20,000–30,000 men, and the rebellion grew into a full-scale war with the rebels capturing even large cities like Perm, Tsaritsyn, Saratov, and Kazan. Catherine was forced to send regu-lar troops released at the conclusion of the Russian-Turkish war to fight the peasant army. In 1775 Pugachov was finally captured and brought in a cage to Moscow, where he was executed.

Bored with the strictures of monastic life / Grigory is preparing a miracle for the world: his ascent to the throne in the guise of the tsarevich Dmitry, risen from the dead.

Monastery of the Miracle / The monastery where Grigory was a monk.

the parable of his life and art / In *The Captain's Daughter* Pugachov tells Grinyov a parable about an eagle and a raven. The raven brags that it lives longer than the eagle, to which the eagle responds that it would prefer to drink fresh blood once rather than feed on carrion for a hundred years.

The fatal scaffold stood / From *Poltava.*

Khlopusha / A historical figure, a "heneral" in Pugachov's army. He was reported to be a convict who had escaped from the mines in the Urals. His nostrils were torn when he was tortured.

I dreamed that a steep staircase / Grigory Otrepev's dream from *Boris Godunov.*

The noise died down. I stepped out onto the stage / The opening line of Boris Pasternak's poem "Hamlet," from the poems of Yury Zhivago, which comprise the final chapter of Boris Pasternak's novel *Doctor Zhivago.*

Having crossed the bridge, Kokushkin / A reference to Pushkin's poem "Kokushkin Bridge" (1829), written as a response to illustrations to *Evgeny Onegin* that were published in the *Neva Almanac.* Sinyavsky also has in mind limericks in which Pushkin's name is often used out of context just for the sake of rhyme. The probable continuation here would be something like, "Tsar Nicholas was shit on by Pushkin."

Tynyanov / Yury Tynyanov was a Soviet critic and theoretician of literature, one of the major representatives of the formalist school. Tynyanov wrote several articles on Pushkin as well as a biography of the poet.

Who do you think I am / From *The Captain's Daughter.*

The rumor . . . grew to a fury / Pushkin married Natalya Goncharova, widely considered the most beautiful woman in Moscow. She caught the eye of Tsar Nicholas I, who decided to transfer Pushkin to St. Petersburg in order to have Natalya nearby. To do that, he bestowed the meaningless title of *Kammerjunker* on Pushkin, forcing him to be present at various court ceremonies. Immediately after their move to St. Petersburg, rumors began that implicated Natalya in affairs at the court. This finally resulted in Pushkin's challenging Baron d'Anthès, the adopted son of the Dutch ambassador, to a duel. D'Anthès mortally wounded Pushkin and was exiled from Russia. Natalya Goncharova remarried several years later.

a coarsely painted ace / A reference to the red diamond shape that was sewn on prisoners' clothes. It served as a target for guards if a prisoner attempted to escape.

Just you wait / From *The Bronze Horseman:* "poor" Evgeny's threat to the monument.

in every existing tongue / In the poem "Monument" Pushkin writes that he will be remembered by every nation and that his name will be spoken in every tongue. Here, however, Sinyavsky uses the words "every tongue" differently: every tongue will spread rumors about Pushkin.

He recognized him in the crowd / From *The Captain's Daughter,* when Grinyov witnesses the execution of Pugachov.

Not for ordinary worries / The concluding lines of "The Poet and the Crowd."

despondent and mute / From "To the Poet" (1830).

Didn't he encourage the Decembrists? Didn't he scorch people's hearts with his Word? / References are to Pushkin's "Epistle to Siberia" ("In the depths of Siberian mines, keep your proud patience," 1827), in which Pushkin rallied the exiled Decembrists; to his ode "Liberty" (1817), which ends with the words, "And now learn, o tsars: . . . You should be the first to bow your heads/To the faithful shadow of Law"; to the poem "To the Slanderers of Russia" (1831); to the poem "The Monument" (1836), in which among his achievements Pushkin mentions the fact that he will be remembered for his appeal for mercy toward the exiled Decembrists; and to the poem "The Prophet," in which the final goal of the poet is to burn people's hearts with his words.

He sings for his own amusement / From the poem "Near the place where golden Venice reigns" (1827).

I write for myself and publish for money / Pushkin was the first Russian writer to rely on his writing as his primary source of income. His civil service posts—first in Kishinyov and Odessa and later in St. Petersburg as a *Kammerjunker*—provided him with very little money. His father (who was the probable prototype for the baron in *The Covetous Knight*) refused to help him financially. Pushkin was in constant need of money, not only to provide for his most ordinary needs, but also to pay his gambling debts.

a smile on lustful lips / The concluding words of the poem "To Turgenev" (1817).

no, not all of me will die / From "The Monument."

a spoiled gentlewoman / Andrei Zhdanov, Stalin's cultural commissar, used these words in 1946 to refer to the poet Anna Akhmatova during the Central Committee's attack on the literary journals *Zvezda* and *Leningrad* for publishing works by Akhmatova and the satirist Mikhail Zoshchenko.

Go away! / From "The Poet and the Crowd."

And I forget the world / From "Autumn. (An Excerpt)."

Along a free road / From "To the Poet."

To wander here and there / From the poem "From Pindemonti" (1836).

ACKNOWLEDGMENTS

We would like to express our gratitude to Richard Borden, Sylvie Richards, Ronald Meyer, Marcus Levitt, Igor Nemirovsky, and Helena Goscilo, who read all or part of this manuscript at different stages of completion, offering valuable comments and providing much-appreciated moral support. Our special thanks go to Caryl Emerson for her encouragement and insight, to Richard Miller for his extraordinary editing, and to Jonathan Brent for his steadfast enthusiasm for this project and for his patience. Michael Robinson helped greatly with the research on the introduction. We are of course grateful to Irina Yastremski and Slava Nepomnyashchy, without whose understanding and support this book would never have seen completion. Last, but certainly not least, we would like to thank Andrei Sinyavsky and Mariya Rozanova for their hospitality and their willingness to take time from their busy schedules to elucidate the text and its history.

C.T.N.
S.Y.